THE
MIND
GYMNASIUM

742
/1549 =

68%

129,000 .
6,800
351,800 — July
(35,500) M.Hole

100,300
(50,000) loan

need 2 months
receive

258,000
6,800
264,800

50,000 Revenue
37,500 Payment

87,500

THE MIND GYMNASIUM

A New Age Guide to Self-realization

DENIS POSTLE

New York St. Louis San Francisco Bogotá
Hamburg Madrid Mexico Milan Montreal Panama
Paris São Paulo Tokyo Toronto

A GAIA ORIGINAL

THE MIND GYMNASIUM

Written by Denis Postle

Editorial
Rosanne Hooper
Jonathan Hilton

Design
Margaret Sadler

Illustration
Aziz Khan
Philippa Beale
Chris Forsey

Production
Susan Walby

Direction
Lucy Lidell
Patrick Nugent

Panel of Consultants

John Rowan is a new paradigm research specialist, psychotherapist, occupational psychologist, lecturer in psychology and psychotherapy, and influential author.
Dr Windy Dryden is a lecturer in psychology at Goldsmith's College, London and author of numerous books and articles.
Dr John Tomlinson is a general practitioner particularly interested in the effects of stress on health and counselling in general practice.
Dick Saxton is a professional counselling tutor and group work trainer.

Dr Robert Young is a psychoanalytic psychotherapist, editor of the journal *Free Associations* and writer on human nature and society.
Anne Dickson is a co-counselling teacher, assertiveness trainer, sex therapist and author.
Jill Anderson is an associate facilitator at the University of Surrey, an interpersonal skills trainer and psychotherapist.

Published 1989 by McGraw Hill Publishing Company,
11 West 19th New York, New York
10011, USA.

Copyright © Gaia Books Ltd 1988

1 2 3 4 5 6 7 8 9 0   8 9 2 1 0 9 8

Library of Congress Cataloging-in-Publication data

Postle, Denis
    The mind gymnasium: a new age guide to self-realization, by Denis Postle.
p. cm.
    Includes index.

    ISBN 0-07-050576-4 (hardcover).   ISBN 0-7-050569-1 (paperback)

    1. Mind and body – Problems, exercises, etc. 2. Self-realization – Problems, exercises, etc. 3. Self-evaluation. I. Title.
BF161.P59 1988   88-27465
153 – dc19   CIP

Typeset in Sabon 10½ on 12 pt by S B Datagraphics, Limited, Colchester, England

Printed and bound in Spain by Artes Graficas Toledo S.A.
D.L.TO.: 1930/1988

HOW TO USE THIS BOOK

It is entirely up to you how you choose to use this book. But to help you keep track of the possibilities, let me just explain how the book is organized. The first chapter, SELF-ASSESSMENT, is a series of self-searching questions that are designed to help you identify your strengths and weaknesses. The middle chapter, KNOWHOW, draws together current knowledge and ideas about the mind. And the third chapter, MIND GYM, is a series of practical self-help exercises.

One way to start is to dip in wherever you like, perhaps to a topic that is of particular interest to you at the moment. From there, you could follow the arrow and references at the foot of the page to take you on to something else. Another way is to begin with the SELF-ASSESSMENT chapter, keep a note of your findings and move on to the KNOWHOW chapter when you are ready. Then finally you can try the MIND GYM exercises that look useful. Or you could go straight from one of the SELF-ASSESSMENTS to the relevant exercises in MIND GYM. Or you could start with KNOWHOW for an overview. Or you could start with MIND GYM and refer back to the SELF-ASSESSMENTS. There are as many ways to use this book as there are people. Feel free to jump backwards and forwards and in and out of the book; it's intended to be used like that.

Before you launch in, you may want to take a look at the Introduction to find out more about the book's attitudes. To get the best out of the book, consider it as the basis for doing some work on yourself. Buy a notebook and jot down what you discover about yourself. Even better, if you don't already, keep a journal (see p. 197). Ultimately what you get out of the book depends on you and the experiences and memories you bring to it.

Is there, as a matter of fact, any better truth about the
ultimate things than the one which helps you to live.
Marie-Louise von Franz

Awe is upmarket fear.
John Heron

As a sword cannot cut itself, or as a finger cannot touch its
own tip, Mind cannot see itself.
Vivekachudamani

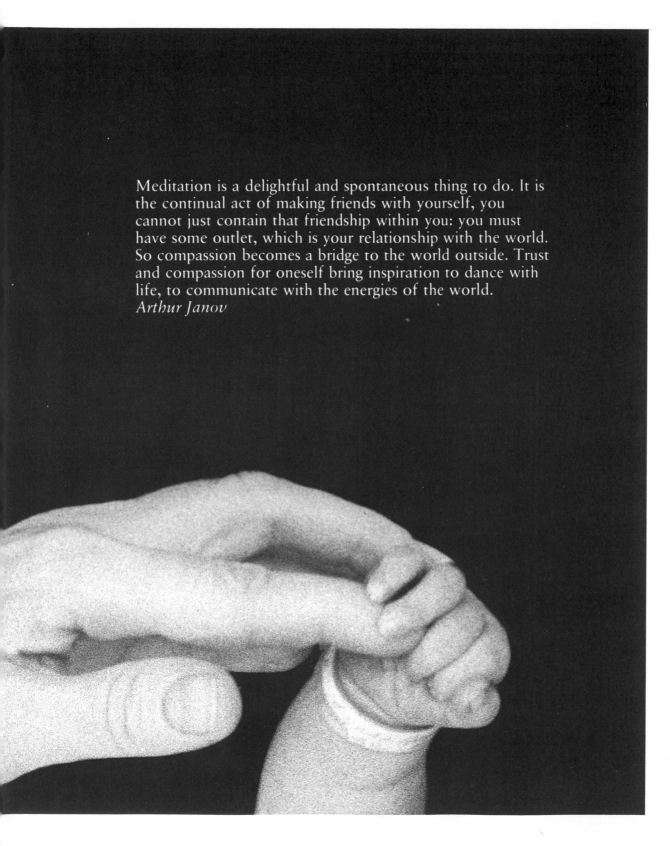

Meditation is a delightful and spontaneous thing to do. It is the continual act of making friends with yourself, you cannot just contain that friendship within you: you must have some outlet, which is your relationship with the world. So compassion becomes a bridge to the world outside. Trust and compassion for oneself bring inspiration to dance with life, to communicate with the energies of the world.
Arthur Janov

CONTENTS

INTRODUCTION

Ah, so there you are. I thought someone would turn up eventually. I've chosen to speak to you directly like this, both to bring the book alive and to draw attention to what is going on in your mind. The mind can seem mysterious. Yet here it is, doing its thing right now. If you hadn't already noticed, these words, these marks on the page, are an event in your mind, an experience which you create for yourself by making sense of what I am writing. So as we travel headlong down the page, we have a relationship you and I – in your mind.

It's up to you

How this relationship goes is your choice. You can pause here, look up, look around the room. You can choose to throw the book away, to skip to another page. You can choose to carry on reading. Choice crops up frequently as a topic in this book, because the amount of choice you have in life seems to be directly related to how well you know your own mind. Once you become aware of the way in which your mind is persistently trying to make sense of what you are doing – as it is now – you can get to know its games and quirks, and the tricks it uses to limit your choice. If, for example, something in your mind tells you that you are stupid, you are not likely to feel free to use your intelligence fully. It's from areas of your mind that you don't know or aren't friends with that hard times and limited choice tend to arise. If you have a skeleton in the cupboard – a part of yourself or your experience that you have disowned – from time to time the door will fall open and the skeleton will fall right out, face-first, into the pudding in front of your most honoured guests. Recognize any of these? 'I don't know what got into me' 'How could I have done such a thing?' 'Why does it always have to happen to me?' 'Why do I do this to myself?' 'Why do I never seem to learn?' 'I must have been out of my mind.' These are your mind noticing that it has been on automatic, and behaving as if it had no choice. With your mind on automatic, choice is crowded out by distress, lack of confidence, lack of spontaneity, low self-esteem, jealousy, envy, anxiety, panic, grief, anger, loneliness . . . But human minds do have the capacity for choice. And it's lack of choice, along with lack of love and understanding, that leads to suffering.

Changing your mind

That's the bad news. The good news is that human minds do have the capacity for choice. And once your mind is out in the open, you have more of a chance to change it. You can learn to work with it yourself and increase your awareness of how much choice you have in your own life. And that's the purpose of this book – to provide an opening, a vision of the possibilities available to you for changing your mind in directions you choose.

Working on your mind isn't easy. And it's sometimes painful. But it can be great fun – and it can change your life. And you can do it if you have a mind to – anyone can. In this book you will find a variety of ways of assessing your mind. Then, when you have a clearer idea of your strengths and weaknesses, you can choose a programme of emotional, intuitive, intellectual and sensory gymnastics.

So is all this for you? If you are curious about your own potential, about how your mind works, about how you came to be the way you are and what you can do about it, the answer is yes. If your mind is presently or frequently flooded with distress, or if you feel it is fragile and could easily shatter, gently draw on this book to build up your strength. You can dive in deeper later, when you feel ready.

You know best

The basic approach of this book is facilitative. It assumes that, as an intelligent, self-directing person, your mind will do what it needs to do to heal itself and increase its potential, given the necessary guidelines. As author, I am responsible for being informative, stimulating and supportive – and you are responsible for being active, creative and enterprising in what you do with what you learn. How does that feel? Does it seem right to you? Or does your mind believe that someone else, an 'expert', should assess you and tell you what to do? Not here. Here, you'll find that your own assessment is the one that counts. Other people may have a lot to contribute, but you are your own best expert. Just as you are making sense of these words in your own way, so you can make sense of your own mind. This approach shifts the balance of responsibility in your favour. Think about it. How could anyone ever know what is going on in your mind as well as, or even better than, you? They never could and they never will . . . It's just that other people, such as doctors, teachers and psychiatrists, have been happy to take responsibility for you. And they will continue to, if you let them. But now you have an alternative: this book and the tradition it comes from can show you how you can begin to take charge of the evolution of your mind.

The value of experience

So facilitation is my contribution, and taking charge of what you do with it is your contribution. But is this enough? Not quite. For what tends to happen when you start to take charge? You buy a book like this one, you start discussing it with a couple of friends, you have a few drinks and you spiral up into some kind of high intellectual speculation that has nothing to do with actual experience. And when you wake up in the morning, you can't remember a word anybody said. Or else, you find you've fallen in love yet again with someone who appears to promise happiness and a solution to all your problems. The best way to avoid these kinds of cul-de-sac is by persistently giving attention to your own experience.

If you ever suspect that what you feel has become separated from what you think, you can put thought and feeling back together by looking at what happened and what went on in your mind. This means looking at the whole of your experience – what you saw, felt and imagined, including any discomfort, pleasure or anxiety – and valuing each part of it as a source of knowledge, an opportunity for insight. This approach pulls you into a deeper, more realistic connection with your inner and outer life. You will be less likely to believe that the world is the way you feel about it, and 'facts' will become no more and no less than someone's personal opinion. It is not unusual to have a mind packed full of 'facts', abstract logic and intellectual reasoning. It pays good money for a start – and it can give a tremendous sense of being in control and of making giant steps for humankind! The trouble with having your mind full of thought to the exclusion of feelings and more down-to-earth experience is that, like the legendary Greek character Icarus, if you fly too near the sun, your wings will melt – and it can be a very long way to the ground.

Learning from experience means looking at your attitudes to all aspects of your life – such as bringing up the children or earning a living – through the whole spectrum of your experience, emotional, physical and intuitive, as well as intellectual. Until you have tested your attitudes against your own experience, you can't know what's good for you. And neither can anyone else.

What effect does all this work on yourself have? You may feel sadder and wiser more often than usual. But you will also come to appreciate that your mind and everyone else's is not a fixed thing that you are stuck with forever, but a process that is susceptible to evolution and change.

The wisdom of the body

For centuries, minds have been baked from the pure white flour of intellect without being grounded in the physical reality of feelings. Emotions and feelings were, and often still are, considered a sign of weakness and inferiority, the preserve of women and children. But we are now seeing how damaging it can be to fear and deny our feelings. Why do you think most men live several years less than most women? Being hard, thick-skinned and competitive can literally take years off your life. And many people on the receiving end of this 'macho' attitude, particularly women, have crushed their rage at what it was doing to them, until it became squashed into 'depression'. If you know someone who often feels depressed, try renaming it anger and see what it tells you.

The Mind Gymnasium invites you to look at the physical reality of your experience, at where in your body the feeling is, so that you can unite your thoughts and feelings. It values the intelligences of the body, the emotions, and intuition as well as that of the intellect.

The key to your mind is in the past

Working on your mind means looking into your past, because that's when those skeletons were locked into their cupboards. To begin with, you may just want to take a peep round the door and shut it again quickly. But gradually tracing the origins of adult distress back to early childhood is the first step, not only to reducing that distress, but to increasing your general intelligence. Ignoring the past, apart from ensuring that you remain a prisoner of your own history, means that there's every chance you will become a prisoner of other people's histories too.

Personal politics

Some people will tell you that recovering your personal history is self-indulgent, that the only way to improve the human condition is through political change – and for oppressed minorities, that is certainly true. There will be others who argue that it's all in the mind, so why bother with politics. But the personal and the political – the distribution of power within organizations and families – are not separate. Keeping them apart sets up a vicious circle in which your abilities are crushed and distorted by oppressive social arrangements. And this means that your mind, having been limited in this way, can see no alternative but to join the oppression or put up with it. It seems to me that the overriding priority is to break into this circle, wherever you find yourself. If this means political action, that's fine, but remember the personal dimension, because otherwise you'll trip over it. If personal growth makes more sense to you, remember the political dimension, so that you don't find yourself engulfed by it.

The Mind Gymnasium emphasizes the value of taking charge of your own choices, choosing to trust, to love and to accept yourself and other people, as well as to choose to become aware of what is happening to you. As you work on this, you'll soon come to see how intimately your personal power is tied up with the politics of the wider world, you'll be less likely to blame enemies or idealize leaders, you'll be more likely to respect your own and others' vulnerability.

Where am I coming from?

What I am offering in this book is the direct result of my own experience and that of people close to me. It is based on what has worked well for us, what has been fruitful, decisive, enlivening and fun and is a direct consequence of taking personal responsibility for working on my mind in the ways that are outlined here. The early tributaries of my own self-enquiry were fed first by one kind of meditation and later by a second. Other streams, based on making films about high-energy physics, about an episode in C G Jung's life and about the mathematics of Catastrophe Theory – led to a deepening study of active imagination, meditation and the primal therapy approach to recovering childhood experiences. This built up until I eventually joined the mainstream of humanistic psychology, including co-counselling, psychotherapy, new paradigm research and professional training. They have worked well for me, and I believe that they help to ensure that what is said here is well-grounded in other people's experience as well as in my own. Alongside this, I was born before World War II, grew up in a steel town, and was one of the first children of the working class to have a full education. I am white, European and a man. All this may lead to some over-heating, some gaps and distortions in my viewpoint, but it also adds insight, ingenuity and vigour, relatively untainted by establishment or institutional inertia or taboos. We are all children of our epoch and books on the mind even more so.

Are you still with me? Oh, good. Well, let's move on.

WHAT YOU MIGHT GAIN . . .

This book offers knowledge and insight that often remain trapped in the professions – in psychiatry, science, medicine and education. It regards working on your mind not as 'therapy' or 'treatment' but as personal education. It's up to you what you make of it, but here are some of the possibilities.

Understanding others

You will gain more understanding of the underlying causes of human behaviour. You will discover that:

Early childhood experiences tend to distort adult behaviour.

The mind and body are not separate. The mind is a property of the whole body.

We communicate as much through our bodies as through words.

Feelings are physical.

We are not responsible for what we feel, but we are responsible for what we do about it.

The split between thinking and feeling can be mended by looking at personal experience.

Old distress squeezes out intelligence.

We often blame other people for what we do not like in ourselves.

Intelligence includes emotional, physical and intuitive intelligence as well as intellect.

Present-day pressures re-trigger the reactions we had to painful childhood experiences.

Domination is not inevitable.

Human beings are naturally intelligent, self-directing and co-operative.

Physical fitness lies at the root of fitness of mind.

Labels that people attach to us limit our freedom.

Memories are stored in the body.

Change is inevitable.

Understanding yourself

You will gain more understanding of your own personal behaviour. You will find out why you:

Lack confidence
Can't concentrate
Feel shy
Feel guilty or anxious
Get depressed
Can't stop . . .
Find it difficult to . . .
Can't make decisions
Get into moods
Don't get promoted
Always arrive late
Feel compelled to . . .
Hate commitments
Feel numb
Can't relax
Don't have many friends
Feel very tense

Can't say no
Never learn
Have a phobia about . . .
Feel misunderstood
Don't understand other people
Feel confused
Feel bored
Daydream
Feel lonely
Can't trust other people
Can't pass exams
Get over-promoted
Get irritated
Can't get round to . . .
Feel you have to be nice
Feel stupid
Think other people know best
Never get your own way
Feel nervous
Feel resentful
Feel misunderstood

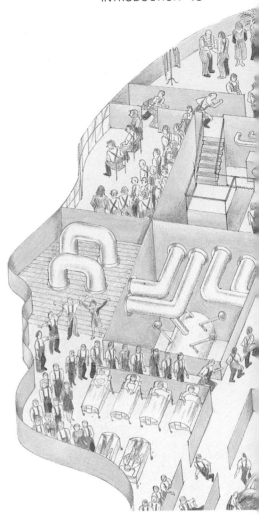

Changing your life

You will be more able to take charge of your own life, because you will begin to:

Accept your strengths and weaknesses.
Realize that other people are different.
Respond to other people with compassion, not criticism.
Accept your own body.
Know the limits to your health and energy.
Make good decisions.
Have more confidence.
Know what you want.
Solve problems effectively.
Make your own choices.
Listen without judging.
Fulfil more of your potential.
Get what you want.

Learn new skills.
Ignore put-downs.
Become more intelligent.
Become more balanced.
Improve your fitness.
Moderate extreme behaviour.
Improve your emotional competence.
Handle conflict more effectively.
Understand other people better.
Handle conflict and achieve win-win situations.
Present yourself well.
Know what you want out of life.
Enjoy more satisfying relationships.
Become more relaxed.
Enjoy life more.
Feel more alive.
Develop your creativity.
Open up new choices for yourself.
See what it's all about.

The Mind Gymnasium does not . . .

Tell you who or how you ought to be.
Invite you to compare yourself with other people.
Show you how to control other people.
Prescribe ideal forms of behaviour.
Support mental mastery.
Tell you how to conduct your life.
Diagnose success or failure.
Provide a ready-made technique for living.
Believe that some people are better than others.

SELF-ASSESSMENT

For many people, looking into themselves has an air of self-indulgence, of something that's not quite right. I disagree. Withdrawing into ourselves as a way of avoiding reality is always regrettable, of course, but there are times – during personal crises, for example – when even this can be necessary for survival. *The Mind Gymnasium* regards looking into ourselves as an honourable activity that is essential for personal wellbeing and growth.

Assessing ourselves is something we all do naturally all of the time. We notice whether we are happy, excited or bored, whether we are hot, cold, hungry or in danger. By monitoring ourselves in this way, we find out how well we are performing, we discover our likes and dislikes; we remind ourselves of what we have learned in the past and prepare ourselves to learn more in the future.

Yet we experience this self-assessing process as no more than an undercurrent in our thoughts. We tend to think of ourselves as stupid, mean or open-minded, for example, without noticing how or exactly when we form such opinions of ourselves. But this is not inevitable, as you will discover.

The benefits of assessing ourselves

We may be so used to being judged and criticized by others at home, at school or at work, that we feel other people's opinions of us are worth more than our own. But although other people may have useful comments to make about how we behave, or about the contents of our minds – whether, say, they find our conversation entertaining or interesting – only we ourselves can really know what is going on in our own minds. Our inner thoughts, images and feelings are unique, and forever private and inaccessible to others. So we are the ones best qualified to assess them.

The guiding principle of this book is that we have the potential to be the world expert on our own minds. This may involve a slight shift in responsibility, but it is a shift towards self-reliance and one that

How this chapter works
SELF-ASSESSMENT is made up of six parts – Personal history, Identity, Bodymind, Intelligence, Relating and Beliefs – each containing questions, feedback and action planning. The questions invite you to look within yourself, FEEDBACK shows you how you measure up, and ACTION PLAN suggests ways to improve. Together they set out to throw light on your dark corners, to get to know your brighter parts even better, and to identify your grey areas. Once you have identified which aspects of your mind need re-training, re-balancing or re-creating, you can begin to gain a more accurate perspective on any problems you may be experiencing, and decide what action to take.

happens quite readily. Learning how to make better use of our minds, working with them, understanding what they are like, how they work and how they interact with other people's minds, is a rigorous personal discipline that can lead to self-realization.

The old dependence on traditional patterns of behaviour to sustain good health and psychological security is crumbling. We now recognize, for instance, that containing our emotions is unhealthy, not a sign of strength. Understanding ourselves is a vital element of survival in a fast-changing, technological world. We urgently need to develop our capacity to 're-create' ourselves continuously in response to changing environmental and economic circumstances. Learning how to assess ourselves honestly and accurately is the first and the most essential stage in this.

The following six self-assessment sections invite you to take a realistic look at how your mind works and how it shapes your behaviour in all areas of life. And they offer practical suggestions about what you can do to 'change your mind' if and when you want to.

Self-assessment guidelines
Before you can decide what you are really like, you need some guidelines to measure yourself against. For instance, if you are working out how physically fit you are at the moment, your guidelines may be your pulse rate before and after exercise, and your weight in relation to your age, height and build. The next stage is to make an honest assessment of how you 'measure up'. Then you can decide what you want to do about it, and finally take some practical action – by, say, taking more exercise.

The secret of successful self-assessment is choosing the most appropriate guidelines. *The Mind Gymnasium* offers some suggestions that have proved effective for many people, but you may well want to adapt them to suit yourself. As you gain more experience of assessing yourself, you will soon find ways of devising your own.

How to use this chapter
The chapter is designed to be used in whatever order suits you – you can start where you like. You may want to work your way straight through all the self-assessments and the relevant feedback sections for a complete view of your strengths and weaknesses, before referring to more in-depth information in KNOWHOW or ideas for self-improvement in MIND GYM. Or you may like to follow up individual assessments by referring directly to KNOWHOW or MIND GYM as you go along, before coming back to the next self-assessment. If you want to start by looking up your own personal preoccupation, you may find the mini menu above a helpful way in. But however you choose to use the book, I suggest you clarify both your strengths and your weaknesses by noting them down as you discover them. To make sure you do not pass over your strong points, you could try listing them on a larger sheet of paper than the negative ones.

PERSONAL HISTORY

As we step across the threshold from childhood to adulthood, we carry forward, along with the genetic material of previous generations, their preferences and wishes too.

How to use this section

The following self-assessments will help you to begin to unravel your own personal history and to pinpoint which of your childhood survival strategies may be undermining your life as an adult. This book can help you make a start on this, but it's *your* history; unravelling it is something that ultimately only you can do. So plunge in and see what you come up with – it may be a pearl.

Work your way through the questions, taking as much time as you like and changing your mind as often as you like. When you have settled on a response, move on to FEEDBACK and make a note of anything significant you discover about yourself. Then continue to the ACTION PLAN and consider what, if anything, you want to do about your new view of yourself. If you do not find what you are looking for in this section, use the marginal references to direct you to another part of the book.

The very nature of human existence endows us all with some kind of burden or hurt, stemming from disappointment, loss or injury in the past. Our personal history – the unique collection of personal experiences during birth, childhood and adolescence – inevitably colours the way we act as adults. In fact, as you sit reading this now, the whole of your history is there too.

How your past affects your present

You don't have to be ill to admit to having awkward corners in your mind – everyone has them, and however much you suppress a part of your personality, it is likely to sneak out and surprise you when you least expect it. How do you identify these shadowy areas? They tend to emerge as an inexplicable anxiety or compulsion that doesn't seem to fit the situation, often as a recurring pattern of over-reacting or under-reacting. A tactless remark, a slight or a rejection, for example, may trigger a massive explosion of jealousy or anger, or a week of gloom and despair.

This kind of mystery has its roots in your childhood. When you were little and impressionable, you did what you had to do to survive in the family, at school and with friends. You learned that it was acceptable to act in some ways and not others, and many of these attitudes, opinions, likes and dislikes will have been carried over into adult life where they are no longer appropriate. This is inevitable, and the same for us all. Learning to smile your way through difficulties may have been the best way to win approval at the age of five, as one of a big family where there was no room for the finer nuances of feeling. But now, as an adult, if you smile through sadness, others may not trust you and you may not react appropriately when faced with a serious situation. There are as many different examples of the way the past affects the present as there are people.

The rewards of unravelling your personal history

Exploring your past can be one of the most rewarding things you will ever do. It can be profoundly liberating to recognize how many of the compulsions, inhibitions and distorted thought processes you suffer from today are a hangover from the past. What often happens is that when you unlock these aspects of your past life, it also releases joy and energy that belonged to that part of your life. Of course, just as your history took many years to accumulate, so unpicking it is not a quick or easy task, but the benefits are considerable. You will find a deeper sense of wellbeing, often better health, and, as you begin to uncover the patterns of your own past distress, you will find that it can be a very humanizing experience to begin to appreciate how much pain and hurt you share with other human beings. Perhaps most important of all, if you have children, you will be less likely to impose on them inappropriate attitudes that have carried over from your own childhood. For me, this is reason enough – to reduce the amount of unnecessary distress and pain that rolls down through a family from one generation to another.

SOCIAL BACKGROUND

Let's begin this exploration of your personal history by tracing the broad patterns of outside events that will have affected your state of mind as you grew up. For example, any small child in Northern Ireland or Beirut or New York in the last couple of decades will have absorbed a whole galaxy of attitudes and anxieties into the grain of their personality. The same is true for all places and all times, though some relics of the past may be easier to see than others. So keeping the enquiries broad (more personal questions will follow), look at the period of your life up to, say, age 16, bearing in mind that the earlier each event occurred, the more general its effects will be.

Consider whether you experienced as a child any of the circumstances shown here. Make a note of any that apply to you and how old you were. How did they affect your state of mind?

Economic background
Always short of money
More than enough money
Unskilled/skilled labour
Tradespeople
Professional employment
Private homes
Rented accommodation

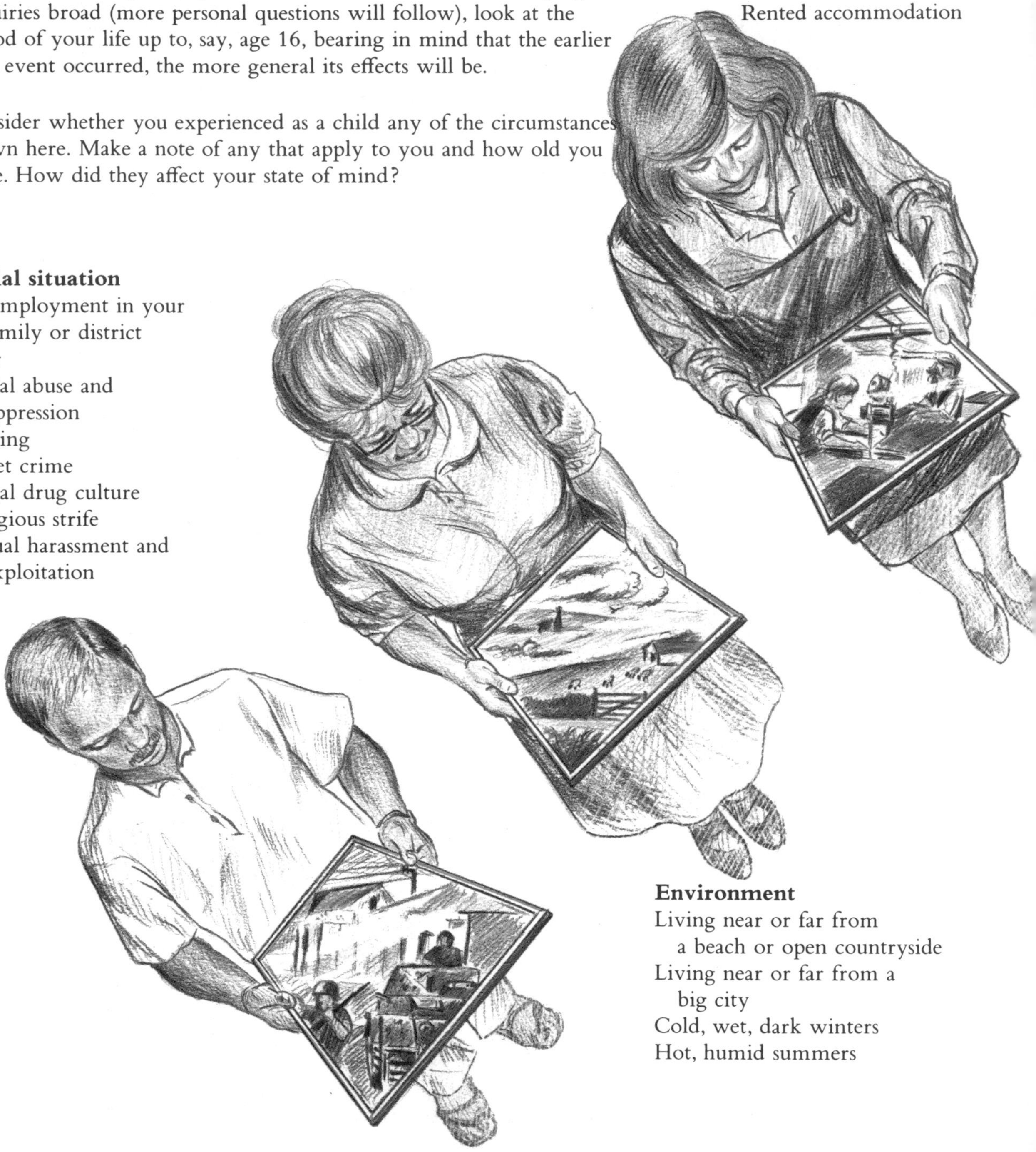

Social situation
Unemployment in your
    family or district
War
Racial abuse and
    oppression
Rioting
Street crime
Illegal drug culture
Religious strife
Sexual harassment and
    exploitation

Environment
Living near or far from
    a beach or open countryside
Living near or far from a
    big city
Cold, wet, dark winters
Hot, humid summers

School-life
Often changed homes and
  schools
Mostly the same home
  and school
Violence at school
Sent away to boarding
  school

Home
Lived mostly in a big
  city, small town or in the
  country
Could run out safely to
  play
Only child
One of a large family
Overcrowding in the home
Plenty of privacy

FEEDBACK
Think yourself back into each life event – one by one or however it seems to work for you – and consider how you dealt with these pressures as a child. There is no right or wrong way to do this. What you are looking for are the unique, personal adaptations you made to survive. Only you or people close to you are going to know what they are.

Here are some examples from my own experience. I was a young child in Britain during World War Two; scarcity and shortage were normal; survival meant learning 'not to want too much'. I grew up in a district where everyone I came across, almost without exception, worked for 'the company'. Survival meant learning that 'you can't do what you like in this life, you have to do what you are told'. Almost all our family friends and relatives were skilled craftpeople. Survival meant 'learning to be very clever and never needing to ask for help'.

Make a note of what you discover and keep it safe so that you can add to it, because often, once you have begun this kind of enquiry, new thoughts pop out later when you aren't expecting them. All the questions about personal history, including those that follow, are very interconnected, and you may find that you have a better idea of how to progress when you have worked through some of the later ones.

ACTION PLAN
Take time over the next few weeks to consider further how any of these life events may be still contributing to the texture or direction of your life. Take time to ask people from that period of your life how you reacted to any of the life events that may seem significant.

LOVING, UNDERSTANDING AND CHOOSING

A very useful way of assessing the relationship between childhood experience and adult behaviour has been put forward by the leading British humanistic psychologist, John Heron. He proposes that human infants have a remarkable, though undeveloped, potential for loving, understanding and choosing and for receiving these same qualities.

The following series of questions invites you to look at how far, when you were a child, your basic human capacities for loving, understanding and choosing were allowed to flourish. When you have considered each of them, move on to FEEDBACK to see how your childhood experiences may have affected your mind as an adult.

Loving

Loving others - *was your capacity to love others encouraged and supported?*

How far were you able to be really close to your mother and father or brothers and sisters?

Were you encouraged to develop close friendships outside the family?

Being loved – *was your capacity to be just who you are allowed full play?*

Were you prevented from going at your own pace as a child?

Were you allowed to make mistakes, to make a mess and be childish, or were you frequently criticized?

How well were you accepted as who you were?

Did you feel that you were not the child your parents had dreamed of, that you were the wrong sex, that you were unwanted or not as lovable as a brother or sister?

Did your parents make their love conditional on good behaviour?

Did you feel responsible if your parents argued?

Understanding

Understanding – *was your capacity to understand what was going on around you supported and encouraged?*

When you were little, did things often happen with no explanation, such as moving house?

Did you feel 'fobbed off' with unsatisfactory answers?

Were you prevented from playing with certain children without knowing why?

Did you never understand what sex was all about or why it was bad to be naked?

Did you often not know why you were punished?

Being understood – *was your capacity to make yourself understood supported?*

Did you have trouble making yourself understood because of your accent, a foreign language or a speech impediment?

Did people give you enough time to explain?

Did your school friends come from a very different social or financial background?

Did you have difficulties that you were too shy to explain or which no one tried to understand?

Choosing

Choosing for yourself – *was your capacity to be self-directing, to make choices for yourself encouraged and supported?*

Did your parents interfere with or control your choice of friends or clothes?

Did your parents make you learn a musical instrument against your wishes?

Did your parents closely control where you went and with whom? Were you over-protected?

Did your attempts to make your own way in the world raise a lot of anxiety in your parents?

Have you always felt that the pattern of your life was pre-ordained by family traditions?

Being chosen – *was your capacity to be chosen by others supported and encouraged?*

When gangs were being formed or groups were getting together to go on visits, play sport or perform plays, or when jokes were told, were you often not included?

When there were perks to be had in class or around the neighbourhood, did they always seem to go to someone else?

Did you feel you were never noticed?

FEEDBACK

If, because of the demands of life, parents or circumstances, your potential for love, understanding or choice gets rejected, blocked or ignored, then emotional distress patterns are likely to be stored in the body's memory. This 'unfinished business' from childhood influences the way you behave, and the choices you make, as an adult.

Love

If, through lack of love, you were never fully accepted for who you were or never had your love accepted, then distress in the form of grief or sorrow will be stored in your bodymind.

Understanding

If, from a lack of understanding during childhood, you never really knew what was going on, if your life was subject to peremptory and inexplicable changes or if you could never get people to listen to and understand your needs, then distress in the form of anxiety, fear or even terror will be laid down in your bodymind.

Choosing

If your parents could never let you choose for yourself, if you were constantly deprived of the opportunity for self-direction as a child or if you were rarely or never selected, then the corresponding distress recordings in your bodymind are likely to be anger, rage, frustration and resentment.

Note: These are, of course, simply rules of thumb, but in practice they prove to be a very useful guide for working out the connection between present difficulties and childhood experience. Take your time and consider how this fits with your own personal experience. The case histories (see pp. 24-5) illustrate how this scheme actually works.

ACTION PLAN

If you often feel anxious or resentful or sad for no apparent reason, or if letting your mind scan across these parts of your history leaves you feeling upset, then something in your past may be living on into the present. It's useful to regard these feelings as an opportunity for healing old hurts. Give yourself permission to feel whatever it is that comes up and to choose to direct it into positive action. If, for example, you can trace inexplicable 'upwellings' of resentment back to events in your past, you will be more likely to be able to transform this resentment into positive energy.

Plan to take time to look in more detail at any feelings that don't seem to be connected with the present. See if you can trace them back to your childhood. Ask yourself who, when, where and what they remind you of. Other items in this section may give you some clues.

CASE STUDY

Loving

Robert grew up in a family where all the children were cared for meticulously. They never went short of anything; nevertheless, it was not the sort of household where emotions were expressed very freely. Robert had always struggled to be a good boy and do as his parents wanted. But whatever he did, it never seemed to be enough and he found himself in frequent conflict with his father who ruled the household very strictly.

When Robert married, his wife Judy complained that he was cold and unresponsive. He felt that this was unfair because he did everything she asked of him and they were never short of money. She wanted children. He didn't. Her criticism threw him into longer and longer silences. Eventually his resentment at her complaints and her dissatisfaction with his coolness and distance led to a crisis in which Judy abruptly left him.

When Robert was able to take the time to look at what had been happening, he realized that, although he had been a 'good husband', who had provided all the material needs of the marriage, he had been recreating the home life that he had grown up with.

He began to see that, while everything in his childhood had been very comfortable and 'reasonable', there had also been a deluge of criticism. Neither he nor his sisters had had any chance of being themselves. They had been forced to fit into the moulds, and even the careers, which their parents had diligently prepared for them. Robert came to see that his coolness and lack of warmth reflected the almost complete lack of love from his parents. They had given him everything materially that he needed, but not love, acceptance, permission to make mistakes, to go at his own pace or to be himself.

In the absence of his wife, Robert's silences pulled him into a further crisis, as his sense of lost love surfaced as sorrow and deep sadness. During this crisis, which to other eyes seemed like a nervous breakdown, Judy returned to care for Robert. As she saw how much Robert had melted and softened, this led to a reconciliation and a new beginning for both of them.

CASE STUDY

Understanding

When Jenny was very small her mother died, and not long afterwards her father disappeared, leaving her in the care of her kindly granny. Jenny had never known why her mother had died, she had just been told that 'her mummy had gone to heaven and wouldn't be coming back' and to 'dry her tears now like a good little girl'. Nor did she know why her father had disappeared. Her granny had simply told her that he was 'working away from home' and this is what she told her school friends. After a few years, when her questions about her father continued to be dismissed with a kindly 'don't worry your head about him', she became increasingly anxious. She didn't like to be in the dark. She slept with the light on. She came straight home from school every day, even when there were things to do and friends to play with, because she had to be sure that her granny was still there.

As a young teenager, Jenny discovered that her father was living in the same city and always had been. She was very upset, because she couldn't understand why her father had never made contact with her or her granny. When Jenny was in her early twenties her granny fell ill and she began to have severe panic attacks. Then her granny died, and at the funeral she discovered that throughout her childhood, her granny had been in regular touch with her father. After the funeral, her attacks became so disabling that she had to seek help.

Over the next couple of years, with the help of a youth leader with counselling experience, she gradually built up a list of events in her life. She found that the common denominator was that she had not understood what was happening to her. She gradually came to see that being uncertain about what was happening in the present tended to remind her of the old feelings of not understanding what was happening to her as a small child and awakened the full force of her childhood fears.

Eventually, as she was able to come to terms with the old fears and to deal with the anger she felt at having been deceived, the panic attacks receded. And while she was still prone to anxiety, she was able to take charge of her life, to make her own decisions, and began to build a career, training to become an interior designer.

CASE STUDY

Choosing

In her early thirties, Amanda was becoming increasingly gloomy and had been described by her doctor as depressed. Her work as a journalist, which had been going very well for ten years, was now lurching from crisis to crisis. Her talents as a writer and an investigator of corporate scandals, in which she specialized, were increasingly at the mercy of a less useful talent for quarrelling with her editors and quitting in high dudgeon.

The more she became regarded as touchy, the less people hired her and the more she felt the articles she wrote had to become big stories. A series of relationships fell apart in the same way as her work. Her gloom and lack of energy gradually took her further and further into crisis. The stories she wrote were usually denunciations, investigative reporting of corruption, but now the big hit was harder to find and she often didn't feel she had the energy even to get out of the house.

The overdose never had a chance to work because at least two people had picked up the surreptitious signals that something was about to happen and had been taking care to check up on how she was. When she was well enough to meet people again, a friend introduced her, despite considerable scepticism, to a women's support group that was meeting in the neighbourhood. Over the next year, Amanda increasingly found this a safe place in which to try to look at how she could have come to want to destroy herself. The answers she came up with pointed first to how angry she was. It leaked out everywhere. She came to see herself as a disaster looking for somewhere to happen.

The hardest thing for her to accept was the damage that her father, who she idolized, had done in the name of good parenting. As she and the other women in the group shared their concerns and their history, Amanda came to appreciate that, as a child, her life had been extraordinarily circumscribed. She had never been able to choose her friends or her clothes, her toys or her dolls. Her father, a middle management corporate executive, was a brilliant organizer who had applied his skills as thoroughly to his wife and children at home as he did to his working life.

Amanda's career had been his idea. Despite her mother's protests, he had chosen her apartment for her and paid for the furniture which a friend of his had got at a discount. For years he had passed his car on to her when he bought a new one. 'It makes good sense' he'd always said. She had been forced to learn to play the piano. She had sweated through years of Italian and Russian, his choice of foreign languages. She had gone to a university where he knew the Vice-Chancellor and had again been able to get a good deal – 'it made sense'.

As she built up the catalogue of over-control, she began to see how much of it had been for *him*. She saw how she had made herself the kind of girl of whom he could be proud, who he could show off to his friends, who he could admire, who was grateful to him for all he had given her. All the angry feelings that she had previously turned in on herself now broke out in the safe custody of her women friends, as the rage she had felt as a child surged through into the light of day.

It was hard at first to feel fury at a man she loved. But then her depression vanished. She knew she was on to something. The rage and resentment at having been moulded like an object to suit someone's whim was gradually – with difficulty at first, but eventually with more assurance – channelled into her work in the form of energy and she picked up the threads of journalism again. And there were new kinds of stories too. About women and women's lives.

Now, some years later, her father has heart trouble and doesn't walk very well. He has occasionally let slip that he feels very, very tired. Amanda sees him most months. She's been surprised to find that, apart from the occasional twinge of irritation when the childhood father tries to get back into harness, what she feels for him now, as she sees his strength receding, is mostly sadness.

LIFE EVENTS

Another way of assessing how far your emotional potential has been supported or denied in your upbringing is to look at the key events in your early life. Think back to how you reacted at the time and consider what influence these survival strategies (see pp. 28-35) may be having on your present life.

Starting at a point in your late teens or early twenties, look back over the whole of your life and make a list of the events. Be sure to include times when you were very happy, when you suffered pain, separation, loss, violence or when you remember particularly strong reactions from your parents, if that's possible. Here is an example of the kind of list you might make: broken leg; grandma moved to Canada; changed schools; horrible new teacher; brother left home; parents started having rows; moved house.

Take your time to make your list and be sure to go right back to when you were very little. This may mean checking with your parents. You might also like to ask other people who know you well what they would put on your list. When you have finished, get some idea of how each of them have affected your life.

Human behaviour is so complex that there are unlikely to be any one-to-one causes between past events and present behaviour. You are more likely to find an accumulation of influences.

Sunken memories

Just as a stone falling into water makes a brief disturbance, then slips from view but remains below the water surface, so our most significant traumas appear to vanish from memory. To survive, we forget them, but in later life they re-surface as out-of-scale reactions. One way of dealing with present-time distress is to recover the detail and feelings of our past life through patient detective work.

Making waves

Like rocks in the path of a stream, early traumatic experiences set up a pattern of emotional reactions that permeate adult life. The earlier the event, the deeper and the more widespread its effect will be.

Deflected pain

If you feel that the waters of your childhood were calm and unruffled, that nothing traumatic enough to have significantly distorted your behaviour happened, consider whether you may be imposing these survival decisions on other people or on your children.

FEEDBACK

Here, and in the following eight pages, you will find some examples of how the strategy chosen to survive an event in childhood can affect adult behaviour. These examples are intended to stimulate your mind to explore its own origins, so beware of too literal a connection between the material here and your own life. If something on your list does not appear, look for survival decisions and behaviour that most closely match your own situation. But as soon as something 'clicks', take hold of it and follow it through. It may well relieve you of a lot of unnecessary stress.

AT ANY AGE

Sexual abuse

Sexual abuse – defined as sexual contact or threat of sexual contact with an element of coercion, which cannot be based on equality or reciprocity because of age differences or of close family relations – is likely to colour the whole of your personality.

Survival decisions

The survival decisions include detachment – forgetting about it; secrecy – choosing to detach the knowledge from other people; presuming that you are the cause of the abuse because you are bad or wicked; presuming that everyone else is bad and will try to hurt or abuse you. These childhood survival decisions may continue into adult life as secretiveness, using sex as a weapon, lots of 'one night stands', lack of openness about sex, actually behaving as though you were 'bad' and 'wicked' or avoiding contact, particularly intimate contact, with other people as far as possible.

Separation from one or both parents

Separation for any reason will have left a long shadow, and, to reverse a common saying, the earlier the worse. The effects on your later life will vary according to the length of the separation, who was with you during it, how early it was and of course how long you were separated. One extreme form of separation is death of both of your parents. Further along the scale is hospitalization for weeks or months. But any separation, the loss of someone you were fond of, even being lost at a big public event or in a department store, can be significant for later adult behaviour.

Survival decisions

The response to loss is first protest – shouting, screaming and crying – then despair, then detachment and dissociation. The survival decision is likely to include hanging on, clinging to what you do have. For this reason alone, childhood separation may make departures and endings, whether of jobs or relationships, very difficult to handle in adult life. Others may feel you are sad, melancholic and withdrawn, due to the grief you carry with you.

Going into hospital

In recent years it has become easier for parents to stay close to small children in hospital and some unnecessary operations have been abandoned. However, the separation that a stay in hospital causes, with or without major medical intervention, appears to generate particularly problematic survival decisions in a child.

Survival decisions

Again the survival decision is likely to be detachment. Bravery, not crying, not being upset, stoicism or being patient are rewarded and admired. As a response to traumatic circumstances, all these are likely to mean dissociation, not feeling. In later life this decision may leave you vulnerable to anything which evokes the buried feelings – the whiff of anaesthetic, or disinfectant, wounds, blood, bandages and so on or to a separation that reminds you of the earlier event.

Abuse/non-accidental injury

Non-accidental injury tends to be associated with parents who unconsciously need to be looked after by their children. When the child fails to fulfil this role, the adult lashes out. Parents who secretly feel that they are incapable of looking after their children may also be led to injure them, so as to get their children, indirectly, the care they need and themselves the attention they crave.

Survival decisions

If you were injured deliberately by your parents, your survival decision may have been to learn not to feel, to suppress your rage or to believe that you were to blame and in some way 'bad' or 'wrong'.

Going to boarding school

If you were sent to boarding school as a child, you may have developed a habit of not feeling as an adult. The separation from home, family, friends, neighbourhood, dolls, toys or bikes and the loss of freedom, all at once, probably forced you into making a whole array of survival decisions.

Survival decisions

This again usually seems to involve learning to conceal feelings, keeping a stiff upper lip, toughness, and drawing warmth and solace from whoever you are close to – which favours homosexual activity.

Being sent to a single-sex boys' boarding school probably also meant a survival decision about women – either to idealize them or to regard them as distant inferiors to be manipulated and controlled.

Being sent to a single-sex girls' school could have resulted in a survival decision about men, leading you to regard them either as protective and fatherly or perhaps as rather dangerous animals, with alarming sexual instincts.

Distressed parents

Growing up in a home where one or both of your parents was very distressed, addicted to drugs, alcoholic or mentally ill presents very severe survival problems.

Survival decisions

If you responded by assuming that children are there to look after their parents, the inappropriate giving you did as a child may now leave you empty and very vulnerable, with no strength to cope with your own difficulties. If the demands on you as a child were very heavy, you may have been left with such a big vacuum that life becomes a nightmare of panic attacks, resentments, jealousies and despair. Alternatively, you may have become very competitive and keen to achieve.

Similarly, growing up with parents who were constantly overwhelmed by their problems may lead you to decide that survival means caring for 'lame dogs'. In adult life this decision may result in self-neglect and the choice of partners who are unable to give in return.

PUBERTY TO LATE TEENS

Parental anxiety at puberty

If sex was a problem for either of your parents, say your father if you are a woman, then your becoming a woman – a sexual being, someone who could become pregnant – is likely to have aroused very deep feelings in him. Apparently reasonable protectiveness, such as caring about where you were going and with whom, may at this age have turned into a compulsively protective shield that distanced you from him.

Survival decisions

This kind of reaction to your femininity is unlikely to have reassured you about the virtues of becoming a woman, although of course it would depend on what other support you had. The amount of coercion used will also have been significant. If you felt pressurized, you may have responded with lying and deception. This survival decision may then repeat itself in adult relationships, if coercion arises.

Parental disapproval of sex

In many families, sex has always been, and still remains, taboo. If everything to do with sex in your family was tinged with disgust or was perceived as dirty, prohibited, nasty, shameful or rude, so that sex was equated with excretion, this may have distorted your view of your body.

Survival decisions

You may have come to see your body as disgusting, shameful and unmentionable. You may also regard your mind as being of a purer substance. Taken a stage further, you may have come to feel that you are personally disgusting and shameful, and as a result, you may decide to detach yourself from your body and go off to live in your mind.

This is recognizable in a tendency to neglect your body – eating junk food, taking drugs, smoking a lot – while being fascinated by highly intellectual pursuits. This may be how you survived the idea that your body was, if not 'bad', then at least some kind of inconvenience.

SCHOOL 4 TO 12

Falling behind at school

If a key life event for you was failing at school, perhaps because of unsympathetic teachers, your survival decision is likely to have taken one of two forms.

Survival decisions

You may have rejected education, learning and study or you may have accepted the failure as an accurate reflection of your ability. As a result, you may have set your personal ambition thermostat according to this view and believe that you are not clever, not talented, not bright. If you knew you were bright but couldn't somehow connect with school work, then your survival decision may have been rebellion. Whichever it was, check out the Intelligence section (see pp. 66-81) for how it might have happened and what you can do about it.

Changing schools frequently

Changing schools means losing friends and making new ones – both very stressful activities. If it happened a lot, you would have had a great deal of grief to cope with and your survival response is likely to have depended on the capacity of those people around you to allow you to be upset.

Survival decisions

If others insisted that you were brave and strong, your survival decision may have been to be distant, shy or diffident and to learn not to feel the loss. This would have made it harder to approach people around you willingly and openly to make new friends and ultimately may have led to a loss of confidence. Alternatively, you may have learned to constantly put on a performance, in order to earn acceptance and approval.

Bullying by staff or others

Learning how to deal with force seems to be one of the key things that we learn at school.

Survival decisions

There appear to be only a few choices of response – to become part of the dominant group, to learn to submit to the dominant group, to learn how to placate or appease the dominant group or to find some way of avoiding the power issue altogether. If you consider what your school-day approach to power was, you will very likely find that that early decision is re-enacted when power issues arise.

Threatened abandonment

If you were repeatedly threatened with statements like 'I'll go away and leave you . . . and never come back', then you were faced with a difficult choice.

Survival decisions

You may have decided that your only way out was to become a 'very good boy' or 'very good girl' who does exactly what he or she is told. You may have also concluded that you really were very 'naughty' or 'bad', for your parents to have made such a threat. Or you may have decided that all adults are bad and unreliable.

Tense, anxious parent or guardian

If your mother, father or guardian felt insecure, they may have leaned on you as a child for support. To survive, you probably learned that you had to care for your mother or father. But too much giving to others, at a time when you needed the strength for yourself, tends to deprive you of a strong sense of self.

Survival decisions

This can lead to compulsively caring for others in adult life, so that you become vulnerable to burnout and collapse.

Cruel and unusual punishments

Being frequently punished until you submit and break down either angrily or coldly, without anger or emotion, can take many forms. You may have been locked in the dark, deprived of food, tied to a chair until you ate your dinner or forced to be absolutely silent for hours on end.

Survival decisions

Survival here is likely to involve detaching yourself from the pain, hurt and fear of the experience, so that you forget it. You may have detached yourself by going off into dreams of being someone else or being somewhere else, perhaps becoming very clever at something like mathematics, music, philosophy or science, so that you could literally inhabit a world entirely of your own making.

The survival behaviour that made sense in childhood may of course seem very bizarre and alarming in adult life. If, for example, you were very successful at surviving these extremes of pain and hurt as a child, as an adult you might find yourself dismissing other people's pain. Paradoxically, you may have become exactly the person you most feared as a child, someone who will tend to bully and use excessive force to get your own way. It is because you have 'forgotten' your own hurt – or defended yourself against it by being tough – that you may find yourself able to do these things.

Neglect

Neglect can take many forms, including not being fed, clothed, housed or kept clean or not being given love, physical contact or attention.

Survival decisions

You may have survived this through deciding that you were undeserving, not good enough to merit proper care or even that you were the cause of the neglect. This can manifest itself in later life as very low self-esteem and a belief that you are a 'bad' person or 'wrong' in some fundamental way.

Excessive criticism

Being repeatedly criticized and put down by your parents, even if the criticism was caringly stated, is perhaps one of the most common and problematic life events children suffer.

Survival decisions

The survival decision that eventually emerges from incessant criticism is acceptance that something is wrong with you, that your opinions don't count, your actions are ineffective, your behaviour is objectionable and your ideas are worthless.

The effect in adult life is likely to be a poor sense of self-esteem, shyness and a lack of confidence, or sometimes a brash 'superiority'. Through sheer repetition, the parental oppressor's voice may have become built in to you as a pathological inner critic. In later life, this critical voice takes every opportunity to sabotage whatever you are doing, telling you that 'it isn't going to work', that 'whatever you do won't be enough'.

Favouritism

If you picked up the impression, or were repeatedly told, that your brothers or sisters were preferred to you, this is highly likely to have shaped aspects of your adult behaviour.

Survival decisions

One survival decision may have been just to accept the inferiority, so that in later life you came to have a chip on your shoulder. Alternatively, you may have survived denigration by seeking your parents' attention in any number of ways, including throwing tantrums, becoming a comedian or a performer, making a mess, tasting petty crime. Anything that reliably restored you to the centre of your parents' attention could have become your survival raft.

Humiliation

If, as a child, you were humiliated, shamed, ridiculed or embarrassed – either intentionally to control your behaviour or accidentally through insensitivity, carelessness or through the viciousness of a parent or teacher – this will have affected your view of yourself.

Survival decisions

Your survival decision is likely to have been to take the shame or humiliation on yourself, perhaps even to see it as something you caused, because you thought you were 'bad'.

Later, if it continued or the humiliation appeared to be unfair or unjust, your survival decision may have shifted towards swallowing the hurt and injustice. You may have encapsulated it in silent fury: inner statements, such as 'just you wait . . .' 'one day . . .' Other common reactions include blaming other people for the pain the humiliation has caused you and even inflicting the pain on your surroundings through vandalism or aggression.

Pressure for premature development

Being coerced into walking, talking, eating or toilet training before you are ready, can cause problems.

Survival decisions

You are likely to feel clumsy or accident-prone, since your muscular co-ordination may have been learned out of sequence, and you may feel 'wrong' in some way. To survive, you are likely to have learned that to get on in this family and in life, you have to be clever and try harder. You may feel that nothing is ever good enough.

Rejection by peers

If you were persistently rejected by your peers because you were 'different' – for example, black, disabled, from a different economic background or the 'wrong' sex – then this is likely to have had a profound effect on the rest of your life.

Survival decisions

You are likely to have survived this kind of rejection by resorting to flattery, bribery, lying, being very entertaining or becoming detached. These survival decisions are likely to have carried over into your adult behaviour.

EARLY MONTHS AND PRE-SCHOOL

Illness

Serious illness at an early age, particularly if it felt life-threatening and involved a stay in hospital, presents a small child with a formidable challenge.

Survival decisions

You may have survived by shutting off or 'smiling through', or, if the original illness was very severe, deciding not to feel. Either is likely to have left its mark in later responses. If you over-react now to being ill or imagining that you are, then you may find the roots in your early experience of illness.

Other decisions in this area are to believe that 'people can't be trusted', to feel angry at being left in hospital by your parents, to absorb your parents' anxieties about your illness without understanding what they are based on, and never to understand what is happening to you. Both types of survival decision tend to lead to accumulated distress such as anxiety, or even fear and terror, if the original illness was very severe.

Feeding difficulties

Early feeding difficulties, such as premature weaning, can provoke a number of survival decisions, including thumb-sucking and nail-biting.

Survival decisions

In adult life these early survival decisions may surface as smoking, gum-chewing, over-eating and being fussy about food. You may have also decided that 'you will never get what you need'.

Lack of bonding

If there was no consistent adult with whom to bond, then you may find commitment and intimacy a continuing area of difficulty.

Survival decisions

Your survival decision may revolve around beliefs, such as 'People aren't to be trusted' or 'I won't ever get what I need'.

BIRTH

'Normal' birth

Whatever your personal history, being born is one life event you share with everyone else. Research in recent decades underlines the view that we all experience being born as a life-threatening event.

The fully grown foetus, which has filled the available space for several weeks, is suddenly compressed even further and then propelled by the mother's contractions through the birth canal. As the moment of birth approaches, the tremendous contractions and squeezing of the baby into and through the birth canal present an enormous challenge to the new human. And it has only one chance to get it right.

Survival decisions

Faced with a life-or-death threat, the foetal body system responds to it, but as the threat continues, the 'pain' – the body's response of rising temperature, metabolic rate and heart rate – reaches a point where it would result in death. The human organism has a fail-safe protection which splits off the experience of this pain from consciousness, so that survival is assured. This is the most basic of all survival decisions. It's built into us and it seems likely that later survival decisions emerge from it. It surfaces in day-to-day experience through statements like 'I just don't want to know', 'in one ear and out the other', 'I just switch off', 'forget it'.

Premature birth

If you were born earlier than expected, there may have been difficulties in bonding due to early weeks in relative isolation.

Survival decisions

In adult life, your response to this early lack of bonding may include lack of trust and uncertainty about commitment.

Caesarean birth

This kind of birth lacks the long and very intense stimulation of the skin of normal birth.

Survival decisions

In later life this may leave you with a feeling that you are never ready and a persistent need for physical contact and stroking.

Difficult birth

The more protracted and life-threatening your birth, the more you will be likely to carry the pain around with you.

Survival decisions

In adult life, this pain may emerge as physical tension, confusion, claustrophobia, tics, foot-tapping, panic attacks, and restlessness. You may have also decided that survival means not feeling.

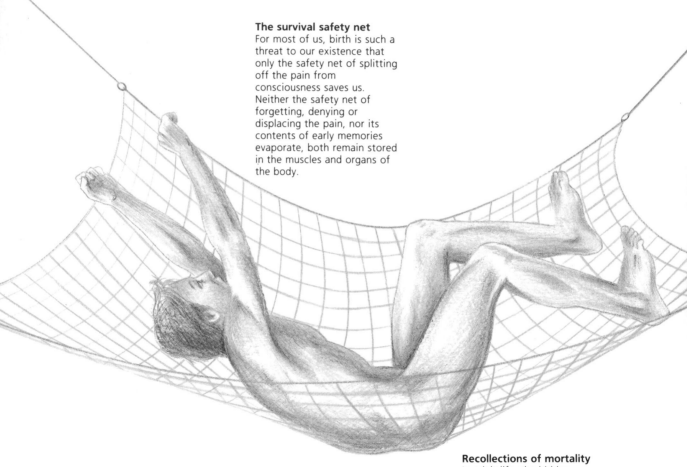

The survival safety net
For most of us, birth is such a threat to our existence that only the safety net of splitting off the pain from consciousness saves us. Neither the safety net of forgetting, denying or displacing the pain, nor its contents of early memories evaporate, both remain stored in the muscles and organs of the body.

Recollections of mortality
In adult life, the hidden memories of birth and the safety net which saved us from them can be reactivated. A present-time event – being crushed by a crowd, trapped in an underground train, locked in a room that echoes the early life-threatening situation – may trigger some of the early feelings of terror.

BEFORE BIRTH

Even during an untraumatic pregnancy, a foetus has intermittent negative experiences caused by occasional shortages of oxygen. But if the mother also smokes, uses drugs, is continually anxious or angry because of threats or marital discord, the foetus will be even more stressed, adding to the overload of birth when it eventually comes. A possible reaction is for the foetus to learn to handle these feelings, by learning not to feel.

Survival decisions

If, in the months and years following birth, threats to the infant continue, he or she is likely to deal with them in the same way – by forgetting, learning not to feel hurt, frightened or alone. To jump on to adult life, after two decades of repeating this survival decision, you are likely to be out of touch with your feelings, to appear hard-headed, thick-skinned and insensitive or you may cling to other people because you feel bad.

Very early experience is a model for dealing with difficult later life events. An early style of defence against hurt and pain seems to form a core around which other defences against feeling increasingly attach themselves as we get older.

ACTION PLAN

Learn to become more aware of your past experiences and how they may be affecting your adult behaviour. You are already making a start by working through this book, but unpicking your life history, although rewarding, can be a long and often arduous task. You will find that the guidance of other people who have been through it themselves, say a skilled counsellor or therapist, can help to speed up the process.

Reassess your attitudes to people in power, and begin to see how you can strive for change at work, in your neighbourhood, state or nation. Laying the ghost of your personal history can be dramatically energizing in terms of political and personal effectiveness. Look to see how you can share power with others rather than accepting dominant or subordinate positions. You may have a false start here and there, but that's OK. It won't be quick, it won't be easy and the horizon may recede from time to time as you make progress. But that's OK too. That's life. So take a risk.

IDENTITY

Concealing feelings of vulnerability behind a mask of superior wisdom or smiling detachment, can come to be one of the major functions of some people's identity.

How to use this section
The following self-assessments will enable you to survey the catalogue of opinions that may have become set in your personality and to pinpoint any that are weakening your health, happiness or effectiveness. The guidelines for assessing your identity focus on the core issues – social identity, personal potential, work, life changes, body image, self-esteem, inner criticism and other people's labels. These are aspects of the mind that many of us find difficult, but they are also the most susceptible to change. The aim is to give an overall impression of the influences that shape and direct the way you feel about yourself, to hold up a mirror that reflects an honest picture of those parts of your mind that are hard to distinguish in the day-to-day rush. This will give you a chance to let go of any that no longer fit or that limit you.

Work your way through each set of questions, taking as much time as you need to think each one through, and changing your mind as often as you like. When you have built up a clear picture of yourself, move on to FEEDBACK and ACTION PLAN and note down what you aim to do about it. If you do not find yourself reflected here, use the marginal references to direct you to another part of the book.

Your personal identity is how you see, feel and think about yourself. It is that unique collection of opinions about yourself and the world that you carry around with you. This identity is always with you; it is woven into your personality. Even if you moved to a different country and culture, and had a complete change of life style, it would be very slow to change.

As you develop through childhood and adolescence, your ability to make decisions, to assess situations, to form relationships and to communicate with other people expands. The ways in which you learn to respond to the opportunities, pressures and difficulties that come your way become a rich mixture of attitudes, habits and opinions which together make up your personal identity. And this identity becomes combined with the genetic attributes you inherited from your parents. Your own personal sense of identity may include innocuous attitudes, such as 'I'm not very athletic' or 'I'm not very adventurous', as well as opinions that make you feel stuck or paralysed, such as 'I'm stupid'. And these labels are often unintentionally perpetuated by other people – by family or friends who brand you as 'bright', 'unsociable' or 'strong'. You cannot avoid this accumulation of beliefs about yourself – we all have them.

How your identity affects your life
The biggest single reason for looking at your ingrained views of yourself is that they are intimately connected to how much choice you feel you have in your life. For example, if you have frequently been criticized as being careless or clumsy, this may have solidified into an attitude of mind, which says that you-as-a-person are careless or clumsy. But the reality may be that, just like anyone else, you drop or lose things from time to time. An attitude or opinion that convinces you that you are careless or clumsy rules out the possibility of change, so that becoming dexterous will be a choice that won't seem open to you. If you can identify any aspects of your personality which may be counter-productive in this way, you can begin to do something about them. But if you are unaware that you are running around with a personality throbbing with a rich mix of self-defeating attitudes, then you are likely to continue to feel undermined.

A second reason for looking at your identity is to demystify some of the beliefs that surround it. For example, is identity fixed? Can it change? The answer is it can change, over time. As the world changes around you and you respond as best you can, there will inevitably be times when the identity you have accumulated up to that point fails to match new opportunities and you find yourself having to change. This is a common, and essential, phase of human development. Going to 'big school', reaching puberty, leaving home, starting a new job, becoming a parent and so on all involve some reshaping of identity. This may occasionally be problematic enough to amount to 'an identity crisis' until your old identity has evolved ways of handling the demands of a new situation.

SOCIAL IDENTITY

To some extent, we all define ourselves by our race, our nationality, our religion, our sex, the socially useful roles we play and the groups we join. Looking at the roles you have already taken on and those you are preparing or planning for is another way of discovering how much you are making of yourself. You may decide that you are already taking on as much as you need to.

Your roles

Draw a circle and write in it the social identity you were born with. This could include your race, sex, nationality, parents' social status, physical characteristics and position in the family.

Now draw a second circle around the first and write in it the roles of *responsibility* you have acquired – those that bring commitment and restriction, as well as privilege. You benefit from the status of the position because you are appointed, qualified or elected, but at the same time you are restrained from acting freely. These could include, for example, wife, husband, company director, doctor, nurse, lawyer, parent, policeman or policewoman, committee chairperson, priest,

Inherited roles

Roles of responsibility

Chosen roles

Role playing
Within a lifetime, we all perform a variety of roles (right). The central, most basic ones we are born with, others we acquire as badges of merit, and the rest we choose for ourselves. For a secure sense of identity, we need a good balance between our different roles. If one begins to take up most of the space in our lives, our personality can become cramped and fragmented.

professor, social worker, soldier, manager, judge, criminal, youth leader or therapist.

Now draw a third circle enclosing the other two and write in this ring the names of the independent roles that you play – those that are largely based on skill. These could include vocational or leisure interests that you can take up and put down. In principle, anyone can have as many of them as they choose. Occupational roles could include taxi driver, shop assistant, researcher or electrician and leisure roles might include golfer, amateur athlete, do-it-yourself enthusiast or gardener.

Now think about each role and how it has shaped your view of yourself. How does each role make you feel? Consider how your roles relate to each other. How do you choose your roles? Do you have a role that blocks other roles? How do roles you plan to take on 'sit' with what you already have? Look at how you indicate to other people that you have taken on a new role. Look at what roles are tied to a particular time of day or week. Look at what happens when someone doesn't acknowledge your role. If they don't defer to you, do you negotiate and modify your attempt at superiority?

FEEDBACK

The roles we have accumulated greatly influence our sense of identity. What we often tend to do is to compartmentalize ourselves in our relationships, so that we only allow people to see us in one role at a time. A teacher, for example, may also be a parent, musician, householder and magistrate, but may restrict many relationships to an impersonal level, so that most people only see the teacher.

Roles of responsibility seem to be the most problematic, because they lend support to a fragile or insecure identity. In late adolescence, becoming a lawyer or a nurse can provide a global solution to not knowing what to make of your life. What you won't be able to see at that point is how much ordinary experience you will miss, because of the way that roles of responsibility block others. This can be seen very clearly in the lives of media megastars for whom life is a mixture of extreme privilege and extreme restraint. All general roles involve some version of the megastar situation. So if you are very ambitious or greedy for fame, watch out!

ACTION PLAN

If you feel your roles are ruling your life, look to see if you could drop some of your responsibilities and take on more enjoyable roles. If you feel a gap in your sense of identity, consider what other roles you would like, and what it would take to get them.

PERSONAL POTENTIAL

First let's look at your own individual qualities and talents and how far you have developed them.

Skills and achievements

Starting today and going back to when you were a child, make a list of your main personal achievements. They might include, for example, qualifications, business initiatives, artistic work, skills, relationships and personal change.

When you have made your list, go back over it and see if you can qualify each item – did you do it for the glory or for yourself as a person? Now look at the balance between them. How many were for 'doing' and how many for 'being'?

FEEDBACK

Whatever you do, all achievements large or small contribute to your sense of self-worth. And it matters how you value your achievements. If you tend to base your sense of personal value on material success and a utilitarian approach to achievement, then don't be surprised if you feel upset at the prospect of failure or anxious that you may be rejected. Also, if the balance between internal and external achievement strongly favours the external, you are likely to be cut off from your body messages and so divorced from your feelings. Feelings tell you the value of what you are doing. If you aren't listening to them, you may drift into a way of life that may be busy and productive but not in your best long-term interests. Conversely, if your achievements are balanced strongly in favour of 'being' rather than 'doing', then you may find yourself over-dependent on others for material support. There is no ideal way of balancing 'being' and 'doing', but bear in mind that a sustained imbalance will eventually lead to difficulties.

ACTION PLAN

Take time to look at how competitive you are. Does achievement mean 'winning'? Do you despise people who reject 'doing' as 'losers'? Take time to listen to what you feel is worthwhile for you, independent of its immediate economic or social usefulness. Take time to weigh up all your external achievements. You might well discover that you have done enough and that it's time to concentrate on 'being' the person you would like to be.

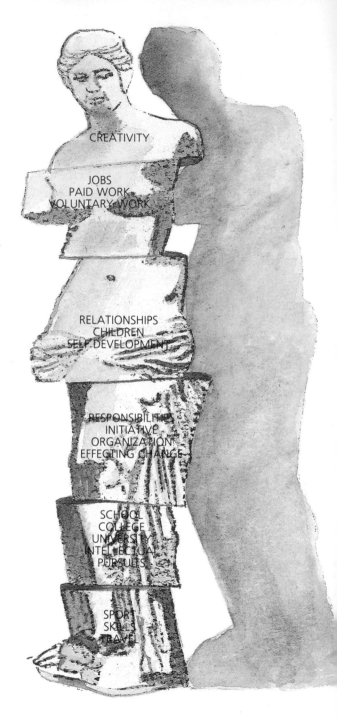

CREATIVITY

JOBS
PAID WORK
VOLUNTARY WORK

RELATIONSHIPS
CHILDREN
SELF-DEVELOPMENT

RESPONSIBILITIES
INITIATIVE
ORGANIZATION
EFFECTING CHANGE

SCHOOL
COLLEGE
UNIVERSITY
INTELLECTUAL
PURSUITS

SPORT
SKILLS
TRAVEL

Building blocks
Think of your achievements as building blocks that have shaped your identity. Do some areas of your life feature more prominently than others? Do you think of yourself as mainly synonymous with your job, your relationships or your major interest? Are your achievements well balanced, are they in proportion with each other? Is this a useful image for you; would interweaving be a better metaphor?

Unrealized potential

Take a long look at what else you feel you could achieve in life. Think of the hidden talents you suspect you may have. Consider the natural aptitudes you know are there, but are not being fully stretched. Reflect about other, more satisfying outlets for your special abilities and qualities. And think of the parts of yourself you have given little attention to so far.

Draw a pool of water and write in it the aspects of yourself that you are not yet using. Think of the aspects you are already using as individual channels running off in satisfying directions and your unrealized potential as the remaining water. How many channels are there and how big is the remaining pool?

Now think what input you would need to channel the rest of your potential. This may include:

Money	Persistence	Confidence	Energy
Talent	Opportunity	Courage	

Draw this input as waterfalls flowing into the pool. How many would you need. And how big are they? When you have added them, review your drawing. Have you forgotten anything?

FEEDBACK

At any given moment, you may be functioning at your full potential – making love, having a baby, playing football, running ten miles (or one mile), painting a picture, running a business or caring for elderly relatives. And for the rest of the time you may be idling along on automatic. But if you are constantly preoccupied with day-to-day living, there may be whole areas of your creativity and energy you haven't yet tapped. If this is true, then it's useful to look at where the responsibility for this unrealized potential lies.

There are two extreme positions, with many in between. At one end of the scale, you cede all the responsibility for reaching full potential to other people or to chance. At the other extreme, you take all the responsibility for reaching full potential on yourself and see merit as all-important.

At the 'helpless' extreme you may feel that taking charge of your potential is impossible or impractical, because you mistakenly assume that total control is essential. It's not. You may have forgotten or never noticed that opportunities can be created. You can do this through groundwork and preparation, through keeping in touch with colleagues and friends or through letting your interests and abilities be known to others.

Similarly, if at the other extreme you believe that you have to be completely in control, you will be limiting your potential by ignoring other people's contributions of insight, experience and support. If your attitude is near either extreme, try to moderate it.

ACTION PLAN

Identify obstacles to realizing your potential. Look at what is keeping these obstacles in place. Increase your knowledge of how they can be dissolved, minimized or removed. If you expect to have total control over your future, let go a little and see what happens. If you leave your life to chance, see how you could create your own opportunities.

See Self-assessment
42-4	Work
45	Life changes
47-9	Self-esteem
50	Inner voices
51	Other people's labels
54-5	Coping with change
60-1	Sex
66-81	Intelligence
82-101	Relating
100-1	Humanity
102-9	Beliefs

See Knowhow
142-3	Intelligence
146-55	Self-defence
156-7	Other connections
164-5	The new paradigm
166-71	Humanistic psychology
180-1	Communication
188-9	Transpersonal psychology

See Mind gym
203-9	Self-esteem
210-13	Priorities
218-22	Emotional intelligence
223-5	Physical intelligence
226-7	Intuitive intelligence
228-9	Intellectual intelligence
231-4	Confidence
236-8	Relationships
238-41	Synergy

WORK

For many of us, work or unemployment represents the most significant single influence on our personal and social identity. The following questions will enable you to review your working life and the importance you attach to work.

Commitment to work

First take a look at how much time you spend working. Work out how many hours you spend, including travelling to and fro, on your job. 0-20 20-45 45-60 60+ hours a week. Note your response.

Now consider how much energy and commitment you apply to your work on a scale of 0-10, with 0 meaning you have no interest in work, and 10 meaning you live and breathe your work.

Extreme responses are likely to be the most significant.

FEEDBACK

High hours, high commitment

If you work a lot of hours with a lot of commitment, this may mean you have a rather lopsided attitude to employment. Your job may delight and satisfy you, but if you are working at this rate six or more days a week, for more than just a few weeks or months at a time, is this too much? Only you can say. If you feel that you can't stop and that it would be a problem to fill the time if you were forced to stop, your work could be health-damaging – you may be heading for burnout. It may also mean that you are strongly identifying yourself with your work, perhaps at the expense of other areas of your life.

ACTION PLAN

Look into yourself and consider whether work is acting as an anaesthetic in some way. Consider whether there is some hidden gain to be had for working this much. Might you, for example, be escaping from your home life? Think about what is driving you; could you be working to please your parents in some way? Consider whether you are indulging in some kind of compulsive helping.

High hours, low commitment

If you are working a lot of hours but with low commitment and energy, then work is probably taking up a lot of space in your life. You may be working in a relaxed way that you feel suits you, but if this has continued for months, perhaps you are working for the money. Do you have a choice? If so, is work unnecessarily limiting your sense of identity?

ACTION PLAN

Consider whether you could move on and take a job that satisfies your mind as well as your pocket. If you are working without energy in response to oppressive working conditions, do you think this is all you really deserve?

Low hours, low commitment

If you work few hours with little commitment, how you respond is likely to depend on your past. If your life has always included long periods of work, then you may feel that you ought to be working harder. You may have made a conscious decision or you may feel that circumstances have forced this upon you. Work often solves the problem of what to do with our lives and without it we tend to feel a great gap in our sense of identity. Yet this can be an opportunity for sideways movement into, for example, the kinds of personal discovery which this book puts forward.

ACTION PLAN

Think about how you use the time spent not working. Is it enriching your sense of identity? If you feel guilty about not working more, do you need to rethink your attitudes to work? If you feel you would like the opportunity to work longer hours or with more commitment, think of what you can do to increase those opportunities.

See Self-assessment
  40-1   Personal potential
  47-9   Self-esteem
  54-5   Coping with change
  56-7   Body signals
  62-3   Physical fitness
  66-81   Intelligence
  108-9   Beliefs at work
See Knowhow
  122-3   School's subtle
            lessons
  142-3   Intelligence
  146-55   Self-defence
  180-1   Communication
See Mind gym
  203-9   Self-esteem
  210-13   Priorities
  218-22   Emotional intelligence
  231-5   Confidence
  238-41   Synergy

Job satisfaction

Consider how your work is organized and how much control you have over what you do.

Read the following statements and make a note of any which apply to you.

List one

Your career structure is determined by your own efforts.
You are expected to contribute to the organization of your work.
You are fully in charge of organizing your own time and tasks.
You have a complete grasp of the purpose of your work.
You check the quality of your own work.
You have and use a broad repertoire of skills.
Your work is always varied.
You are free to redefine the job if you choose to.
You are self-employed.
You can decide your own hours of work.
You can set your own salary through the amount of work you do or by the rate you charge.
You can refuse work you don't want to do.
You head your own business, department or section.

Unemployment

If you are out of work, unemployment may be creating an opportunity which could take you into new and exciting orbits – if you can only let go of messages telling you otherwise. Work brings you into contact with other people, gives a structure to the day and affirms your sense of self-worth. When this disappears, you are likely to feel demoralized, but unemployment can be a challenge and can lead to a new start. If you hate being unemployed, use the time to take a close look at how much your sense of self has been moulded by your work. This is a chance to make your identity more your own. A person is never obsolete, but a mind shaped to suit an employer's demands can easily become redundant. If you would prefer not to be unemployed, the information in 'Job satisfaction' may help you find a way forward.

List two

Your work always involves meeting targets, deadlines and quotas.
Your work involves competing against others for the highest rating,
bonus, commission or results.
Your pace of work is determined by the production line and how fast
it moves or by other people.
You use a narrow range of skills most of the time.
You clock in and out at regular, predetermined times.
Your work is often or seasonally repetitive.
The quality of your work is checked by others.
The career structure of your work is predefined.
Someone higher up makes all the significant decisions about how you
organize your work.
You have little idea what your work is for or how it is used.
The career structure is frozen or nonexistent.

FEEDBACK

If you have answered more yes's to the first list than to the second, you
have considerable autonomy in your job, which probably gives you a
lot of job satisfaction. This may mean that although your identity has
not been frozen by your job, your work still has a significant effect on
your sense of self-worth, not least because of the attention you give it.

If you have answered yes more to the second list than the first, you
probably have little control over how your work is organized. If you
work for a hierarchical institution or company, it may echo the kind
of structure you grew up in, with 'daddy' in charge and everyone else
doing what they are told. If this is true of your workplace, your life
may revolve around giving and receiving orders and avoiding
admitting mistakes, weakness or failure. Your identity may have also
been influenced by the notion of competitiveness, and its related ideas
– ambition, promotion and productivity. Competition for power may
not only be a major source of stress, but may be squashing your
imagination, commitment, energy and creativity, except to the extent
they are demanded by other people. Denying your capacity for self-
direction in this way may mean you are accumulating cynicism,
boredom, apathy, depression, bloody-mindedness, complacency or
envy of people who have more power than you.

ACTION PLAN

If you have a lot of autonomy in your work, consider whether it may
be unduly stressful. If so, explore some stress-release techniques. If you
have little autonomy at work, look into ways of confronting
oppressive management demands. Build up your fitness to cope with
the inevitable stresses of such a change. Find out more information
about self-employment, job-sharing and co-operatives.

LIFE CHANGES

Major changes in life inevitably challenge our sense of identity. Important life events, whether it means becoming a parent, giving up smoking or moving to another country, involve adopting new roles and discarding old ones. This disturbance to our view of ourselves can lead to feelings of confusion and vulnerability that at times may be hard to cope with.

Make a list of the major landmarks in your life.

Each major life event can make you feel that you are temporarily off course, while you try to reshape your identity. Times when you changed direction in your life might include: leaving school and home; starting or ending a job, a course or a relationship; setting up home, moving house or emigrating; getting married, separated or divorced; changing careers or going back to work; and becoming a parent.

Beside each event write down how you managed the change. Think back to how you responded to the challenge of a major change. You may, for example, have taken a risk and plunged in. You may have withdrawn into yourself. You may have asked for advice or watched what other people did and followed suit. Did this reaction work? Did the change enhance your sense of identity or diminish it?

FEEDBACK

Each of the events on your list probably amounted to an 'identity crisis'. An identity crisis is characterized by a major life change that involves the reshaping or modification of your identity. Usually there is an ending, an in-between stage that feels awkward or uncomfortable and then a new beginning. When you are in the midst of the crisis, it is easy to get into a panic and to feel that you will never come out of it, but people usually do. Being able to weather these identity crises is part of developing a strong sense of identity. If you accept the need for these periodic shifts in your identity, it will be better to view each change as an opportunity rather than as a disaster. If you can avoid approaching an identity crisis as a catastrophe, you will have more influence on the outcome – you can choose to reject change or insist on a slower pace of change.

If you are in the midst of an identity crisis, think of it as a painful launch upwards into new and challenging experiences, rather than a descent into the mire. Find a good counsellor or therapist (see pp. 246-7) and use their help to find a new stability on the higher level.

ACTION PLAN

If you are planning a change in your life, concentrate on all you could gain, as well as on what you may lose. Look at how you usually react to change and how this makes you feel.

BODY IMAGE

Another aspect of your identity is locked into your relationship with your body.

Dear body . . .

Write a letter to your body, briefly outlining first the parts you don't like, then the parts you do like. Apologize for any neglect, abuse or injury and express appreciation for devotion to duty. Before you sign off, suggest some plans for pleasure, exercise and coping with stress.

Dear . . .

Now write a letter from your body in reply, covering the following points: What I need is . . . What I want is . . . Please reduce or stop . . . You don't seem to realize that . . .

FEEDBACK

Feeling comfortable with your body and having a good, healthy, close relationship with it is very likely to be reflected in a positive self-image, good self-esteem, a sense of belonging inside yourself and of being somebody.

Feeling uncomfortable or critical of your body tends to accompany poor self-esteem and usually results in some distortion of your identity. You may, for example, be keeping up a false front to hide the body you are unhappy with, or you may tend to overvalue your place in the world, in compensation for your inner reproach. You may even feel like a nobody.

ACTION PLAN

If you feel physically at ease, trust this bodily well-being as a secure base for reaching out into more risky, less comfortable areas of your mind. Transfer the knowledge and skills you have about your body to adjoining areas, to, say, your personal relationships or your work.

If you feel uncomfortable in your body, increase the amount of attention and care you give to your body. Organize your time so that you have the opportunity to listen to what your body wants. Begin to notice how often you override the signals from your body which say stop, or more or enough. If you think of your body merely as a means of transport for your mind, take time to reflect on what this may be depriving you of in the way of physical intimacy, companionship or sensual pleasure.

SELF-ESTEEM

Your sense of self-worth is influenced by how you believe others see you, how much you value yourself and how much other people seem to value you.

How do you think others see you?

First let's look at the image you believe you project to the world.

Imagine you overhear a close friend who has a reputation for honesty and insight describing you to someone else.

What would be the key points that you think they would make about you as a person? What would they praise? What would they caution them against? Write down their description of you.

Then write down how you feel about being described in this way. Do you like the person they have written about?

FEEDBACK

The aim of this self-assessment is to hold up a mirror in which to see yourself more clearly. If you feel that your 'friend' has done a good job of describing you, then we can move on to your reactions to the description. If you can hear what your friend says and accept the good with the bad then you probably have a good level of self-esteem. If the description is a catalogue of faults, shortcomings and inadequacies or that's how it seems to you, then your sense of self-esteem may have been undermined or disrupted to such an extent that you may have settled for a rather negative view of your value as a person. If, on second thoughts, the description does not really seem to fit you, re-write the description.

If you recognize and are happy to be the person your friend has described, and you can live with it, then fine. But ask yourself if this means keeping some area of yourself quiet, out of sight and so out of mind. If you suspect that this is true, try to look into what that area might possibly be.

If you are not happy to be the person described, then you have work to do. This means discovering where and when you learned to be dissatisfied with yourself. It also involves resolving the tension between you and your opinion of yourself, because if you don't like yourself very much, your whole identity will be under strain.

ACTION PLAN

If you are discontented with your friend's description, think about people who you are friends with in spite of their unfortunate habits. Try adopting the same attitude to your own undesirable traits – make friends with yourself.

See Self-assessment
42-4	Work
51	Other people's labels
66-81	Intelligence
82-101	Relating
107	Beliefs at home
108-9	Beliefs at work

See Knowhow
146-55	Self-defence
166-71	Humanistic psychology
176-7	The workshop
178-9	Co-counselling

See Mind gym
203-9	Self-esteem
214-17	Transformation
218-22	Emotional intelligence
231-4	Confidence
234-5	Projection
236-8	Relationships

How do you see yourself?

Now let's consider the 'self-image' you have imprinted on your mind. How do you feel about yourself and what do you think are your good and bad points?

Make a list of your positive points, your virtues and your strengths as a person under the following headings.

Appearance
Personal manner
Work
Home life
Relationships
Social awareness
Self-awareness
Sexuality

Now make a list of your negative points, your vices, bad habits and weaknesses under the same headings.

FEEDBACK

These lists should provide two useful sources of insight into your identity. Which list is the longest and how are the negatives distributed? If the list of negatives is longer then this probably indicates a low sense of self-esteem. Conversely, a longer list of positives probably corresponds to good self-esteem. If your negatives are clustered in just one or two areas then you may have good self-esteem generally but have one or two areas that need attention.

ACTION PLAN

Go back over your list and look at how realistic your impressions are. Cross out put-down words like 'stupid', 'unsociable' or 'forgetful' and replace them with more specific words, so that, for example, 'stupid' becomes 'lacking information', 'unsociable' becomes 'independent' and 'forgetful' becomes 'remember faces not names' and so on. Now look at your list. How does it feel? Make a note of the areas you need to attend to. Bear in mind that you *can* change, and the first step is to shift your opinions about yourself.

See Self-assessment
40-1   Personal potential
50   Inner voices
66-81   Intelligence
82-101 Relating
102-9   Beliefs
See Knowhow
142-3   Intelligence
146-55 Self-defence
166-71 Humanistic psychology
178-9   Co-counselling
See Mind gym
203-9   Self-esteem
214-17 Transformation
231-4   Confidence

Do you feel valued?

Another way to approach self-esteem is to look at how highly valued you feel in other people's eyes.

Make a list of situations in which you feel valued.
Make a list of situations in which you feel devalued.
Add to these the names of people who contribute to either feeling.

FEEDBACK

Again, the length of each list is likely to reveal how your self-esteem affects your identity. If the list of people who make you feel devalued is much longer than the other one, it may be that you have inadvertently found yourself living or working with people who are hostile, critical and uncaring in their attitude to you. Perhaps you never really noticed that this was happening but it has. How come? Did you resist? Did you perhaps unintentionally invite the invalidation? There is often some kind of a pay-off in staying around people who undermine you. It may be horrible but at least it's familiar, whereas confronting or moving away from these people may seem ungrateful, too risky or economically impossible. Sometimes people can make you feel invalidated without intending to – by, say, not selecting you for a task. If this neutral intention is confirmed by other people then you will need to turn to your personal history to find out where the feeling of invalidation comes from.

It is useful to consider that if you like yourself, others will like you. If you care for yourself, others will care for you. If you love yourself, others will love you. If you value yourself, others will value you. But if you hate yourself, others may hate you.

ACTION PLAN

When you respond very emotionally to a put-down, check out what or who it reminds you of. This will probably bring to the surface some association from your personal history. You can tell if you have found the right association because the emotional charge is likely to subside, leaving you free to act. Say, for example, you feel devalued by a man at work who is very blunt in the way he gives you instructions. When you discover that he reminds you of a teacher you had at junior school who constantly picked on you, you may be able to ask him to be more careful about how he speaks to you.

See Self-assessment
42-4   Work
51   Other people's labels
60-1   Sex
66-81   Intelligence
82-101   Relating
102-9   Beliefs
See Knowhow
166-71   Humanistic
          psychology
174-5   Starting points
176-7   The workshop
178-9   Co-counselling
See Mind gym
203-9   Self-esteem
214-17   Transformation
218-22   Emotional intelligence
231-4   Confidence
234-5   Projection
236-8   Relationships

INNER VOICES

When you have to act or make a choice, do you sometimes have an inner voice that influences you – criticizing, urging, inspiring, directing or commenting?

Try to identify your inner voices and write down what they say to you. Are they helpful or undermining? Examples may include:

Conscience   you should . . . you really ought . . .
Critic   you're no good . . . that won't work . . .
Inspiration   why not try . . .? you could ask for . . .

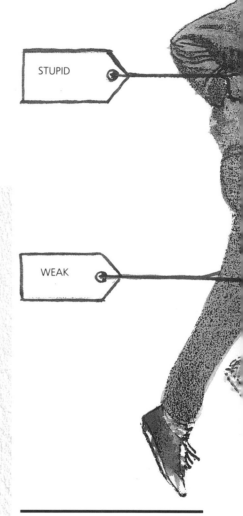

FEEDBACK

Although you may not be sharply aware of them, it is not unusual to have a whole chorus of voices. For some people these voices can be no more than occasionally disruptive or encouraging, for others they can become a long-playing record. Even though your personal range of voices may be very diverse, you may be aware of only one or two. Either way they are likely to amount to a very active part of your identity. It is very important to get to know these inner voices, because they are very likely to be running your life.

If the inner orchestra is harmonious, it can be highly motivating, but if the voices are disruptive or simply confusing, you will find it very helpful to examine them. You may find, for example, that you are receiving conflicting advice from half a dozen different voices.

One of the most powerful and damaging influences on the human mind is the voice of the 'inner critic'. If it is allowed a free rein, it can cast an all-pervasive blanket of gloom and derision on your every action. It distorts both your perceptions and your responses, leaving others disappointed and yourself feeling uncomfortable or cheated.

The inner critic usually derives from the past, linking you to earlier authority figures, across time and space, as if by remote control. Almost always, this voice is an internalized version of one or both of your parents, or people who made themselves responsible for your behaviour when you were younger.

ACTION PLAN

If you have an inner critic, give it some conscious attention. Try to find out who it reminds you of by listening to its tone of voice as well as what it says. Concentrate on what the other voices say too. Consider whether they argue with each other. Identify which voices are the loudest or most frequent, and whether, on balance, they are positive and supportive or negative and undermining. Learn how to develop a dialogue between these inner voices and learn to let them speak out, so that you can choose to accept or ignore what they say.

OTHER PEOPLE'S LABELS

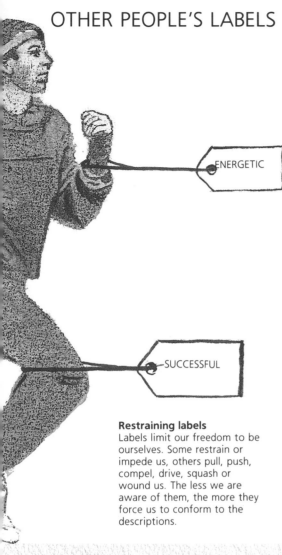

ENERGETIC

SUCCESSFUL

Restraining labels
Labels limit our freedom to be ourselves. Some restrain or impede us, others pull, push, compel, drive, squash or wound us. The less we are aware of them, the more they force us to conform to the descriptions.

One of the most formative influences on our minds is the kind of labels that other people attach to us. Other people often unwittingly hypnotize us into a quite mistaken opinion of our value or worth through repeatedly telling us that we are 'stupid', or 'lazy' or 'depressed'. As Philip Zimbardo says in his book on shyness: 'once labelled is twice proved'.

There may be some truth in the description, but it is the all-embracing nature of the label that can be so damaging. If someone repeatedly says that you are a 'good girl', or that you are a 'good laugh', there's a good chance that the repetition and the application of an impossibly generalized description is likely to stick. Even if you know it's wrong to begin with, your inner conviction may dissolve in the judgement. Like the roles we accumulate, the labels we wear can make a sizeable contribution to our identity.

Make a list of the labels other people have attached to you. They may include some of the following:

Depressed	Strong	Kind	Unreliable
Loser	Cheerful	Weak	Thick-skinned
Failure	Mean	Quick	Incompetent
Lazy	Patient	Slow	Aggressive
Generous	Selfish	Clever	Irresponsible

Against each label note which works in your favour and which works against you. Then add where you got the label, when and from whom.

FEEDBACK

If you have adopted a large pack of labels chosen by other people, you may need to reconsider whether they really belong to you. If you feel they do belong, how far have they become self-fulfilling prophecies? Labels are often there as a way of controlling you or limiting your personal power.

ACTION PLAN

Listen out for people making statements about you that are too general to be accurate. Reject their label, then try asking them to be specific. Ask them to keep statements about you as a person separate from statements about your behaviour. Be an example yourself: 'I'm not a stupid person but I sometimes have clumsy fingers'.

When people give you a label, it is often for their own convenience. Try to notice who benefits from any label you are invited to wear. It can be useful to think back to a time when a label first came into use. Consider how it happened and how you now keep the label in place.

BODYMIND

We are brought up believing that body and mind are independent units, whereas actually they are different aspects of the same thing. The body throbs with thought and emotion, while our physical condition influences the way we think and feel. If you are nervous before an exam or an interview, you feel butterflies in your stomach. If you are depressed, your posture reflects it in hunched shoulders; if you are happy, your body walks tall.

How mind and body influence each other

This inseparable connection between body and mind means that you probably have less conscious control over your behaviour than you might think. The self-aware part of the bodymind, the individual 'I' that is reading this, does have the power to direct your activities, but it is not autonomous. It is bound up in layer on layer of interdependence with the intelligence of the rest of the body. This intelligence not only regulates temperature, digestion and defence against disease, but registers sense impressions, comfort or discomfort and, not least, your feelings. Regardless of your conscious purposes, the bodymind patiently pursues its own purpose. For example, specialized forms of white cell in your blood are at this moment diligently producing antibodies to fight infections while others are engulfing and destroying harmful microorganisms. If your bodymind is subject to high levels of stress, however, these cells may give up on the task or become less effective. At a more visible level, specific parts of your bodymind may be spontaneously expressing unacknowledged emotions as physical tension, or 'body language'.

Cultivating a healthy bodymind

The whole structure of the bodymind has evolved from centuries of challenge. Each succeeding wave has sculpted, eroded and sedimented itself into the bodymind's central nervous system. Biologically, we are well equipped to cope with a wide range of problems, and the bodymind usually responds creatively. However, the biological base is always interwoven with inherited patterns as well as with the accumulated experience of daily life.

You can improve your mind by working on your body – mental and emotional wellbeing, for example, improve demonstrably with regular exercise, deep breathing, plenty of sleep and periods of complete relaxation. Avoiding cigarettes, alcohol and other stimulants and tranquillizers and eating a healthy diet also free the bodymind from unnecessary interference. Likewise, you can improve your physical wellbeing by working on your mind. The old attitude towards health and wellbeing emphasized a repair shop approach in which the doctor 'fixed' the illness lodged in the patient.

A more appropriate way of caring for the body is to prevent a health-damaging build-up of stress. Dealing with the relics of your personal history, identifying and expressing feelings and boosting your self-esteem, for instance, can dramatically lower your stress levels and so encourage the bodymind's healing processes and enhance your feeling of general wellbeing.

While emotional distress is often a bodymind response to oppression, it can also be the outward sign of an inner healing crisis.

How to use this section

The following self-assessments will enable you to estimate how much your life is being influenced by the belief that your mind and body are separate. The guidelines for assessing your bodymind focus on your awareness of body signals, and your attitudes to sex, feeling of general fitness, diet, drugs, symptoms and change.

Work your way through the assessment items, taking as much time as you need. Make a note of your response, then move on to FEEDBACK and ACTION PLAN. If you do not find yourself reflected here, turn to the index and use it to direct you to a different starting point.

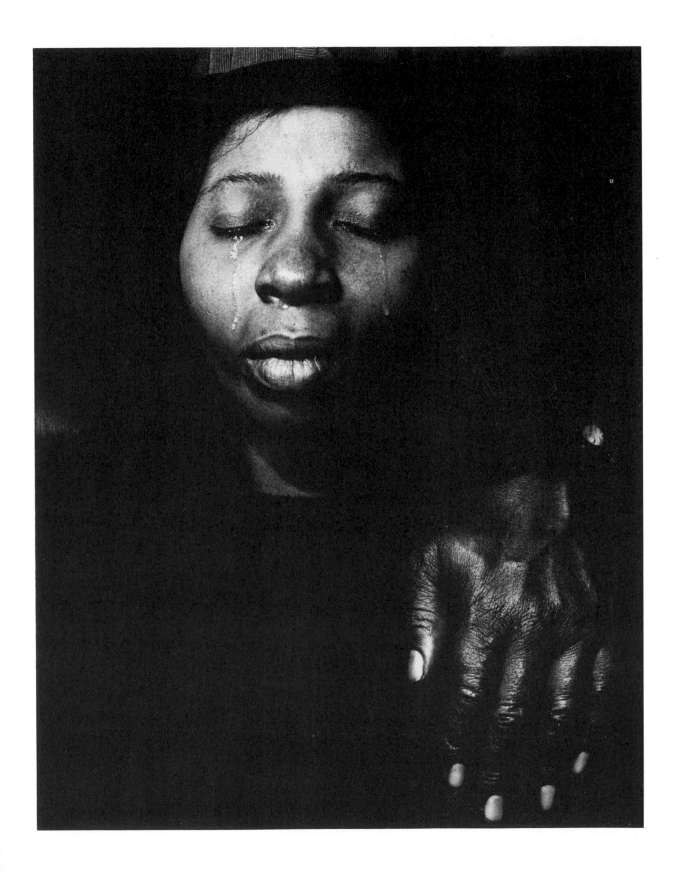

COPING WITH CHANGE

The human bodymind has a built-in ability to cope. And it is this adaptability that enables us to find a niche for ourselves in almost any climate and under very diverse social conditions.

Most of us face such a high rate of change in our daily lives that the ability to respond well to challenge is essential. If we are adaptable, we are also more likely to be able to handle the pressures or tedium of work, family, school or college life.

But human adaptability also has its disadvantages. As individuals we may come to believe that we should be able to cope with anything that life – circumstances or society – throws at us. If we fail to cope, we often tend to absorb the blame personally and not notice how some of the demands we face are unreasonable and overwhelming.

How much challenge are you facing at the moment?

Time pressures

Time pressures and commitments can make us feel that we are in the grip of a vice that is squeezing out our freedom of choice. We feel as if we are always running to catch up with ourselves until we run out of energy and slip into 'burnout'.

Make a list of the 'inescapable' time pressures that you find yourself dealing with in a typical month. Examples could include:
Attending meetings, functions, conferences, assemblies
Taking children to and from school
Preparing reports, audits, plans, strategies, proposals, analyses, lectures, lessons
Meeting deadlines and quotas
Getting to work on time
Preparing meals for the family
Sitting tests and examinations
Attending to sick relatives
Coping with colleagues' demands

Responsibility without power

If you feel you are responsible for the outcome of a situation, yet you do not have the power to influence it, you are likely to feel as if the ground you stand on may cave in at any moment.

Make a list of the situations where you feel you have a lot of responsibility without much power. Examples might include:
Coping with adolescent children
Doing a good job in a subordinate position
Sitting on voluntary committees
Handling relationships

Relying on people

Depending on other people for the success of any event or piece of work can make you feel like a juggler or trapeze artist. You may be in a constant state of suspense, because if one small part of the sequence fails, the whole enterprise might collapse.

Make a list of the situations where you have to depend on other people to 'get it right'. Examples could include:
Making appointments
Avoiding management crises
Meeting target production figures
Organizing events, such as presentations, conferences, public events, entertainments, weddings, services
Entrusting children to school, friends or relatives
Driving
Maintaining high standards
Getting repairs fixed and goods delivered

Poisonous people

People who undermine, confuse or hurt us, either deliberately or unwittingly, can drain us of our resilience and create additional stress, so that our ability to cope is severely threatened.

Make a list of the people you come into contact with who are 'poisonous'. This could include people who seem to be:
Undermining
Malicious or wounding
Blaming
Abusive
Capricious and contradictory in their demands
Harrassing and unwilling to take 'no' for an answer
Manipulative

How well do you cope with challenge?

Do you experience times of gloom and low energy and times when you are very alert and excited? Draw a large square on a piece of paper, divide the square to make two rectangles representing the amount of time you feel you spend in each state. Do you know how you get from one state to the other? Write down how you do it. Draw two arrows indicating the directions of movement – 'From excitement' and 'To excitement'. Do you get stuck in either of the two states? If so, which one do you get stuck in the most? Put a thick line around the one you get stuck in. Looking at the thick line, how is it made? Is it a person or an attitude or a lack of material resources?

FEEDBACK

Coping is a complex human phenomenon in which inner resources, such as ingenuity, a sense of humour, stamina and fitness are mobilized in response to outside demands. If your ability to cope collapses or is threatened, the bodymind's state of *arousal* is affected. When faced with a challenge, the bodymind responds by mobilizing your energy reserves. Adrenalin is released into the bloodstream, digestion shuts down, the heart rate increases and breathing quickens. The result is a heightened state of arousal. Coping well depends on managing your arousal well. Under poor management, you can become stuck in high arousal – when you feel restless, excited, elated, sleepless, anxious or hyperactive. Alternatively, you may become stuck in low arousal – often as a result of insufficient challenge – and feel depressed, lethargic, and despairing. Both limit your freedom of choice. In sustained high arousal, calm, quiet consideration becomes difficult or impossible. With sustained low arousal, opportunities slip by, attention is unfocussed, and 'everything seems to be too much trouble'.

You can significantly improve your ability to cope by noticing how much pressure you feel comfortable with, and by adjusting the load. You could be trying to cope with too much, or not enough. Taking charge of the load may mean choosing to resist, avoid or confront 'people poison', delegating more responsibility and simply finding the time and space to look at the world – sitting in the park or walking by the river. Once you are aware of how much of a challenge you are dealing with, it is easier to assume the power to moderate it.

ACTION PLAN

Good management of your state of arousal means being able to raise or lower it at will. Typically, you can raise your arousal level by playing or watching competitive sport, going to parties or listening to loud music. Conversely, you can lower arousal by resting, meditating or listening to calm music. Plan to improve your coping ability by learning how to recognize your arousal level and practise changing it at will. Recognize and deal with exhaustion, sleep deprivation and self-destructive tactics. Become fit enough for your chosen lifestyle.

BODY SIGNALS

Your bodymind communicates with you through the language of body signals. How aware you are of them, and how you respond to them reveal a lot about how you relate to your body.

To begin, here are some questions about your body signals. Draw a clock face with the hours from one to twelve. If any of the following statements are true for you, ring an hour on the clock.

You are good at staying up late at night.
You can easily ignore tiredness.
You frequently have less sleep than you need.
You frequently stay up all night then go to work the next day.
You work nights and look after your family during the day.
You often work hours that have little relation to day or night.

You find it easy to do without breakfast or lunch.
You often just grab a sandwich between meetings, classes or jobs.
You find it easy to forget that you are hungry.

You regularly work through a whole morning or afternoon without taking a break.
You regard yawning as something to be suppressed.
You get high on your work because it's so pleasurable and keep on going, then eventually collapse.
You work very intensively for weeks or months and then have difficulty relaxing when you stop.

Body codes
Think of your bodymind as layer upon layer of electrochemical circuits, alive with messages about your physical state. Do all the messages get through? If you hear a message saying, 'I'm hungry', 'I'm exhausted', 'My head aches', do you take the message and give it due attention? Or, if the message is inconvenient, do you sometimes block it, so that the body condition continues, but news of it doesn't get through?

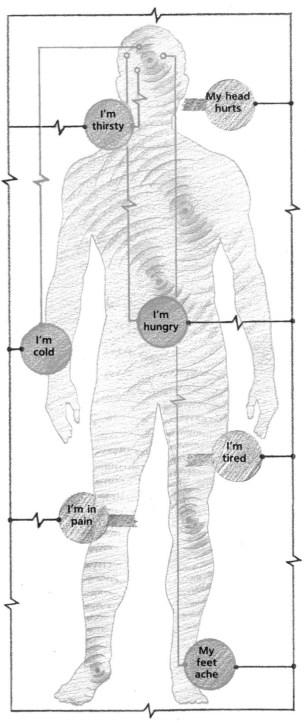

FEEDBACK

A score past four on the clock face suggests that you may have got into the habit of over-riding many of your body's subtle time signals.

If the demands that you make on yourself or accept from others are so great that they make you feel you 'need to sleep for a week', then your body will soon realize that it isn't going to get the help it needs to work properly. Those of us who would never for a moment drive a car with no air in the tyres are sometimes prepared to live for months on less than half the sleep we know we need.

The processes that keep you alive and well operate in a continual ebb and flow of different rhythmic cycles. Sleep, for example, frees the bodymind from the need to respond to external stimuli, so that digestion, elimination and healing can proceed at their own rate.

When you persistently ignore the underlying rhythmic cycles of your bodymind, it will initially manage to adapt. Your kidneys will continue to purify the bloodstream, bone marrow will generate new blood cells and your stomach will go on extracting nutrients. But some of the body's processes will be weakened, reducing resistance to disease and laying the ground for ill-health or psychosomatic ailments.

A low score below 4 on the clock face probably indicates that you are not presently ignoring your basic biorhythms to any great extent. At best this may mean that you are already accurately tuned to the needs of your body; at the very least it means that your lifestyle is free enough from stress to enable you to learn to take account of your biorhythms.

ACTION PLAN

Identify and follow your body's rhythms. Learn to 'listen' to your body signals and to act on them. Become more disciplined in the way you treat your body's messages. This doesn't mean giving in to every flicker of fatigue or muscular twinge that you feel. Choose to override fatigue or other body signals for only limited periods and afterwards follow your body signals. Let them lead you to rest, exercise or recuperation.

SICKNESS AND HEALING

One of the more subtle interconnections of the human bodymind is the capacity to interpret and respond to the body signals that indicate that you are not well. How do you deal with them? Do you take responsibility for them, or do you delegate responsibility for your wellbeing to the professionals? Or both?

Divide up a piece of paper into six columns and write in the following headings.
1 Warning signal – actual or potential imbalance in the body
2 Fault condition – body function requiring correction
3 Evidence of healing – that the body was healing itself
4 Nuisance – to be controlled or eliminated
5 Doing too much
6 Accident

Now make a list of the things that have been wrong with you for the last few months or so, under the appropriate headings. It doesn't matter if you can't remember them all, but include spells of unhappiness, anxiety, irritability and generally feeling unwell, as well as coughs, colds, aches and pains and more serious illnesses.

FEEDBACK

If most of your symptoms were in the second or fourth column, you may have absorbed the somewhat mechanistic approach to the bodymind espoused by the medical profession. Doctors remain our best source of help when serious illness arises, but biomedical knowledge has, until recently, been entirely based on the idea of ill-health rather than wellbeing, emphasizing cures rather than prevention. Many of us have learnt that to get our practitioner's attention, our symptoms need to be physical rather than psychological. An earache, backache or headache will be more acceptable than 'feeling low' or 'feeling strange'. However, the assumption that doctors can bring disease under control is meeting increasing resistance. How often have you been to your doctor and then failed to take the medicine prescribed? A more holistic approach to health, which keeps the best of the old and includes the psychological dimensions of wellbeing, is making steady progress. It emphasizes health maintenance, self-diagnosis and self-healing, and puts the responsibility for health on a more co-operative footing.

If most of your responses were in the first and third columns you have probably already begun to absorb and act on this more holistic concept of health and wellbeing. If so, you probably regard symptoms as messages, saying, perhaps: 'Look, something is off-key' or 'Please be patient. All will be well soon'. This approach opens up a whole new range of choices for improving your health.

Symptoms of emotional problems
A significant number of physical symptoms are caused not by mechanical problems, but by emotional aches and pains. Different emotions can affect specific parts of the body.

A headache may be a signal that your bodymind has had enough of being overworked.

A pain in the neck may reveal unexpressed resentment or frustration with someone or something.

Backache may be reminding you that your sex life is unsatisfactory.

Heart palpitations may be drawing attention to your over-stressed lifestyle.

Stomach pain, especially centrally under the ribs, may be warning you of underlying anxieties.

Stiff joints could indicate unsatisfactory relationships.

If you had a number of responses in the fifth and sixth columns, you may already realize that a number of your symptoms are related to excessive challenges in your life, such as sleep deprivation, increasing demands on declining personal resources, time pressures, threats of violence or physical danger.

ACTION PLAN
If you don't already do so, consider your body signals as a warning sign that something is out of balance and as an opportunity to find out what is happening and why. The best way to begin to do this is to ask yourself what a symptom might be trying to tell you. Try to trace each symptom back to its root cause and, having identified the cause, give it the attention it needs. Don't ignore warning signals; seek medical advice promptly.

See Self-assessment
26-35   Life events
54-5   Coping with change
56-7   Body signals
64-5   Diet, drugs and alcohol
See Knowhow
144-5   Feelings are physical
166-71   Humanistic psychology
See Mind gym
194   Arousal
214-17   Transformation

SEX

Sex reveals very clearly how well you balance the conscious and automatic processes of your bodymind. The last twenty years have seen a transformation in attitudes towards sex. And this, in turn, has made contraception more available and abortion and homosexuality legal in many countries. This has undoubtedly generated a lot of physical delight. However, each generation of young people have to work their own way through the experiences of developing their sexuality. Older guidelines which are evidently obsolete make emerging sexuality more difficult to cope with.

The degree to which the sexual revolution has affected you will depend on your age and where you live. But, whatever your experience of sexuality, living in your body, being at home with it, is important in all sexual activity.

Do you recognize any of the following statements as true for you? Make a note of how many you agree with.

You have a clear idea of what your sexual needs are.
Your sexual feelings often lead you to initiate sexual activity.
You allow yourself to fulfil your sexual needs.
You can ask for what you need and specify preferred times and places.
You take the trouble to find out what your partner needs and likes.
You can choose to refuse what your partner wants.
You frequently need to suppress your sexual arousal.
You choose to retain control or let go of it in a sexual situation.
Given the foreplay that you need, you can readily reach orgasm.
Orgasm is accompanied by a profound switch of bodily sensation –
    from excitement and arousal to deep relaxation.

Now make a note of how many of the following statements are true for you.

You usually rely on your partner to arouse you.
You need a drink before you can abandon control of yourself.
When making love you have to be in control throughout.
You only become sexually aroused through creating or recreating
    special roles or situations.
You are unable to accept masturbation as an alternative to sex with
    another person.
You rely on pornographic material to become aroused.
You have had some experiences, perhaps as a child, that make sex an
    on-going problem.
As a child you were discouraged from masturbating.
You worry about sex a lot.

FEEDBACK

If you responded mostly with 'no' to the first set of statements and mostly with 'yes' to the second set, then your sexuality may be unnecessarily distorted. Because our culture tends to devalue feelings, the powerful sexual urges that seem to threaten our self-control can make us very anxious. And sexual feelings can become even more worrying if they echo the cultural attitude that sex is 'bad', dirty or 'sinful'.

Distortions of your sexuality are most likely to derive from:

Domination – the desire to impose your needs on others.

Submission – sacrificing your personal needs, perhaps because you don't feel you deserve anything better.

Fear of failure – perhaps through an over-emphasis on measuring up to some ideal.

Overwork – allowing the excitement and stress of work to squeeze out sexual activity.

Compulsive need for approval – doing whatever it takes to get it from your partner.

Memories from the past – a sense of freezing, blocking or numbness

Harmful beliefs – thinking that your body is ugly, bad, disgusting, animal or sinful.

A mechanical attitude – you think that sex only means a penis and a vagina.

A desire to hurt or humiliate.

If you find yourself struggling with sexual difficulties, they may be part of a difficulty with feelings in general. Developing your ability to care and respond and becoming more in touch with your body can be better ways of transforming your sexuality than trying to confront it directly. Non-sexual touch, massage, hugs and listening to what your body has to say across a whole spectrum of experiences can begin to support an open, caring approach to sexuality.

If you had a majority of 'yes' responses to the first set of statements and a majority of 'no' responses to the second set, then you are probably well along the way to bringing your sexuality in from the cold. If this meant shutting off from earlier negative attitudes, perhaps linked to religion, you may find that they are still lurking and occasionally re-emerge. You may find it very useful to unpick some of the early history that put these attitudes in place.

If you found yourself neither disagreeing nor agreeing with a majority of the items on the two lists this may be a sign of either an underdeveloped or suppressed sexuality or a serious lack of information about sexual matters.

ACTION PLAN

If you have recurring problems with sex, learn to get in touch with your own feelings and your body, develop a caring approach to your partner and look into your personal history for memories or beliefs that may be blocking your spontaneous responses. Psychosexual counselling can also help to solve recurring difficulties.

PHYSICAL FITNESS

Fitness is a measure of how well the bodymind is tuned to cope with the demands of life. In its traditional sense, it may reflect a narrow view of people, but it does provide an essential set of guidelines for wellbeing. The following assessments will reveal whether your fitness level is within these guidelines or outside them.

How efficient are your heart and lungs?

You can measure how effectively your heart pumps blood around your body simply and adequately, by taking your pulse rate at rest.

Pulse rate at rest

One of the best signs of peak fitness is a strong, slow and regular resting pulse rate. Any sort of emotional or physical activity, however, will raise your pulse rate, so check it when you wake up in the morning. Women tend to have a slightly faster pulse than men, and in most people, pulse increases a little with age, although rates vary from individual to individual.

Using your fingertips, feel your pulse at your wrist, your temple, your elbow or in your neck – about two inches below your ear – for one minute. If you are unsure, try again for another minute as a double check.

How active are you?

Write down your own assessment of how much exercise you take in an average week.

Do you jog, swim or workout?
Do you do a lot of walking?
Do you climb a lot of stairs, do a lot of lifting and carrying or other manual work?
Do you play sports regularly?
Do you have an active hobby, such as gardening or DIY?

Now write down how you feel about the amount of exercise you have taken, and how active you think you are for your age.

If you are in doubt about your overall activity level, take a look at the following list:

You take physical exercise, vigorous enough to make you sweat, less than once a week.
You walk less than half a mile a day.
You travel to work by public transport or car.
You take the lift (elevator) rather than the stairs.
You watch TV most of the time at weekends.
You get other people to go shopping or run errands if you can.

Can you find yourself in here somewhere?

FEEDBACK

If you find your pulse is between 60 and 85 beats per minute, this indicates a good general fitness level. Even lower is excellent. If it is over 85, this may be an early indication of risk and your heart may be under strain.

Caution: consult your doctor immediately if your pulse rate is consistently over 100 beats per minute.

Secretly, most of us know if we tend to be a bit sluggish, but find it difficult to change our habits. If this is true for you, you would be well advised to rethink your attitude to exercise. Once you've gained first-hand experience of the increased energy and enthusiasm, reduced stress, improved self-image and general health that come with even modest amounts of exercise, you'll probably never want to stop.

If you are fit you probably know it and may already monitor how much exercise and effort it takes to become or stay fit. If you don't know whether you are fit or not then monitoring your fitness level is an important first step.

ACTION PLAN

Start some kind of aerobic exercise routine, or book into a gym or exercise class. Monitor your fitness level through graded exercise and pulse checks. Put aside the time to take more exercise every day. While exercising with other people can be very supportive, it's important to find a form of exercise that is easily accessible. Arranging partners, making bookings, travelling to venues, can all increase the chances that regular exercise doesn't happen. If in doubt, run!

DIET

At the most basic level, we each owe our existence to food. And, in a very literal sense, 'we are what we eat'. But, perhaps because eating is so repetitive, it tends to become a habit, so that we sometimes come to view meals as a refuelling exercise in which one kind of fuel begins to seem much like another. Another tendency is to go for food that is cheap and convenient but not necessarily very wholesome.

Healthy eating

Following a healthy diet means paying constant attention to what you eat and how you eat it. Do you know? Start a list right now for the week ahead of *what* you eat. Be sure to include everything—both healthy and unhealthy foods, and snacks.

Make a parallel list of *how* you eat in the week ahead, including rushed, snatched or missed meals, social occasions and treats.

When you come to review your lists, if there is a serious imbalance in either of them, it will probably be immediately obvious. If you are not sure if your diet is healthy or not, do you recognize yourself here?

Have snacks three or more times a day.
You eat fruit and fresh vegetables and salads three times or less a week.
You eat fried food most days.
You add salt and sugar liberally to food.
You eat chocolate, biscuits or cake most days.
You regularly eat butter, cream and full-fat cheeses.
You eat fish once a week or less.
You eat wholemeal bread less than two or three times a week.
You never remove the fat from the meat before cooking it.
You have three-course meals every day.

You eat only one meal a day.
You often eat standing up or in transit.
You eat while reading or watching TV.
You often eat when you are tense, bored or depressed.
You usually have a second helping.
You frequently reward yourself or your children with food.
You rarely have time for breakfast.
You often eat when you're not hungry, just to be sociable.
You eat quickly without chewing.
You often survive on 'fast' or junk food for days.

FEEDBACK

If several of the above statements apply to you, then giving more attention to how you eat will bring many benefits. Raising consciousness about what and how you are eating is the first step towards improved fitness and an essential part of good bodymind housekeeping. Although in the past it has been difficult to live without industrially produced food, increasing consumer awareness of the problems arising from artificial additives, preservatives and flavourings is gradually changing some manufacturing priorities. However, it is as important to eat a balanced diet as it is to avoid 'unwholesome' food.

ACTION PLAN

Eat more slowly and be more aware of what you eat. Make several meals a week into a mini-occasion. Look at your knowledge of nutrition and improve it if it is inadequate.

See Self-assessment
26-35 Life events
46 Body image
47-9 Self-esteem
50 Inner voices
54-5 Coping with change
56-7 Body signals
58-9 Sickness and healing
62-3 Physical fitness
102-9 Beliefs
See Knowhow
118-21 The early years
See Mind gym
223-5 Physical intelligence

DRUGS AND ALCOHOL

Living in a competitive world and enduring boring, repetitive or dehumanizing work is, in itself, extremely stressful. But this can also breed with the pain of your individual personal history to produce an intolerable degree of stress. Surviving the rejections of unemployment, for example, is infinitely more difficult if you suffered rejection as a child. Drugs that promise to alleviate the daily pain of living can be very attractive. The extent to which you use drugs, in the broadest sense, is likely to point to areas of your life that need attention. When you want to alter your mental state, do you often reach for some form of drug? How easy would it be to do without it?

The medicine test

1. Start by going to your medicine cupboard and counting how many different kinds of medicines you have there. Include those bought without a prescription.

2. Now make a list of the drugs you have used in the last 12 months. It doesn't matter whether you know the names -'the spray I had for my throat' will do. Include alcohol, tobacco, stimulants, such as tea and coffee, and any other harmful substances you use.

3. Rate each drug according to the part it plays in your life. Draw a circle for each drug. Start with a tiny circle for a minor drug and build up to the more prominent ones.

4. Keep a record of your drug use for a week. Draw a 24-hour chart using different colours for different drugs so that they can overlap. Drugs remain in the body for different amounts of time. So coffee at 8.30am starts solid green and fades towards 10am; cigarettes start solid red and fade after an hour. An alcoholic drink fades after four hours; a sleeping pill after seven.

5. Consider how much of your experience is altered by drugs. To what extent do they influence your working life?

6. Now ask yourself whether the drugs you use support the body's natural healing abilities or whether they suppress symptoms that would otherwise interrupt your lifestyle.

FEEDBACK

The invention of drugs that promote healing is one of the great achievements of scientific medicine, and there are undoubtedly occasions when prescribed drugs ensure survival. But using powerful medicinal drugs to suppress symptoms, so that you can continue to pursue a health-damaging lifestyle, is inevitably self-defeating because the original cause remains unresolved.

If you use drugs when you feel 'low', unhappy, anxious, tense or unable to sleep, they will simply disguise the personal or social reasons at the root of these feelings. Using any kind of drug, including tea or coffee, to alter or improve your daily experience may be a sign of pain. It may be pain stemming from your childhood, still living on in your bodymind, or the pain caused by the intolerable pressures inherent in the way you make a living. Whichever is true for you, using drugs will not only damage your health in the long term but will undermine your ability to change your life.

ACTION PLAN

Identify situations or people that trigger your need for drugs, cigarettes or alcohol. Where does your need to anaesthetize yourself come from? Look at how you came to be so tense that you need chemical tranquillity. When did it start? Search for other ways of increasing or reducing arousal, such as hypnosis, meditation, fitness and diet.

See Self-assessment
22-5   Loving, understanding and choosing
26-35   Life events
45   Life changes
47-9   Self-esteem
54-5   Coping with change
58-9   Sickness and healing
60-1   Sex
102-9   Beliefs
See Knowhow
124-5   The television 'I'
140-1   Paying attention
146-55 Self-defence
166-71 Humanistic psychology
See Mind gym
195-6   Healing and distress
203-9   Self-esteem
214-17 Transformation
231-4   Confidence

INTELLIGENCE

Intelligence is a fundamental property of all life. In this basic sense, it means the capacity to adapt, survive and flourish – not just in humans, but in animals, plants and microorganisms. It takes intelligence to adapt to changes in temperature, to survive infections and to grow. The human mind extends this basic definition to include the nurturing of children, animals, crops, other people, ideas and technology, so that they too can prosper and develop.

Idealizing intellect

Even though we all inherit intelligence and prove it by surviving from one day to the next, some of us are given the impression that we are not intelligent enough. This is because intelligence is equated with intellect. At school, our minds are constantly tested and examined for evidence of intellectual intelligence. If we prove to be intellectually clever, we are likely to be separated out to have our intellect further enhanced at college or university. But without this official endorsement we are likely to feel deprived or inferior and our choice of career may be automatically restricted.

This form of grading and examination not only assumes that intelligence and intellect are interchangeable, but makes intelligence seem like a raw material to be harvested, refined and marketed – and one that only the favoured few can enjoy. Children whose parents talk a lot, think a lot, write a lot and read a lot count as more intelligent than children who belong to a different, less intellectual background. In promoting the supremacy of intellect over all other aspects of the human mind, current Western education is reinforcing cultural beliefs that were held 2000 years ago by the Greeks and strongly reinforced by Descartes and others after the 16th century.

Redressing the balance

A more modern view of intelligence, which takes into account the tremendous developments in psychology and biology over the last few decades, shows that the old view is seriously deficient. When we take as a yardstick for intelligence the natural ability to adapt, survive, and flourish, four things become clear. First we see that, as well as representing a pinnacle of human achievement, thinking skills such as deduction, inference and reasoning are just one of several, more or less parallel styles of intelligence – including emotional intelligence (see pp. 69-70), physical proficiency, intuition and learning from experience. Secondly, we find that the powerful self-healing, self-stabilizing, self-regulating intelligence of the human body has been grossly under-valued. Thirdly, it becomes easier to see that the tremendous attention given to intellect over the last few centuries is an accident of history, a side-effect of the dominance of men (see pp. 162-3). Finally, we realize that our excessive respect for intellect reflects a dangerously one-sided view that, far from supporting human survival, now threatens it. Hundreds of thousands of people devote their working hours to planning the last day of life on earth – a catastrophic memorial to intellect divorced from feeling.

The confident physical co-ordination and accurate judgement of time and distance needed to rig industrial structures safely, amounts to a whole branch of intelligence.

How to use this section
In the following pages we look at intelligence as a changing process, as a landscape to be explored. These self-assessments will help you to discover your particular style of intelligence – whether, for example, your predominant strength is emotional, intuitive, physical or intellectual. It will also reveal how far you have absorbed the conventional and limiting wisdom about intelligence. Work your way through the material that follows, taking as long as you like and changing your mind as often as you like. When you have settled on a response to each set of questions, record your assessment of your individual strengths and weaknesses. Then continue to FEEDBACK to find your style of intelligence and, using ACTION PLAN, note down what you plan to do about it. From there you can go on to LEARNING FROM EXPERIENCE and INTELLIGENCE REVIEW. If you don't find yourself reflected here and you think you know what you are looking for, turn to the index and use it to direct you to another starting point in one of the other assessment sections.

OTHER PEOPLE'S OPINIONS

Before you assess your real strengths and weaknesses, let's consider how other people have rated your intelligence, rightly or wrongly.

Using the kinds of feedback you had at school, from examinations, teachers or other people, estimate how intelligent other people think you are. Where do you believe you come on a scale of 0 to 200, with 0 as very low intelligence, 100 as average and 200 as high intelligence.

Now make a list of your formal qualifications in academic subjects, such as science, mathematics, computer science, history, languages, economics, politics, medicine or other equivalent subjects. Be sure to include the following levels.

GCSE, GCE O or A levels/High school diploma or SAT
Other diplomas, such as a technical qualification
College/university degree
Master's degree
Doctorate

FEEDBACK

Academic success tends to be equated with developed intellectual intelligence. If your list of qualifications represents three or more levels of further education, and other people say you are of average or above average intelligence, your intellect – your ability to organize your thoughts, collect information, make deductions and construct reasoned arguments – is probably a core strength of your mind.

If your list was short and you have picked up the idea that you are of average or below average intelligence, this may have several meanings. Perhaps you have tried to adapt to the Western intellectual tradition's train of thought and failed. Perhaps you rejected it. Perhaps you felt intuitively that it wasn't right for you. Perhaps you never had the opportunity to try, maybe it was rejected by your family and friends, so you never considered it.

ACTION PLAN

If you have done well in the Western intellectual tradition, consider whether this leads you to ignore other styles of intelligence and some of the more subtle feelings. If you have done poorly in the intellectual tradition or have rejected or been rejected by it, then look at how this may have happened. You may find you want to adopt some parts of the tradition while rejecting others.

EMOTIONAL INTELLIGENCE

Now let's explore other ways of looking at intelligence. Run through the following statements and see if you find yourself there.

You radiate warmth and pleasure in human relationships.
You know your own feelings and relate to the feelings of others.
You handle relationships according to emotional values which may be traditional.
You have lots of words for different nuances and shades of feeling.
You work to bring about harmony and good feeling between people.
You enjoy nurturing others.
You can manage with a few firmly held beliefs.
You make friends easily.
You have few illusions about people.
You find that you can arrange your life so that in general you can get what you want.
You can easily 'put yourself in someone else's shoes'.

Make a note of whether these statements are largely true of you or not, if possible making it an either/or decision, and make a note of your response for future reference.

View of reality
Look at the picture below. Which person do you identify with most? Do you tend to see details and concentrate on the 'foreground' of life (far right)? Or do you prefer to focus on the future and more distant horizons (far left)? When you think about your life, do people and 'shades' of feeling feature most prominently (second from right)? Or are logical connections, abstract thoughts and finding order in chaos more important to you (lower left)? To find your thinking style, read the following 10 pages.

Now let's approach your emotional reactions from a different point of view. Read the following list of feelings and think about how you tend to respond when others express them. Consider each one and note how many you can tolerate when someone else displays them.

Sadness	Energy	Fright	Hate	Boredom	Vulnerability
Grief	Enthusiasm	Regret	Dislike	Excitement	Weakness
Sorrow	Sexuality	Guilt	Irritation	Elation	Joy
Anger	Frustration	Resentment	Impatience	Confusion	Contempt
Disgust	Irritation	Jealousy	Anxiety	Embarrassment	Tenderness
Appreciation	Fear	Envy	Apathy	Hurt	Pleasure

Look at the list again and note which feelings you yourself can express freely, in appropriate circumstances. Now observe the broad pattern. In most cases can you openly express your feelings?

Now take a final look at the list and make a note of any feelings – positive or negative – that you are able to contain at the time and express at a more appropriate moment. In general can you 'hold on' to your feelings?

FEEDBACK

The first part of the assessment reveals how much you value emotional intelligence. If you recognized most of the statements as very true of you, then feeling is probably the way you instinctively understand and respond to the world. The second part of the assessment should reveal how far your emotional intelligence has been developed. If you noted down a large number of feelings and more or less the same ones for each of the three questions, this indicates developed emotional intelligence (see p. 69). Other results, such as if you only noted down a down a few feelings for each of the three questions, are likely to indicate a relatively underdeveloped emotional intelligence. In this case you are reflecting the prevailing Western cultural attitude to feelings and emotion, believing them to be associated with weakness and irrationality. This cultural snobbery has begun to break down in recent decades as it becomes increasingly clear that repressed feelings remain active in distorted behaviour and psychosomatic ailments.

ACTION PLAN

If the list of feelings that you can't express coincides very closely with the list of feelings you can't tolerate in others, look at how this is limiting the choices in your life. If your list of the feelings you can hold on to is much longer than the list of feelings you can freely express, consider if this is impoverishing your relationships. If you have only a light scattering on each of your three lists, begin to give more attention to your feelings.

See Self-assessment
  22-5   Loving, understanding and choosing
  26-35   Life events
  47-9   Self-esteem
  66-81   Intelligence
  84-6   Self-presentation
See Knowhow
  118-21 The early years
  122-3   School's subtle lessons
  142-3   Intelligence
  144-5   Feelings are physical
  146-55 Self-defence
See Mind gym
  195-6   Healing and distress
  203-9   Self-esteem
  214-17 Transformation
  218-22 Emotional intelligence

INTUITIVE INTELLIGENCE

Intuition, like feeling, is often thought to be a female quality and so tends to be valued less than intellect, a traditional male preserve. However, with this sexist labelling removed, intuition turns out to be a distinctive form of intelligence with its own special virtues.

Do you see yourself here? Look through the following list of statements and see how many you agree with.

You are good at 'smelling a rat'.
You often have 'hunches'.
You are good at picking up future possibilities of a situation.
If you are in business, you are at home with speculation and investment, new projects, or new inventions and innovation.
Many people feel you can be a reliable guide to what will be popular next year.
You often prefer to look at things from afar or vaguely and dislike being overcome with too much fine detail.
You tend to sow more than you reap.
You tend to be vague about facts and details.
You can be unaware of the mundane facts of daily existence.
You quite often don't notice what is under your nose.
You quite often leave things unfinished.
You value autonomy and independence.
You are inclined to change jobs frequently, especially if the work becomes mechanical or routine.
You are more willing than most to take risks.
You enjoy using your imagination.
You are interested in or have had experience of ESP or telepathy.
You are good at inspiring others.
You are easily bored with routine.
You could imagine yourself as a journalist 'with a nose for news'.
You could imagine yourself as a revolutionary.
You tend to be inefficient at managing money.
You have often neglected your body.
Your appetites, including sex, sometimes give you great difficulty.

Here is another way of looking at intuition.

You are choosing pictures for your home.

Look through the following images and make a note of any that you feel reflect your preferences or personal style and that you could enjoy living with.

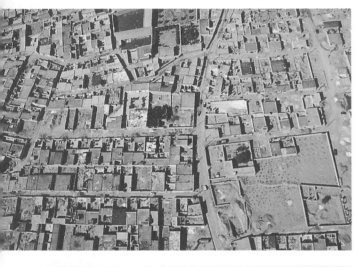

FEEDBACK

In the past, psychologists regarded intuition as being flashes of insight from the unconscious mind. This may well be so. However, over the last twenty years or so, considerable evidence emerging from neuro-psychology has indicated that there is a specific form of intelligence associated with the right side of the brain. People with a high level of intuition are those who are good at tuning in to this right brain intelligence. The right side of the brain, generally influencing the left half of the body, appears to be an organizing centre for visual and spatial discrimination and also music. It also appears to perceive things as a whole, with an emphasis on analogy, metaphor, myth, mapping and networks. By contrast, the left side of the brain, generally influencing the right half of the body (1) appears to be the organizing centre for speech, linear thinking, logic, analysis and calculation.

If you found the majority of statements were true for you and most of the pictures represented your taste, you probably have significant access to the right side of your brain. If you know and value your intuition that's fine. But if you have often fought against your tendency to day-dream and to see things as a whole, then you would gain a lot by valuing your intuition more and learning to use it consciously.

If you agree with only a minority of the statements and like very few of the pictures, there are two possible implications. You may have access to the right, intuitive side of the brain but be rather sceptical of the value of this kind of intelligence. If you have rejected intuition as vague, indistinct, impractical and, above all, irrational, you are unnecessarily limiting your intelligence. The other implication is that you have never given attention to your intuition and so access to the right side of your brain is underdeveloped.

ACTION PLAN

If you recognize yourself here as strongly intuitive, look at the other forms of intelligence in this assessment section. They might not feel immediately appetizing but you may find echoes that will give you an idea of what you could usefully develop. If you don't see yourself strongly represented in this assessment, then give some time and attention to developing some of these intuitive attributes, seeing things whole, using your imagination.

PHYSICAL INTELLIGENCE

Another strand of intelligence that is frequently undervalued is body intelligence – you may be surprised to see intelligence described as physical at all. This includes the physical aptitudes displayed most dramatically by virtuoso pianists, jugglers and champion pool and darts players, but which we all have to a considerable extent. Use this assessment to discover whether it is one of your natural strengths. Look at the following list and note how many describe you.

You have driven a car for five or more years without an accident.
You are good at do-it-yourself and household repairs.
You can sew and/or knit if you need to.
You know how to maintain a garden.
Farm work is something you could do if you had to.
You know how to do home decorating.
You can do basic carpentry.
You can type if you need to.
You enjoy cooking a variety of appetizing meals.
You can ride a horse.
You can play rugby, soccer, badminton, tennis, golf, water polo, hockey or squash.
You can ice skate, roller skate or ski.
You know how to rig and sail a small boat.
You are good at gymnastics.
You take a lot of exercise, such as running over five miles a week.
You are good at caring for small children.
You are able to give a massage.
Your work constantly involves agility, physical precision or stamina.
You like to touch, grasp and physically act on your environment and the people in it.
You have a good memory for details.
You notice and appreciate the texture of things.
You enjoy working with tools and materials.
You could have had a career in selling.
If you are in business you are good at marketing or production.
You have great respect for people who are sensible.
You can, on occasion, go over the top in pleasure-seeking.

Now look at the following signs of physical intelligence.
Would you say you tend to be:

Strong	Poised	Vigorous	Facile
Tough	Relaxed	Virile	Handy
Energetic	Hardy	Dexterous	Quick
Agile	Rugged	Adroit	Well co-ordinated
Nimble	Muscular	Deft	Sexual
Graceful	Athletic	A dab-hand	Elegant

Make a note of any that describe you.

FEEDBACK

If you agree with thirteen or more of the statements and align yourself with many of the positive physical attributes, your physical intelligence is probably well developed. You have an accurate idea of your strength, agility, precision and dexterity and you know how to organize training so that you can learn new skills. Unless you were very lucky, however, you probably gained the impression that your physical ability was not especially valuable, unless you excelled in competitive situations. This is partly because the status quo, particularly when reflected in schools, tends to favour physical intelligence only if it is linked to competitive success.

If you found that few of the statements and physical attributes described you, physical intelligence is probably not your strong point. Whether this amounts to just an underdeveloped part of yourself or a serious weakness should become clear by the time you have worked through all the intelligence assessments. It may be that if you failed to compete your confidence was undermined, until you felt that physical intelligence was not for you. The way that many of us have been brought up to believe that the body is bad, sinful or at least a problem also limits the development of physical intelligence.

ACTION PLAN

If your physical intelligence is well tuned, you can afford to consider what this excellent ability might be excluding from your life. Typically this may mean that you tend to be overtaken by other people's ideas and imagination because you are so much drawn to present-time excitement that you don't have time for, or give much value to, the way things are going. Looking through the attributes of intuitive intelligence may give you some clues to what you are missing. If this seems a bit black and white, remember it is the overall balance between the different modes of intelligence that matters.

If you are dubious about your physical abilities, then plan to look at the increasing number of ways in which you can develop your physical intelligence without having to become involved in competition. Dancing, running, swimming, yoga, aikido and t'ai chi all offer ways of developing your physical intelligence.

INTELLECTUAL DEVELOPMENT

Although most schools emphasize intellectual development above all other skills, vast numbers of people are excluded from the higher levels because of the way subjects are taught. This assessment will help you to assess whether intellect is your basic style of intelligence, and how far it has been developed.

How many of the following do you feel at home with?

Deduction and inference (combining rules or principles to produce new conclusions)
Induction (discovering the general from the particular)
Reasoning
Problem solving
Finding order in apparent chaos
Philosophy
Logical principles
Data collection
Instrumentation
Facts
Systems
Abstraction
Analysis
Mathematical calculation
Proof
Argument
Being objective
Solving problems
Formal logic
Learning a new subject or language
Analyzing facts carefully before reaching a decision
Theoretical explanations

Write a brief report on your intellectual development, covering the following points:

Parents' attitude – was learning encouraged or deprecated?
Discussion – were work, business or intellectual interests talked about freely at home?
Reading matter – were there always books, newspapers and magazines available at home?
Parents' education – did your parents receive higher education?
School – was the teaching good, poor or a mixture?
Continuity – did you change schools a lot?
Pressure from friends – did your school friends accept or reject schoolwork?
Disabilities – did you have time off school because of illness, deafness, poor eyesight or dyslexia.
Special abilities – were they recognized and valued?
Highs and lows – were there critical points of success or failure?

Affirmation – was your attitude to school work tolerated or rejected?
Gender discouragement – were you steered towards or away from certain subjects because of your gender?
Personal judgement – was your overall assessment of your intellectual development strong, moderate or weak?
External judgement – do you agree with other people's views on your intellectual development; are they accurate or inaccurate?
Potential – how far has your intellectual potential been fulfilled?

FEEDBACK

If your report indicates that your family and school background encouraged intellectual development and you also felt at home with the first list, you probably have a core strength in intellect. Your ability is favoured in business, in the professions and in conventional circles of success. However, your education may have excluded other forms of intelligence, and you may well find yourself doing well at work at the cost of your personal life. You may, for example, tend to suppress your emotions and unconsciously project them on to others.

If you give yourself a low rating in both parts of the assessment, it may be because conventional teaching never really seemed to make sense. This could be because it wasn't very good or because it didn't favour your particular style of intelligence. You may have found the tone and style of teaching unappealing and that your interests were poorly represented, if at all.

If your response to the two parts of the assessment conflict, it could mean that you felt pressurized to compete intellectually but felt it wasn't you. Or you may have developed your intellect in spite of lack of encouragement.

ACTION PLAN

Consider whether you have paid the price of intellectual development in terms of suppressed feeling. Is the price too high? If so, think about how you can redress the balance by learning to be more emotionally competent. If your intellectual development never really took off, is this a constant source of frustration and regret? If so, think about the possibilities for taking up further education.

BALANCED INTELLIGENCE

What do you do with all your assessments? Keep them. Together they should have helped you to form a broad view of your intelligence.

You may find it useful to recreate it as a shape. Draw four skyscrapers, one for each aspect of your intelligence, with the height representing how well you function in each mode.

FEEDBACK

The style of intelligence that feels most comfortable is the one we use most frequently because it supports our survival at home and at work. What we often find, however, is that one dominating form of intelligence overshadows the others. A scientist, for example, may strongly favour intellect. But without something of each, a farmer might not make it through the winter. When we come to rely too much on one aspect of intelligence, say intellect, we often find ourselves behaving 'irrationally' – unable to change to intuition, feeling or physical intelligence when the need arises. Behaving 'rationally' means deliberately using the form of intelligence most appropriate to the situation.

This is not always easy because many of us have struggled to develop intellect to conform to the demands of Western society. Intellect is great for calculating how to maximize the profits of a department or analyzing how to make a new product for less than your competitor, but it isn't a lot of use in, say, helping a young child through the aftermath of long hospitalization or comforting a woman who has just lost her husband.

Conversely, there are people, for instance in the caring professions, whose emotional intelligence is well developed but who, when they reach the age for promotion, do not make good departmental managers. Organization and planning need intellect as well as interpersonal skills.

So how rational are you? Can you consciously move from intellect to feeling to intuition to physical intelligence? Or is one mode awkward, uncomfortable and inaccessible? Do you depend on one familiar comfortable mode too much of the time?

If you find all your intelligence 'skyscrapers' seem to be low, this does not mean you have no strengths. Instead, you are likely to be suffering from low self-esteem, probably through no fault of your own – see Personal History (pp. 18-35) and Identity (pp. 36-51).

ACTION PLAN

If one or two styles of intelligence are dominant, concentrate on developing the others, one by one. Practise moving consciously from one style of intelligence to another, so that in the space of a day you may, for example, talk sympathetically to a friend, imagine what you will be doing in five years time, solve a problem at work and sew on a button. If you lack confidence, concentrate first on your strong points, even if they are undeveloped.

INTELLIGENT GUESSING

Now we'll take a look at your intelligence as a whole, at how good you are at 'guessing' – how well you make use of the information you receive, how well you perceive new connections in it, and how well you apply those connections – regardless of your predominant style.

During the next week keep a note of any situation in which you have to make a guess. Here are some suggestions about what to look for.

What would she/he say if . . .
The best way to approach this is by . . .
What's going to happen is . . .
The best choice would be . . .
How long would it take to . . .
There isn't going to be enough time to . . .
She/he is the right/wrong person for . . .
She/he is going to want to . . .

When you have done your list, rate the items on it according to how close your guess was to the final outcome. Look down the list at how conscious you were of guessing.

How often do you learn from your mistakes?
What is your long-term pattern of guessing?
On balance do you tend to get it right?

Make a note of any areas where your guesses turn out to be more often right than wrong.

Make a note of any areas where your guesses turn out to be more often wrong than right.

FEEDBACK

This aspect of intelligence involves a) formulating possible guesses, b) noticing what works and what doesn't and c) learning from that experience. Intelligence, then, depends on coming up with a flow of viable alternatives, and choosing well between them. It is a skill that applies across any kind of cultural boundary and across all types of intelligence. You are best placed to evaluate how easily you come up with solutions and how well you choose between them. But whatever your self-assessment, your guessing ability will improve if you continue to review each guess.

ACTION PLAN

Continue to notice how well you guess. If your guesses are sometimes adrift, consider whether you could use a more intellectual, emotional, intuitive or physical approach. Are you switching from one to the other when necessary? Which of the four do you never use? Try it. Where you find you guess wrong, consider why. Think about what you may have overlooked.

INTELLIGENCE REVIEW

This is an assessment to try after you've been through the book once or after a few weeks when you have started to digest what it has begun to reveal. You might find it very useful at this stage to try repeating a couple of earlier assessments.

Look back to page 68 and your first assessment of how you thought other people rated your intelligence first time around. Now looking at it again, do you agree with their opinion? Do you secretly suspect that you are more (or less) intelligent than this? What would that estimate be now?

On a scale of 0 to 200 where do you now believe that you come?

0 means very low intelligence
100 means average intelligence
200 means very high intelligence

Now take a look back to page 79 and redraw your skyscrapers, showing the proportion of your intellectual, emotional, physical and intuitive intelligence. If you don't feel that it has changed enough yet to be worth redrawing, draw it as you would now like it to be.

FEEDBACK

If your private, personal estimate is that you are more intelligent than other people give you credit for, then your core intelligence probably lies outside the intellectual, thinking domain. It may also mean that you either never had the opportunity to develop intellectually or that you chose not to take it.

If your assessment agrees with other people's, then this may mean that you are sure they are right or that you had no way, until now, of knowing whether they were right or wrong.

If there is a large difference between your own and others' assessments you have probably realized that other people's views of you were wrong, premature, inaccurate or irrelevant and that you are intelligent in ways that are not visible or valued by other people.

If some time has passed since you first read this section because you went on to work your way through the rest of the book, you are very likely to find that you are more intelligent than you thought you were.

ACTION PLAN

Continue to review your own estimate of your intelligence. Begin to work on the areas of your intelligence you feel could be enhanced, and allow yourself to feel confident of your strengths.

See Self-assessment
40-1   Personal potential
47-9   Self-esteem
66-80   Intelligence
102-9   Beliefs
See Knowhow
122-3   School's subtle lessons
182-3   Shared assessment
184-5   Work without experts
See Mind gym
198-9   Life review
200-2   Identity
214-17 Transformation
218-22 Emotional intelligence
223-5   Physical intelligence
226-7   Intuitive intelligence
228-9   Intellectual intelligence

RELATING

Being in touch with other people is founded on being in touch with yourself and on how easy and open you are about physical contact.

How to use this section

The following self-assessments turn the spotlight on your relationships, and will help you to identify your strengths and weaknesses in connecting to people – within your usual repertoire of behaviour patterns. Typically, the strengths will feel familiar, reliable and comfortable, and the weaknesses will be those connections with others that you always try to avoid or feel compelled to enter into, with the result that you feel trapped. Taken together, the following guidelines dealing with self-presentation, introversion and extraversion, personal responsibility, conflict, intimacy, control and love, assertiveness and communication style will help you to illuminate the way your mind makes connections.

Work your way through the questions, taking as much time as you need. When you have settled on a response, move on to FEEDBACK, and record both your positive and negative assessments, such as 'I have a developed capacity for love' but 'I tend to avoid conflict situations'. Then move on to ACTION PLAN and decide what, if anything, you want to do about your new view of yourself. If you do not find yourself reflected here, turn to the Index and use it to direct you to a different starting point in another assessment section.

Your connections with other people – how you relate to them and how they react to you – are central to your sense of self and your view of the world. By relating to other people you become who you are, and you can, if you choose, continually redefine yourself. Yet your approach to your relationships and the value you place on them vary from day to day and depend on your personal history.

The different layers of human connectedness

Your connections to others reveal themselves not only in your close personal relationships and friendships, your working life and your social encounters, but extend also to your sense of belonging to the human race and your connection to the phenomenon of life itself – to time, space and death. Keeping death and dying hidden from view, for example, has a fundamental effect on our connection to the phenomenon of life.

How you relate to others

Some people tend to give priority to their inner world, seeing their relations with others, though important, as secondary. Other people find their exchanges with others take up most of the space in their lives, leaving inner preoccupations low on the daily agenda. How you relate to others is influenced not only by these fundamental tendencies, but by your self-esteem and social skills.

As you develop through childhood and adolescence you acquire a rich and intricate web of skills for relating to other people. Some of these will be serving you well. You may, for instance, be good at absorbing and interpreting other people's ideas – as you are doing now. You may find communicating your own ideas comes easily. You may feel confident among strangers or in social situations. You may find you 'tune in' quickly to the needs of close friends. But other skills may be less well formed, or missing altogether. What often happens is that we come to rely on a communication style that works well for us in one part of our life and fail to notice when it becomes inappropriate in other areas. The logical thinking and determination that sustain you at work, for example, may not help when it comes to sex or childcare. Equally, the softness needed for nurturing and caring for family and friends may be inadequate for managing a business or a whole building full of people.

Can you improve your relationships?

The external expression of your connections with others – the requests, moods, arguments, kisses, caresses, instructions, orders and jokes – are usually easily identifiable. But the inner thought processes that influence how you connect to others are less visible. Changing how you relate involves learning to notice your attitudes towards others and the manner in which you approach and communicate with them. Once you have unravelled your interpersonal style – how you deal with conflict, intimacy and responsibility, for example – you can begin to improve your relationships.

SELF-PRESENTATION

How you come across to other people is one of the most telling ways in which your mind reveals itself. When you meet someone for the first time, you give an immediate first impression. How well do you present yourself? What are your social strengths and weaknesses and in what situations do you present yourself at your best?

Strengths

Look through the following list of self-presentation qualities. How many apply to you?

Witty
Enthusiastic
Able to hold people's attention
Humorous
Able to maintain eye contact
Persistent and tenacious
Patient
Knowledgeable
Confident
Able to make myself understood
Able to stand my ground

Articulate
Sympathetic
Perceptive
Quick-witted
Sincere
Able to raise my voice if necessary
Able to show empathy
Capable of speaking clearly
Able to relax people
Able to put my point across

Calm and composed
Lively
Friendly
Sensitive
Cheerful
Easy-going
Able to establish a good rapport
Good at reassuring people
Able to overcome nervousness
Approachable
Able to make official complaints

Make a note of the qualities you select, and any others of your own that are not included on the list.

Weaknesses

Now consider the following weaknesses in self-presentation. How many tend to be true of you? Are you often . . .?

Unable to think logically, step-by-step
Unable to keep to a train of thought – go off at tangents
Not good at 'selling myself'
Dour
Hesitant
Unable to think while holding eye contact
Long-winded, unable to be pithy
Too forceful
Tactless
Easily pressurized
Judgemental

Obstinate
Opinionated
Easily embarrassed
Slow to come to the point
Sarcastic
Unable to raise your voice
Pompous
Unable to disagree or argue
Hostile
Unsympathetic
Impatient

Do you often . . .?

Suffer mental blocks
Have to have the last word
Have to be nice
Ramble on or become incoherent
Finish in mid-sentence
Talk monotonously
Talk too much, too loud or too fast
Become tongue-tied
Underestimate yourself
Avoid direct eye contact
Lose concentration
Mutter or mumble
Lose your thread if interrupted
Become muddled

Make a note of those you select and add any others that occur to you.

Situations

Like most people, you are probably better in some circumstances than others. Do you know where or when you are at your best and when you tend to get into difficulties? Take a look at the following situations and make a note of which you feel most comfortable with, and which cause you problems.

One-to-one conversations
Technical discussions
Giving formal talks
When you are at home
Formal settings
When you are with complete strangers
Meeting new people
Informal situations
Being with people you know
Instructing somebody one-to-one
When you are well prepared
When you have to talk about yourself

Confronting people
When you are unjustly accused
Speaking to large groups
When you are in the presence of authority figures
Addressing public meetings
Talking to more senior people
When you are reluctant to speak your mind in public
When making personal requests
Social gatherings
Being with aggressive or abrasive people
Approaching strangers

When you feel younger or older than everyone else
Initiating a conversation
When you are with highly educated people
Breaking into a conversation when someone is monopolizing it
Talking to rude people
When you are with people you admire, respect or fear
When you are not sure of your facts or opinions
With the opposite sex

Feelings

Feelings are always involved in self-presentation. Anxiety, contempt, remoteness and pleasure are often instantly communicated, and if you conceal them they may come across as caution, confusion or vulnerability.

Make a note of how many of the following responses you have when you are presenting yourself.

Inability to contain emotions
Nervousness
Anxiety
Palpitations
Fear of going blank
Fear of criticism
Panic attacks

Tension
Discomfort
A tendency to blush
A tendency to dry up
A tendency to get a dry mouth
A tendency to talk too much
Fear of saying the wrong thing

A tendency to become flustered
Fear of hurting other people
A tendency to become easily upset
Panic under pressure
A racing pulse when waiting to speak

Confidence

If you have problems with presenting yourself, why do you think this is? Is it because you see yourself as any of the following?

Shy
Nervous
Self-conscious
Humble
Aggressive
Modest

Unassuming
Detached
Self-critical
Inferior
More of a listener than a speaker
Lacking confidence

FEEDBACK

If you consistently had a much longer list of strengths than weaknesses, you already know that you come over well to other people, that you can explain yourself clearly and that you can hold people's attention. You probably have a healthy sense of your own value and are not afraid to show it. If, despite this strength, you know there are one or two circumstances in which you don't perform so well, consult the ACTION PLAN and marginal references for suggestions for improvement.

If you noted considerably more weaknesses than strengths and if you recognized yourself in the Confidence assessment, then you have work to do. The quality of anyone's self-presentation is usually directly related to two main considerations. The first is present-time causes, such as haste, poor preparation, inadequate briefing, unreasonable demands, reporting too soon and lack of experience or practice. Any of these can easily lead to confusion, anxiety and incoherence. And they can all be readily changed once you learn to spot them in time.

The second consideration is self-esteem. If you don't like yourself or feel that you are inferior, inadequate or unintelligent, then your self-presentation is going to reflect this. It will tend to emerge as shyness, lack of confidence, excessive self-criticism, and very often a flush of self-conscious feelings. It follows from this that the most effective way of improving your self-presentation means doing something about your self-esteem. Your low self-esteem was learned, probably as a way of surviving as a child where being too bright or too assertive was not acceptable, so perhaps you learned to be meek and unassuming. You can unlearn it. It takes time and effort – but it can be done.

ACTION PLAN

If you rate your self-presentation as poor or bad, look at where and how you came to have such a poor opinion of yourself. Find out whether this low self-esteem has some kind of unseen benefit, either for you or somebody else – in what way does it keep you comfortable or please someone else? Look at how your self-esteem is affecting the rest of your life. Consider whether, by putting a lot of energy into remaining or appearing invulnerable, you may be setting yourself up for a psychosomatic ailment. Spoil yourself. Give yourself some treats. If you rate your self-presentation as good or very good, plan to take on further responsibilities – you might enjoy the risks. If your confidence is well-founded, it should also allow you to make mistakes and ask for help from time to time. If it doesn't, give yourself permission to feel vulnerable now and again.

See Self-assessment
20-1   Social background
22-5   Loving, understanding and choosing
26-35 Life events
38-9   Social identity
40-1   Personal potential
42-4   Work
46   Body image
47-9   Self-esteem
50   Inner voices
51   Other people's labels
66-81 Intelligence
82-101 Relating
102-9 Beliefs
See Knowhow
118-21 The early years
134-5 Map of the mind
136-7 Going into your mind
138-9 The shifting spotlight
140-1 Paying attention
144-5 Feelings are physical
146-55 Self-defence
156-7 Other connections
164-5 The new paradigm
166-71 Humanistic psychology
172-3 The new paradigm leader
180-1 Communication
186-7 Resolving conflict
See Mind gym
203-9 Self-esteem
214-17 Transformation
218-22 Emotional intelligence
231-4 Confidence
234-5 Projection
236   Self-disclosure
236-8 Relationships

COMMUNICATION

There are many different styles of communication. Do you know which personal styles come easily to you, which you overuse and which you find completely impossible? This assessment will help you to identify your communication strengths and weaknesses.

Personal communication style

When you are communicating with others, do you have a wide range of different approaches or do you tend to stick with one or two 'safe' ways of putting across your point of view?

Consider the following modes of communication:

Giving instructions
Giving information
Confronting people about their behaviour
Helping people to deal with their feelings
Drawing people out
Being supportive – listening to and accepting someone
Asking for information

Now divide them into those you usually find relatively easy, those you often find difficult and those you avoid where possible.

Assertiveness

When you make a request, express an opinion or take a decision, which of the following statements best represents your approach?

'You know better than me. You're the expert, I'd rather take your
    word for it.'
'I just thought we might try a different place, but it doesn't really
    matter.'
'If it's not too much trouble, if you don't mind, could you just leave
    the letters on the table by the door.'

'That's enough of that. Just do what you're told, all right?'
'How stupid can you get. What makes you think anyone will take any
    notice of what I say?'
'All right, have it your own way. See if I care.'

'Wouldn't you like to try that new restaurant again? You know how
    much you enjoyed it before.'
'While you're there, could you pass me the milk please.'
'If you really loved me, I wouldn't need to ask you at all.'
'I understand you object to giving me the extra day off and I still want
    to say that I feel entitled to it.'
'I have looked into the problem you raised and I would like you to
    stop what you are doing immediately.'
'I appreciate that you have a policy of no returns but the quality of
    this rug is unacceptable. I'd like my money back.'

Make a note of the ones you select.

Now look at the following statements. How many do you respect in yourself and others? How many do you find difficult or impossible?

You have the right to state your own needs and priorities as a person, whatever other people may expect of someone in your position.

You have the right to be treated as an intelligent, capable, equal human being.

You have the right to express your opinions and values.

You have the right to say yes and no for yourself.

You have the right to make mistakes.

You have the right to change your mind.

You have the right to say you don't understand.

You have the right to ask for what you want.

You have the right to decide for yourself whether or not you are responsible for someone else's problem.

You have the right to deal with people without needing them to like you.

FEEDBACK

If, in the Personal Communication assessment, you found that you can easily shift between all the styles of communication, then you are well equipped to work with people. If you rely on one or two styles, you and the people you live and work with would benefit if you learned to expand your communication repertoire. For most people, confronting others is the most difficult style, and helping people with their feelings is a close second.

In the first Assertiveness assessment, if you identified with the first three statements, you probably communicate submissiveness. If the second three seemed more your style, you may come over as aggressive. If you recognized yourself in the next three, manipulation is more your style. If you selected any of the last three statements, you are already familiar with clear, direct, assertive communication. In the second Assertiveness assessment, if there are any statements you feel are difficult or impossible for you, you would gain a lot from learning to be more assertive.

ACTION PLAN

Make a special effort to practise the styles of communication that do not come easily to you and try an assertiveness skills training course.

INTROVERSION AND EXTRAVERSION

Some people seem very outgoing and are primarily concerned with, and interested in, other people. Others seem very withdrawn and preoccupied with themselves and their personal interests. Although, like most people, you may be a mixture of both tendencies, one or other probably remains in the foreground.

The following statements will reveal whether you are leaning in one direction or alternating between the two. How many apply to you?

List one
You spend a lot of time reflecting before deciding what to do.
You feel you need to be independent.
You can happily concentrate on a job alone for long periods.
You need a lot of time alone with your thoughts.
You often prefer reading and relaxing alone to meeting people.
You get lost in thought and forget about what's going on around you.
You would enjoy a project that involved a lot of research.
People say you are a dreamer.
You have a few, deep friendships.
You find speaking in front of a lot of people difficult or impossible.
You enjoy books on serious philosophical subjects.
You would be more inclined to use a map than to ask the way.
You often feel ill-at-ease with people.
The world of people and obligations is a disagreeable distraction.
Your interpersonal relationships are often difficult.
You are often awkward in social situations.
You feel undervalued by others because you fail to communicate the
    richness of your ideas and imagination.

Now look at these statements and note which apply to you.

List two
You are positive towards other people's ideas and views.
You are very sociable and would not want to lose your social contacts.
You are confident in action and prefer 'doing' to studying.
You communicate expressively and like people to be open.
You are happy-go-lucky and easy-going.
You enjoy buying small gifts for people between celebrations.
You tend to believe that analyzing yourself is fruitless.
You have many acquaintances but few deep friendships.
You are likely to introduce yourself spontaneously at social events.
You want to be liked and hate to offend people.
You enjoy joining in amateur theatricals or musical groups.
You are relaxed and confident in a crowd.
You find it difficult to concentrate for long periods alone.
You often need understanding friends to cheer you up.
You prefer to be with other people than on your own.
You enjoy working with others in a group.
You feel at home in most surroundings.
You like variety in your life and enjoy going out with people.

FEEDBACK

If you selected more from List one than from List two, your basic orientation is *introverted*. This means that you find it easy and comfortable to be alone with yourself, you have many different approaches to spending time on your own, and you are probably more interested in ideas and things than in people. Your inner convictions, which tend to be clear and strong, influence how you conduct your life, so that your mind is probably rarely out of tune with your interests. You know what you like, which is a considerable inner strength. But because you are uncertain what other people want or like, this quality may not earn you much money. You may, for example, be plagued by the failure of impractical projects. You probably have great difficulty making life decisions that involve understanding the finer nuances of other people's wants and needs.

If you selected more from List two, your basic orientation is likely to be *extraverted*. This means that you will find being with people easy and comfortable and have many different ways of approaching and responding to them. The very strength of your feelings for other people will ensure that your mind is rarely out of tune with the people around you. Knowing what people want and being able to give it to them not only gives you pleasure but is also likely to help you to make money. But you are probably less certain about what you personally want and like. As a result, any life decisions that involve your innermost convictions and your inner thoughts, feelings and intuitions are likely to be difficult and you may be plagued by obsessive thoughts, jealousies and perhaps a deep sense of emptiness. You may find yourself slipping into a state of compulsively helping other people.

Neither of these two tendencies is better than the other. But believing that your own style is superior may be damaging, because it under-values a fundamentally different way of experiencing the world. The aim is to achieve a balance between the two.

ACTION PLAN

If you are predominantly introverted, give yourself a chance to expand a little more into the world of people. Learn to give more time to the outer world of people and to be more realistic about your projects. Spend more time away from your personal interests and try taking on work that involves working closely with others for extended periods.

If you are predominantly extraverted, give yourself a chance to be more in touch with your inner life. Explore your inner thoughts and find new ways of handling the fantasies that take hold of you. Spend more time alone and try taking on work that means you have to work alone for extended periods.

Inner world, outer world

In the garden of life the extravert lives in an outer world – a fascinating tangle of relationships and events – while the inner garden lies hidden in the shade. The introvert lives in a rich, self-contained inner garden, intertwined with an absorbing array of personal thoughts, feelings, ideas and convictions, which cast the outer world of people in shadow. These two fundamentally different ways of approaching reality were elucidated by the Swiss psychiatrist C.G. Jung. You can recognize your primary mode, because it tends to feel comfortable and offers a wide and subtle range of behaviour styles. Your secondary mode has a clumsy, rather awkward quality to it. Unfortunately, as these labels have come into general use, their original meaning has been distorted and, perhaps because of the rise in global communications, extraversion features far more strongly in business, the media and the entertainment world than is wise or appropriate.

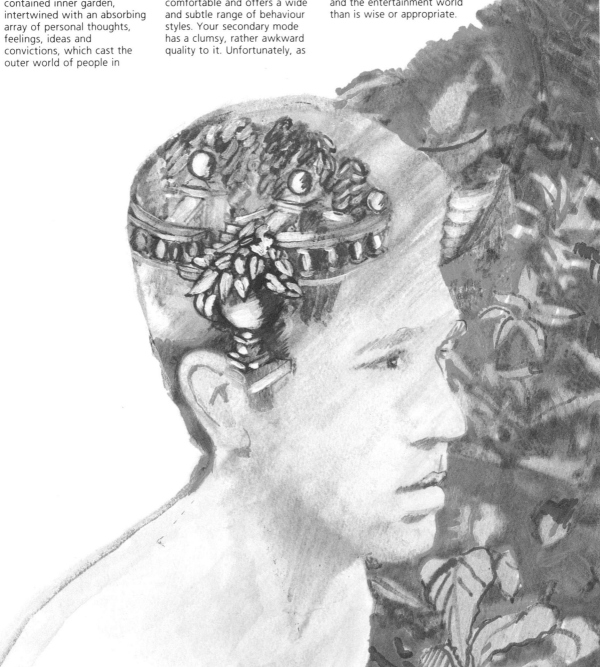

PERSONAL RESPONSIBILITY

One of the ways in which your mind can become unhappily
enmeshed with others' is through insisting that other people are
responsible for how you feel.

Read through the following mini dialogues. How many of these
comments are similar to your own? Taking them as a whole, make a
note of whether you are like this most of the time, frequently,
occasionally or never.

Amy comes home very late from work. Her husband, Hamish, says:
'God, you make me angry, coming home so late. I've been waiting for
hours.'
Amy: 'Oh, shut up, you're always complaining. It makes me sick.'
Hamish: 'Well I wouldn't need to complain if you didn't do these
things. If you really loved me, you'd think about my feelings.'

Later that evening Amy confides: 'Look, the reason I was late was
because I went to see Jane. I thought she ought to know how angry
she had made you.'
Hamish: 'You shouldn't have done that. Oh God, you've really put
your foot in it now.'
Amy: 'Oh, for heaven's sake, it was for your own good. Somebody
had to put her right.'
Hamish: 'I wouldn't mind if she wasn't so bossy.'
Amy: 'Well, it's your own fault really, you asked for it.'
Hamish: 'It wasn't my fault. She made me look such a fool, implying
that I was too fat to fit into the suit I was married in.'

Later still. Amy is noisily stirring an aspirin in a glass of water.
Hamish: 'Oh, do stop that, it's annoying me.'
Amy: 'Take this, it'll make you feel better.'
Hamish: 'It's your fault, you know – you should have had more sense.'
Amy: 'I only did it for your sake.'
Hamish: 'There you go again, you love embarrassing me, don't you.'

When you are not responsible
Taking full responsibility for what
you feel is a necessary step toward
making your mind work better for
you. But there are occasions when
you may not be responsible. If, for
example, you work with six other
people in a badly lit, poorly
ventilated office that is really only
suitable for half that number, then
many of your feelings will be
directly related to these oppressive
conditions. But if you know which
feelings you carry around with you
belong to you and which don't, you
will be more able to devise effective
ways of improving your working
environment. You will be more able
to determine whether any distress is
based on feelings you always tend
to have, or whether they are caused
by the conditions.

FEEDBACK

If you tend to make these kinds of remarks, you probably believe that other people often cause your feelings. Although some feelings arise from other people's actions (see box, left), it makes very good interpersonal sense to assume initially that what you feel comes from you not from them.

There are three very good reasons for doing this. First, because it keeps areas of personal responsibility clear. If, for example, you say: 'You are driving very fast and I am feeling uneasy,' you are giving the driver more freedom to choose to slow down than if you say, critically: 'The way you're driving really frightens me.' Secondly, much of what you feel now is likely to be a replay of past experiences. Feelings that we blame on other people – especially very intense ones – are likely to be caused by old and painful memories, triggered by present situations. Finally, if you really believe that other people are responsible for the way you feel, you can come to behave like a puppet, dancing to other people's actions and reactions.

If you don't identify with any of the comments in the dialogue, you may have already rid yourself of these entanglements. If you know when and how this happened, fine. If not, there is a chance that some concealed version of this kind of blame is still lurking around. It's worth looking into.

ACTION PLAN

The best way of clearing out the junk from any relationship is for both people to acknowledge that their feelings belong to them personally. This is the first stage of being able to take charge of them. Explore the idea that feelings are body messages and take time to listen to what your body is saying. Try taking more responsibility for the way you express your feelings.

CONFLICT AND COMMITMENT

Conflict seems fundamental to human existence. It appears to be an inescapable part of life. Use this assessment to identify your basic approach to conflict and to consider how much choice you have in the way you handle it.

Interests

First, look at how you generally balance your own and other people's interests. Where would you put yourself on this scale?

Own interests	*Own and others'*	*Others' interests*
predominate	*interests balanced*	*predominate*

The balance between these two will vary from time to time, but see if you can detect a general tendency. You may want to mark ranges of movement within the two extremes.

Energy

Another influence on how you deal with conflict is the amount of zeal, energy and commitment you apply to what you do. Where would you put yourself on this scale?

Very little energy	*Considerable energy*	*Enormous energy*
and commitment	*and commitment*	*and commitment*

Again, you will vary from day to day, but see if you can make out your long-term pattern. Again, you may want to mark a range of movement within the two extremes.

Interests and energy

The combination of these two basic personal priorities tends to define how you behave in conflict situations. Trace your position on the map right. If, however, your interests and energy vary considerably, you may want to trace a path of your various positions on the map.
For more information see pp. 186-7.

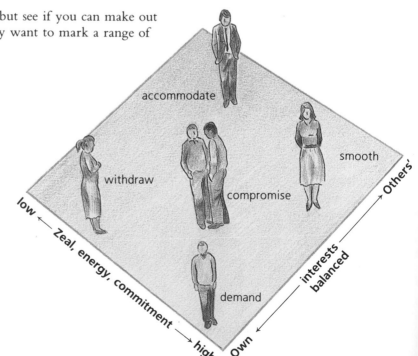

FEEDBACK

Without special training in conflict resolution, most of us are limited to the following five, broad kinds of behaviour, although we may use different ones depending on whether we are already in a conflict or can see one coming.

1 If your own interests strongly predominate and you put little energy into what you do, you probably *withdraw* or avoid conflict.

2 If your own interests predominate and you put a lot of energy, zeal and commitment into what you do, this is likely to result in *confrontation, rebellion and attack* – a combative response.

3 A low to moderate level of energy, zeal and commitment, coupled with a balance between personal and other people's interests, means that you can probably reach a *compromise* in most conflict situations.

4 A high level of energy, zeal and commitment, coupled with a devotion to other people's interests, usually results in a *smoothing, collusive and conformist* approach to conflict.

5 A low level of energy, zeal and commitment, coupled with a devotion to other people's interests is likely to result in an *accommodating and obliging* attitude to conflict.

Each of these groups of conflict behaviour is relatively uncomfortable, and moving from one to the other tends to feel like jumping 'out of the frying pan, into the fire'. So much so, that you may intentionally fall back on only one or two of these choices.

Out of all of them, compromise is the most usual approach for resolving disagreements, but because it is only accessible at quite low levels of commitment, it often feels rather unexciting.

However, when energy, zeal and commitment are high, compromise disappears. And, as those who have lived through industrial conflicts or divorce know, moving across the middle line, from an other-interested, smoothing approach to self-interested confrontation, brings a catastrophic collapse in rapport between those people involved.

To improve significantly your skill in handling conflict, you need to reach a sixth area on the map, to create a new form of compromise, known as 'synergy' – in which both your own and other people's needs are in constant balance, while everyone maintains high levels of energy, zeal and commitment. To create synergy and to stay with it requires a considerable amount of emotional competence (see p. 186).

ACTION PLAN

Get to know which conflict territory you move through best and plot your progress on the map for a few days or weeks. Make a note of any recurring patterns. Notice how compromise becomes more difficult when people increase their levels of energy or commitment. Look at how reaching a compromise often requires a 'cooling-off' period, while people let go of their previous high energy.

INTIMACY

Exploring the connection between your own and other people's minds involves taking a look at intimacy. Intimacy here means the close physical contact, openness and affection that comes from living with someone or caring for someone's physical needs. It means the kind of intimacy that arises within a sexual relationship, childcare, nursing or therapy. At its most intense, it involves all the properties of mind – perception, imagination, attitudes and fantasies. Perhaps because it is so close to home, it can bring both ecstatic peaks and despairing troughs.

Distress

First, let's look at feelings of distress around the prospect or the fact of intimacy. It is not unusual to experience anxiety about loss of control, embarrassment or fear of rejection and, with sexual intimacy in particular, underlying worries about commitment, disease or pregnancy are not uncommon.

Reflect for a moment on how you tend to approach intimacy in your present situation. How much of a problem is it for you personally?

How much distress do you feel about intimacy?

Intimacy is satisfying			*Intimacy is very difficult*	
1	2	3	4	5

Make a note of your rating.

Desire

Now we'll move on to consider the strength of your desire for intimacy. This means a combination of your need for physical and emotional contact and/or for a confirmation of your personal value.

Take your time and reflect for a few moments. How strong is your need for intimacy?

Little need for intimacy			*Strong need for intimacy*	
1	2	3	4	5

FEEDBACK

Our attitudes to intimacy are ultimately traceable to childhood experiences. If there is a tremendous tension around intimacy, this is probably an echo of how you were brought up. Your distress could arise from a lack of intimacy when you were a child – perhaps a lack of touch and cuddles. Or it could be a reaction to painful memories of childhood intimacy – sexual abuse, for example, or acting as a comforter to a parent.

Trace your ratings of your desire and distress levels on the map (below) to find your position.

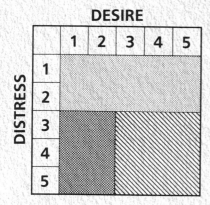

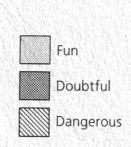

If your position is in the Fun range, then far from causing you problems, intimacy is likely to bring you plenty of fun, if you can find others to share it with you.

If you are in the Doubtful range, then your mind is probably burdened with a lot of unfinished business from childhood. Although it can be painful, it is possible to 'change your mind' and to learn to let go of the restrictions or anxieties you picked up in childhood. This may well increase your interest in intimacy, as you find there is no need to keep your desires out of sight.

If your position is in the Dangerous range, it may be wise to take this as a warning signal. A high level of distress around intimacy, coupled with a high desire for contact may lead to inner pressures to use force to get the closeness you seek. This is not dangerous if other people are not involved, but the move from low to high desire often leads to sudden loss of control, with an incident of, for example, soliciting, flashing, sexual assault, rape or incest.

ACTION PLAN

If you are in the bottom right area of the map, you would be well advised to seek counselling help or psychotherapy right away.

LOVE AND CONTROL

Another big influence on the way your mind connects with other people's minds lies in your attitudes to love and control.

Make a list of situations in which you can tolerate and accept surprise, change and disorder. Examples might include enjoying getting lost in a strange part of a city or not being concerned about punctuality.

Now make a list of situations in which you try to eliminate surprise, change and disorder. Examples might include devoting a whole day to a prescribed series of tasks, or insisting that children are obedient.

Making model people
Controlling and manipulating people to be as we want them rather than as they are, denies them the right to be themselves. And it deprives you of the chance to experience the extraordinary diversity of human individuals. It also excludes love. Do you shape other people, in ways that limit or distort their growth, in order to fit a stereotype of what you want them to be? Do you cultivate yourself to fit somebody else's idea of how you should be?

Love

Love, as defined by this book, means a capacity to celebrate and enjoy difference in others, to let them be just who they are. It means actively supporting other people's capacity to grow and change in their own way, and not needing to force them to collaborate with you. This involves constantly reviewing the urge to control, to command, to insist and to mould others for your own convenience. At times it may be appropriate to guide people, but rigid and compulsive control excludes love. Uncertainty about being loved or lovable often leads to a fear of chaos and unpredictability, which in turn develops into the need to control.

Affection

There is a great deal of confusion about what love is, how to love and the way love grows and dies. This will be clarified if we distinguish between love and affection, renaming the feeling in a dominant/subservient relationship as 'affection'. If you employ me as a servant, we may feel affection, but love is ruled out. Dominance and subservience, both between two people and between people and the human environment, occur often, but they are by no means inevitable. Calling love which has an undercurrent of coercion 'affection' may not ease the ache for the love that's missing, but at least you know when true love is not around.

FEEDBACK

If the first list is, or feels, longer than the second, this implies that you have a high tolerance of change, surprise and disorder. Being able to live with the chaos of human affairs in this way suggests that you may have a well-developed capacity for love.

If your second list is much longer than the first, this may mean that you are very intolerant of chaos and need to be in control most of the time. If this is consistent across the whole of your life, this may mean that you have an underdeveloped capacity for love. Despite often feeling compelled to control other people, you may feel you do love them and that you are only controlling them 'for their own good'. If this rings true, what may have happened is that your love has become watered down into affection. This is outlined in an excellent book by Yi Fu Tuan, who suggests that we reserve 'affection' for the state of feeling between people in dominant/subservient roles and 'love' for relationships free of coercion.

ACTION PLAN

If you have a strong need for control, discover when and how you learned to coerce people. Try letting go of part of your urge to order your surroundings. Learn to 'go with the flow' and welcome more chaos and surprise in your life. Try to be less judgemental and critical with people and learn how to love them even if you object to some or even all of their behaviour.

HUMANITY

There are now something like five billion people alive on this planet
of ours. As a result, most of us find ourselves in very close contact
with large numbers of other people and perhaps because of this
closeness we sometimes lose our sense of wonder at the very
phenomenon of human life.

We rush past each other, averting our eyes from strangers in the
street, connecting to many people only through radio, TV or
newspaper images. Perhaps not surprisingly we have become blind to
the miracle of others' existence. This is great loss, not just because we
are depriving other people of our appreciation of their existence, but
because we are depriving ourselves of the life-enhancing sense of
wonder at our own and other people's existence.

How many of the following experiences are familiar to you?

Have you:

Seen or lived through the kind of crisis that comes to many people
    when children leave home?
Seen or lived through the kind of crisis that arises when work begins
    to seem stale and old interests feel drained of life?
Seen the shock, anger and then resignation of someone who has been
    told they have only a few weeks or months to live?

Seen the delicate and courageous way that many elderly people
    gradually readjust their lives to fit their capacity?
Sat with someone who was dying?
Seen a lifeless corpse?

Been close to a woman who is pregnant and felt or seen the foetus
    moving in her belly?
Seen in real life or on film the birth of a child?
Been close to and held a newborn baby?

Held an infant's hands in your own?
Seen a baby at the point of discovering walking?
Seen a baby learning to smile?

Listened to very young children talking to each other?
Seen the pleasure on a child's face on discovering a new skill?

Shared baby talk with a small child?
Seen the mixture of fear and excitement on the face of a small child
    being left at school by its parents for the first time?
Noticed the new calm and poise of girls when they become women?

Noticed the vulnerability of boys when their voices change at puberty
    and they start to know their own strength?
Seen the sweet tenderness of two young people who have become
    lovers for the first time?

FEEDBACK

If most of these experiences have somehow eluded you, you are being deprived of life at full strength. This may not be surprising, since many families live far apart and the majority of elderly people do not live in cities. Death and dying seem increasingly to be a taboo area, and the caring professions often collude with the rest of us in keeping dying out of sight and out of mind.

Yet delivered from its taboos, the experience of another person's dying can melt the hearts of relatives and friends hardened by the demands of work and survival. Thus melted we can find time for the gentler things of life, taking time to be with people we care about.

Sharing grief and the pain of losing someone close to you and witnessing the delight and freshness of young children can cement connections and bridge the divide of family feuds and disagreements. If you can allow yourself to feel both delight and pain you will find a new and rich connection with other people. If most of the experiences on the list are accessible to you then you are already in touch with much of the full beauty and tragedy of human existence.

ACTION PLAN

Spend more time with the young and the old, particularly with your own relations.

See Self-assessment
    18-35   Personal history
    102-9   Beliefs
See Knowhow
    146-55   Self-defence
    156-7   Other connections
    160-1   Potential for change
    164-5   The new paradigm
See Mind gym
    195-6   Healing and distress
    242-5   Our fragile future

BELIEFS

Beliefs lie at the root of your life. A belief that you can't . . . limits. A belief that you can . . . expands your possibilities. So it makes a lot of sense to treat your beliefs temporarily as objects, to take them out into the sunshine to examine them and see what they are doing for you.

The layers of our beliefs

You may feel that beliefs are too intangible to be scrutinized in this way. It is true that they are intangible and yet they mould the way you view reality and you live by them. You believe that you will receive an electric shock if you put your fingers in a live power socket. You believe it is dangerous to run out into the road without watching the traffic. These kinds of beliefs constantly preoccupied your parents when you were young. And after you had learned the beliefs needed for basic survival, other layers were added – beliefs about trust and morality, about how to succeed and how to live with people.

Our perceptions of reality

Developments in physics and psychology have now thrown into question many of our inherited beliefs about the nature of reality. They show in particular that the separateness we believe exists between one person and another and between organic and inorganic are not facts but *perceptions*. We tend to see reality as continuous and solid, but research in sub-atomic physics has evolved the idea that what we actually see is 99.99% empty space. When we experience things as hard, soft, gas, liquid, metal or stone and when we see colours – the blue of the sky, the green of trees – we are, according to this view, seeing the result of energy exchanges within a relatively small number of different fundamental fields. So reality, far from being fixed in solid, present-time objects, is instead made up of 'fields' of time, energy and space. Within these fields, pockets of energy can become so concentrated that they have mass, they appear to have form – like another person, for example. But the remaining 99.99% of the space is empty. It is the subtle exchange of energy that decides whether something is liquid, solid or gas.

Reality and experience

What you *experience* is a matter of belief too. Your mind draws on what it has learned to believe over the years and recreates in every living moment the outer world that you see and hear, and the inner world that you feel. Whatever seems personally true for you – all your beliefs, large and small – profoundly influence the way you live your life. They decide what you do and how or why you do it – and equally what you don't do. Since these attitudes affect how much choice you feel you have in your life, there is an enormous amount to be gained from identifying the beliefs you are committed to and recognizing who benefits from them.

Beliefs can be difficult to identify, however. Some are more conscious than others. It's useful to remember that the ones you may be embarrassed about, those most difficult to acknowledge, are often the ones with the greatest effect.

What you see in this picture is a matter of belief. Is it police facing up to trouble-makers? Is it a repressive arm of the state? Or is it someone's dad trying not to look frightened?

How to use this section

The following self-assessments invite you to venture down into the basement of your mind and look at some of its unconscious contents. They will enable you to begin to pinpoint the personal beliefs that are running your life, as well as the cultural beliefs that could be influencing your expectations at home and at work.

Work your way through each set of questions, taking as much time as you need to think each one through, and changing your mind as often as you like. When you have built up a clear picture of your own collection of beliefs, move on to FEEDBACK and ACTION PLAN and note down what you aim to do about it. If you do not find yourself reflected here, use the marginal references to direct you to another part of the book.

PERSONAL BELIEFS

The beliefs that most affect your life are likely to be quite well buried, but a bit of patient digging around will bring them to the surface. This assessment begins with several different ways of identifying what you believe in. Use whichever seems to work best for you – all that matters is that you get your beliefs out into the light of day.

Complete these sentences – in several different ways if you are able to.

It's not natural to . . .
It's easy to tell whether someone is normal or not because they . . .
It goes against nature to . . .
I'm religious/not religious because . . .
When making decisions, it's important to be objective because otherwise . . .

Complete this sentence in ten ways. Do it fast without censoring.

Because I'm a woman/man I must always . . .

Complete this sentence ten ways. Again, do it fast without censoring. If only I was a man/woman I would be able to . . .

Identify three beliefs you hold that agree with current orthodox opinion. Three things I believe to be true are . . .

Identify three beliefs you hold that run counter to current orthodox opinion. Three things I secretly believe to be true are . . .

Now that you have warmed up a little, see if you can bring to mind any other remaining beliefs. Use the list opposite to jog your memory.

When you have your list of beliefs, begin to evaluate them.

Check through them to see whether or not you chose each belief consciously or whether it has more or less always been there. Add a 'C' if you can remember when and how you chose the belief.

Now consider which beliefs are most important to you. Number them in ascending or descending order, starting from either end. Which would you find hard to relinquish – and which do you believe are absolutely essential?

Next, try rating your beliefs in a different way – you may find it very revealing. You'll find, opposite and overleaf, two boxes concerning the way that dominance, blame and idealization may have infiltrated your beliefs. Read each box carefully and then go back to your catalogue of beliefs and mark each of them with a 'D', a 'B' or an 'I'.

Progress
The prevailing belief in progress is rooted in the idea that all human problems are ultimately solvable through science and technology. It is a belief which is rapidly becoming both dangerous and obsolete as the limits of sustainable growth are reached on many fronts.

Objectivity
This is the mistaken notion that it is possible to exclude completely personal and emotional influences when evaluating, and so create value-free facts.

Normality
A particularly common belief is that if a phenomenon or way of behaving or living is widespread, it is therefore normal and anything else is deviant. This is a belief that continues to oppress those who don't feel they belong to the 'middle ground'.

Beliefs

Progress is inevitable.

Some people are born lucky.

The conquest of nature is one of man's greatest achievements.

There should be fair play, democracy and justice for everyone.

Progress through life should be based solely on merit.

Everyone should have equal opportunities regardless of race, sex, class, marital status or age.

If you care for yourself, other people will care for you.

There are no free lunches.

You have to learn to control yourself.

Men are natural leaders.

Women should stay at home and look after their families.

It's a man's world.

In today's world, it's every man for himself.

You can't afford to be kind, generous or soft in business.

If you show weakness, people always take advantage.

You have to be prepared to fight for what you want.

Nobody loves a loser.

There's nothing to stop women and members of minority groups from getting to the top if they have talent.

There's always a minority that tries to stir up trouble.

People can't be trusted.

Men do most of the work, so they should have most of the power.

Boys will be boys.

Women like to be dominated.

Men should be tough, strong, courageous, unafraid, decisive, responsible, unemotional, objective, wise, intelligent, worldly, good in action and work well with things.

Women should be soft, compliant, shy, sympathetic, affectionate, supportive, patient, family-oriented, caring and good with people.

The head of the family should be a man.

A good wife will look after everyone's needs and put herself last.

Some people are really evil.

All societies have been stratified and always will be.

Jesus lives.

There is only one God.

There is only one way to Heaven.

There can only be spirituality where there is enlightenment.

I believe in God the Father, God the Son and God the Holy Ghost.

To interpret and carry out the word of God needs an all-male clergy.

Communism is evil.

Sinners go to Hell.

Only those who repent of their sins go to Heaven.

There is life after death.

God will provide.

The spirit is willing but the flesh is weak.

Blame

Many beliefs revolve around responsibility and blame. If you blame someone else for a problem or a bad feeling it means that you do not have to take personal responsibility for what has happened. On the other hand, it is equally common to blame yourself when you are not responsible at all, or only partly. This can impose a big burden of guilt.

Examples of blame include:

People get what they deserve.

Some people are just born lazy.

There is always a minority that tries to stir up trouble.

Man is 'fallen' and so forever in sin.

Some people are just naturally wicked and cruel.

Idealization

Idealization involves a different kind of responsibility. It means seeing a person or a group as so overwhelmingly good, wise and intelligent that they seem beyond criticism. Taken a stage further, responsibility for the whole human condition may be attributed to an all-powerful deity, who is far above reproach. Another kind of glorification belief involves taking credit for far more effectiveness or virtue than is your due.

Examples of idealization include:

It's important to have someone to look up to.

Everyone needs heroes.

Capitalism or communism is the only way.

Leaders deserve loyalty from their followers.

Patriotic duty should override family and other ties.

Dominance

The belief that might is right – that the strong have the right to subjugate the weak and that this is in some way natural to human beings – is a very common one. The idea that comes with this belief is that some people have to be prepared to put up with being submissive and subservient. These beliefs cluster around racial, sexual and class differences.

Examples of a belief in dominance include:
Winning isn't the most important thing, it's the only thing.
Some people's lives are devoid of value.
Somebody has to be in charge.
You have to show people who's boss.
Life is about the survival of the fittest.
Somebody has to be at the top.

Examples of a belief in submissiveness include:
You can't do what you like, you have to do what you are told.
Whatever will be will be.
Some people have all the luck.
Experts know best.
Nothing I can do will make any difference.
That's the way it is – you can't change human nature.

The belief that dominant and subservient behaviour is 'natural' probably originates in our childhood experience of being dependent on our parents. Surviving as a child often means deferring to superior force and this submissiveness is often carried over into adult life. It may bring with it a determination never to be in that position again. But since this decision about who is in charge is learned so early, it often appears to be innate and 'natural'.

The most dominant human beings at the moment are white, Western and men. However, increasing numbers of women, and many men, now regard the belief that 'male dominance is inevitable' as a self-fulfilling prophecy. It keeps women 'in their place' and ensures that men continue to arrange human affairs to suit their comfort and convenience. One of the great achievements of the twentieth century may well turn out to be the beginning of the end of the belief that domination is natural.

FEEDBACK

If this is the first time you have really looked closely at your beliefs, then your personal list probably contains a lot that are based on dominance, submissiveness, praise or blame. There are probably not many that you have chosen consciously for yourself. If this seems a bit worrying, don't be alarmed, because the whole of human reality is constructed out of accumulated beliefs – we can never be free of them. However, you can benefit greatly by systematically withdrawing beliefs that inaccurately assign responsibility and by letting go of beliefs that tell you that you have to dominate or submit. This is no easy task, but it is an honourable one. Learning to discard a belief that has been unnecessarily warping your life can bring an enormous sense of liberation.

ACTION PLAN

Continue to probe your beliefs and uncover some of your more deep-seated unconscious convictions. Learn to identify and withdraw an excessive tendency to praise or blame either others or yourself. You may find this easier with the help of a counsellor.

BELIEFS AT HOME

Here is a series of common human situations where what you believe influences how you act. Note what you and your partner or your friends or relations do and then check out the feedback.

Holidays and trips

Who decides where to go?
Who carries the money?
Who packs the bags?
Who books the tickets?
Who checks the car?
Who drives on long journeys?
Who decides what route to take?
Who decides where to eat?
Who buys the drinks?
Who drives after a party?

New relationships

Do you ever make the first approach?
Does your existing relationship exclude the
   friendships you would value and enjoy?

Work

Whose career prospects determine where you live?
Whose working hours does family life tend to
   revolve around?

Chores and child care

Who does the housework over half of the time?
Who prepares meals?
Who mends fuses?
Who does minor household repairs?
Who takes the children to school and collects them?
Who decides which school the children will attend?
Who buys the children shoes and clothes?
Who does the ironing?
Who keeps track of birthdays and buys presents?
Who disciplines the children?
Who usually does the shopping?
Who puts the children to bed?
Who cares for the children when they are ill?
Who washes up?

FEEDBACK

Instead of considering whether your home arrangements work well or not, think about how much choice you have in the matter and how much force is being used. How much of an undercurrent of coercion is there in the arrangements as they stand? Do you both suffer equal inconvenience and gain equal benefit?

You can test this out with a little experiment. What would happen if you were determined to change the arrangements? Would she/he put up with it? If he/she insisted, what sanctions would be brought to bear? Would you risk losing your job, your partner or your home?

When one of you does want to change the arrangements and give up the supporting role after many years of collusion, it can be a terrible shock to discover how much coercion and even physical force suddenly come into play.

ACTION PLAN

If you find yourself playing traditional roles in relationships and would prefer to have more choice, explore ways in which you could change the balance. You may like to consider an assertiveness skills training course or counselling to see how best to handle it.

BELIEFS AT WORK

This assessment will help you to look at the way your own and other people's beliefs affect your life at work.

How fair is the organization you work for?

Prejudices

Do supervisors or others who control your working life hold a prejudiced belief that you . . .

Lack commitment to work?

Have outside commitments that take priority over work?

Are inferior mentally or physically?

Are not very literate?

Tend to provoke an unfavourable reaction from other staff, customers or members of the public?

Are unsuitable because you don't belong to the favoured group?

Have no ability to supervise?

Are not interested in a career?

Have limited mobility?

Aren't interested or willing to be trained?

Have poor standards of dress or conduct?

Have limitations because of so-called female interests and experience?

Make a note of how many apply to you.

Discrimination against women

If you are a woman, are you restricted by your employer's and your colleagues' beliefs that women . . .

Should only have a 'caring' job, such as personnel, staff welfare or dealing with the public?

Are good at detailed case work, but are not suited to work with broader scope, such as policy-making or planning?

Should not do outdoor jobs?

Are incapable of doing strenuous jobs?

Should not be considered for jobs that involve substantial travelling or moving home?

Can't represent the company because clients or customers would not like it?

Cannot or will not work with numbers?

Are not worth promoting because they will probably leave to have a baby?

Make a note of how many apply to you.

Indirect discrimination

Perhaps the most common way in which beliefs will affect you at work is through indirect discrimination. This happens when there is a stipulation for the job that is unfavourable to certain groups. Where you work are there . . .

Rules about clothes or uniforms which put a racial group at a disadvantage?

Unnecessary or excessive physical requirements, such as height, which could operate against women, the disabled or certain ethnic groups?

Demands for a standard of English beyond that needed for doing the job safely and effectively?

Unnecessary age limits, for example, restricting women who have taken time off to have children?

Deliberate attempts to screen off certain racial groups by advertising to specific areas only?

Unjustifiable demands for full-time work?

Rigid stipulations for educational qualifications that are irrelevant to the job?

Make a note of how many apply to you.

How fair is the organization you run?

The fair manager

If you are a manager, supervisor or employer, do you have unexamined beliefs that restrict the choices of your co-workers? Look through these statements and see how many are true for you.

You are involved in recruitment and selection, but have not personally received training in your legal responsibilities about discrimination.

You or your organization does not run anti-discrimination training courses for everyone who makes key decisions.

You or your organization does not monitor the composition of the workforce to ensure that it reflects the composition of the population.

There are areas in your company where sex, race, marriage or age discrimination still operates.

Neither you nor your organization regularly reviews existing anti-discrimination procedures.

Self-discrimination

If you are relatively free from other people's prejudices and beliefs at work, you may want to consider your beliefs and expectations. Are you unwittingly limiting your prospects for jobs you would like? Think of the work you would like to do and consider what is holding you back. Is it . . .

Low self-esteem?
Lack of experience?
Lack of qualifications?
Poor self-presentation?
Lack of confidence?
Lack of contacts?
Fear of competition?
Lack of opportunity?
Lack of knowledge?
Poor communication skills?

FEEDBACK

If any of the statements in the self-discrimination list applied to you, you are probably more submissive than you realize. If any of the statements in the next three lists applies to you, you may well be suffering from discrimination, perhaps even illegally. If you agreed with any of the statements in the last list, then you are being discriminatory. It's hard to change; you can't do it overnight and you may hate it. But increasingly large numbers of women, racially disadvantaged people and other groups are refusing to stand for it.

ACTION PLAN

What can you do about discrimination? If you have been aware of it for a while, then you may already be doing what you can. If you didn't realize what was going on until now, move with caution. Dealing with discrimination can be risky because it arises out of domination, blame and idealization – a very potent mixture. The first step is to find out your rights. Alongside this you should give some serious attention to assertiveness training. When opposing any kind of oppression, it is important not to become hostile, aggressive or manipulative, or just to give up in submissiveness. More public solutions may include joining campaigns and support groups for people in similar situations. If you have been discriminating against yourself, consider specific training courses, assertiveness training and ways of improving your self-esteem.

If, as a manager, you find you are unintentionally endorsing discriminatory policies, begin monitoring recruitment and selection areas, gather information that will reveal obvious areas of discrimination, and take steps to introduce an equal opportunity programme in your organization. If such a programme is already in place, check that it is running well.

How to tell a businessman from a businesswoman

Here is an example of prejudice at work.

He is aggressive: she is pushy.
He is good on details: she is picky.
When he seems low (or hungover), everyone tiptoes past his office: when she seems low (or moody), it must be her time of the month.
He follows through: she doesn't know when to stop.
He stands firm: she's tough.
His judgements are her prejudices.
He is a man of the world: she's been around.
He drinks because of work pressures: she's a lush.
He isn't afraid to speak his mind: she's aggressive.
He manages diligently: she is power mad.
He's discreet: she's secretive.
He's climbed the ladder of success: she slept her way to the top.
He's a hard taskmaster: she's difficult to work for.

See Self-assessment
42-4   Work
47-9   Self-esteem
51   Other people's labels
84-6   Self-presentation
87-8   Communication
See Knowhow
122-3   School's subtle lessons
146-55   Self-defence
162-3   The old paradigm
164-5   The new paradigm
182-3   Shared assessment
184-5   Work without experts
See Mind gym
203-9   Self-esteem
218-19   Emotional intelligence
226-7   Intuitive intelligence
228-9   Intellectual intelligence
234-5   Projection
238-41   Synergy

KNOWHOW

What do most of us want to know about our minds? KNOWHOW illuminates what is useful, what enhances our personal understanding, what opens up our choices and what helps us to become more self-directing. It does not set out to be a comprehensive survey of the scientific approach to the mind.

Scientific mind research

This part of *The Mind Gymnasium* aims to redress the imbalance that has come out of the mind research industry. Research has brought to light much that is vital, including the whole concept of stress. But a great deal of mind research continues to be driven by the drug and defence industries. Both the funding sources and the biomedical approach have led to distortions and omissions that have only recently become apparent. It is now, however, becoming increasingly easy to see how mind research emphasizes control – either control of distressed, diseased or injured minds, or control of man-machine interaction, as in jet fighter aircraft. It is also clear that the expertise gained is used exclusively for corporate profit or professional power and that this kind of research concentrates on knowing more and more about less and less, and ignores the significance of the personal dimension in all research work.

The value of personal enquiry

The industrial approach to mind – with the exception of the attention given to stress and productivity – entirely neglects the development of personal resources. But in the last thirty years or so a new tradition or paradigm of mind, which is centred on humanistic psychology, has emerged, almost haphazardly. It owes little or no allegiance to academic and industrial research and focusses on the inner personal enquiry that supports self-help, self-direction or self-management. In pursuing this new tradition, KNOWHOW favours the crossing of the boundaries of academic specialization without inhibition. By leap-frogging over the inertia of psychiatric medicine and drug research which continues to move, it seems, away from innovation, this chapter aims to present a coherent and helpful view.

The choice of material

Since the information in this chapter has been selected on the basis of its relevance to our whole lives, there are, inevitably, omissions. There is little about the anatomy of the brain or nervous system, nor anything about where specific areas of human behaviour are located in the brain, which is now quite well understood. Nor does it include the evolutionary history of the brain and its reptilian and mammalian ancestry. All these have been extensively explored elsewhere.

Instead, this KNOWHOW chapter underlines the approach of *The Mind Gymnasium* as a whole, taking as its paradigm the central need to create, develop and maintain bodymind wellbeing. It will enable you to exercise a greater degree of choice in the process of understanding yourself and being understood by those around you. It presumes that, given support for your intuition and insight, you are the world's greatest expert on your own mind.

How to use this chapter

You can read KNOWHOW as a book within a book, or use it as a reference source for the other two chapters. You will find it full of references back to SELF-ASSESSMENT for an estimate of your personal strengths and weaknesses and on to MIND GYM for practical self-development exercises. You will also find liberal references to other resources, both inside and outside this book, to enable you to follow up areas of special interest.

THE MAKING OF THE MIND

The mind is inseparable from the body. To try to divide them, to regard them in isolation is, in a sense, to do violence to both. The mind is also a person, a unique combination of inherited characteristics and experience.

When is the mind born?

We enter life as a bundle of genetic instructions. As we grow, becoming daily more complex, more subtle, more able to adapt to our surroundings, our capacity for richer, more diverse experience develops. From well before birth we are intelligent, able to learn. By just two years' of age, we are able to understand and be understood – a phenomenal feat. And ten years later we are capable of conceiving a new individual.

Within the first year, we begin to realize that we are separate from our mother. A few years later we know that we exist. Decades later we may come to discover that our mind has a history of accumulated experiences, some of which act across the years to limit our choices.

Over the last twenty years or so, psychological research has progressively pushed the onset of formative experience back further and further – from the first weeks at the breast, to birth, then to life in the womb, and now right the way back to conception.

Why explore the mind

As we grow, as our needs are met or denied, we accumulate a complex network of unconscious memories. These universal foetal and infantile experiences form a collective unconscious memory that spans races and continents. Some experiences are exquisite, some excruciating, but all are stored as body memories – latent, slumbering, awaiting a trigger to set them off. They reveal themselves in the fundamental human capacity for 'projection' – the tendency to see in others or in places echoes of our inner experiences that we disown.

Foetal memories can give rise to group fantasies of Heaven, Paradise, Hell, Evil and the Devil (see p. 154). When projection happens on a large scale, an intense early experience such as pain may also be collectively projected as evil – in medieval times on to the women labelled witches, for instance, and before and during World War II on to the Jews. When these unconscious early memories are echoed in the group fantasy of religion, we call them spiritual. When they are projected on to nations, we call them politics.

Taking responsibility for the pain and hurt we have each suffered as our minds came into existence, and learning not to project them on to other people, will do more to rid this planet of war and destruction than anything we can presently imagine. Only with the projector turned off do we have the possibility of entering a new age, of creating a new paradigm.

This part of Knowhow looks at some of the key experiences that help to form the mind – the memories that make us recognizable as ourselves. It presents a series of snapshots of the most formative experiences – from conception, foetal life and birth, to the early years with the family, and of outside influences, such as school and TV.

This 10-day-old child nestling in her father's hand is wide open to her world. Recent research shows that, through choosing, making requests, responding, accepting, rejecting and recognizing, she also shapes her world.

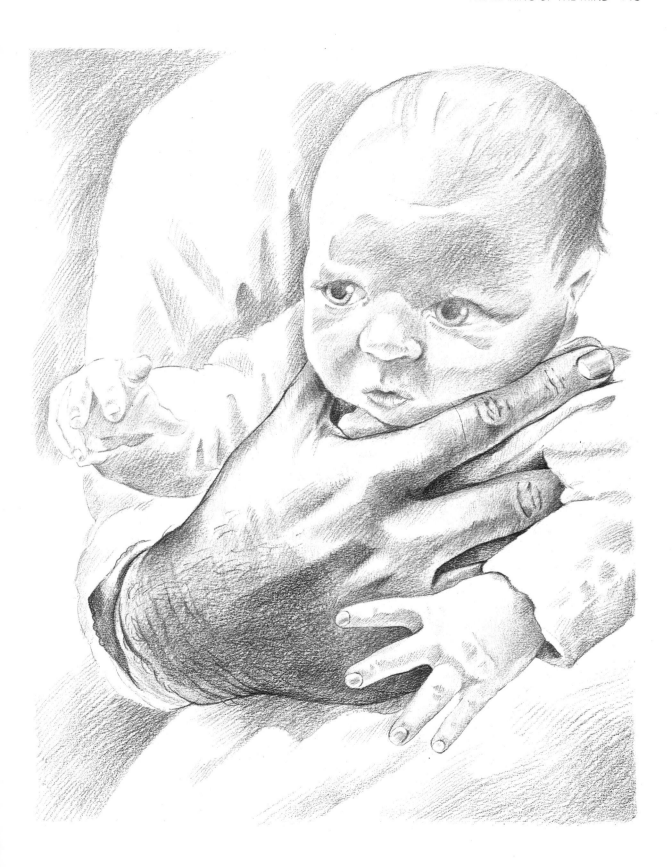

LIFE BEFORE BIRTH

There is a widely held misconception that no aspect of mind is present until after birth. Some people even believe that there is no mind to speak of until not only language but also abstract reasoning is present at around age six or seven. Such a view assumes that a foetus and a newborn baby are unintelligent. But while this may be true in terms of adult intellectual abilities, at an emotional level, the newborn is acutely aware of feelings and emotional messages. From conception on, the baby receives, reacts to and remembers both positive and negative stimuli. And if we take intelligence to be the capacity for love, understanding and choice, then even a very young child is intelligent (see pp. 120–1).

Understanding early experience

The newborn is a visitor freshly arrived from inner space. Yet we know more about outer space, beyond the solar system, than we do of the experience of the foetus. If we want to understand how the core ingredients of the human mind are formed, however, it is essential to get close to these early impressions. An increasingly well-understood way of doing this is through therapeutic regression, which can help to recover these early experiences. This may sound difficult or even threatening, but in recent decades research using LSD and hypnosis has enabled large numbers of people to re-experience their own births and some aspects of their time in the womb through primal and rebirthing techniques. This work has coincided with an explosive growth in research into embryology, neuroscience and psychology. The newborn baby is now described as 'an extremely competent social organism, an extremely competent learning organism and an extremely competent perceiving organism'. Anyone who looks at the accumulated evidence cannot fail to realize that a human baby is in fact already intelligent at birth – able to learn, remember, respond and decisively influence other people. Indeed, these abilities are so well developed at birth that it is reasonable to suppose that they are also present, to some extent, during gestation. This means that the foetus experiences, responds, learns and remembers, too, and that the quality of life in the womb has a profound effect on later abilities and expectations.

First impressions – feeling good

If the needs of the developing foetus are well met, its first experiences are of feeling good. And memories of contentment, perfection and oceanic bliss are laid down in the core mind. The feeling of contentment comes not only from good nourishment and elimination but also from a reassuring relationship with the mother. This bonding develops as the foetus internalizes the mother's lack of anxiety and is also strengthened by the mother stroking her belly when the foetus kicks. If the birth process is triggered at the appropriate stage of foetal growth, this bonding is further strengthened.

First impressions – feeling bad

If the needs of the developing foetus are frequently denied, then it will feel bad, laying down habitual reactions such as anxiety and panic. Alcohol, drugs, over-eating and periodic shortages of oxygen caused by smoking in pregnancy can contribute to this feeling. And if the mother is resentful or worried about being pregnant, if she is consistently angry, anxious or depressed, the foetus will be awash with these feelings too, but without the capacity to make sense of them. The effects of deprivation can also have tangible results. Such is the pace of the unfolding growth of the foetus that if the mother persistently smokes, for instance, the baby may not grow to full size, predisposing it to health problems. Or if she contracts German measles at around the third month, the baby's sight and hearing may be permanently impaired.

Pre-birth memories and identity

Researchers such as Stanislav Grof, Frank Lake, William Emerson and Thomas Verny see the foetal experience as a framework or armature around which later experience is organized. They have found that a relatively constant experience of feeling good as a foetus predisposes the newborn to expect this of life. A mixture of good and bad feelings may tend to undermine later hope and trust, while a predominantly bad experience of life in the womb predisposes the newborn to expect this to continue.

The everyday life of the growing foetus has a tremendously strong, formative effect on our predispositions, expectations and attitudes in later life, as well as on our more diffuse feelings and sensations. At this early stage of development the young child is especially vulnerable, for it only has a limited number of ways of dealing with feeling bad – with the result that these responses are usually carried through into adult life. Some people retain the negative feelings inside their bodies, so that the world of inner thoughts and feelings appears to be bad and frightening, while the outer world provides props to hang on to, such as alcohol, drugs, TV or promiscuity. Others locate the bad feelings as a terror coming in from the placenta or umbilical cord, with a corresponding adult fear of snakes, for example, or spiders. The continual invasion of bad feelings can also result in a sense of persecution, where the outside world seems hostile and dangerous. When the negative feelings pervade the whole body, overwhelming it, in later life the only safe refuge may appear to be the head, so that only thought seems real. And if there is a mixture of feeling good and feeling bad, perplexity and confusion is stored in the bodymind, and often emerges in adult life as depression – often a state of arrested rage. In fact, it also becomes increasingly apparent that what we often refer to as 'instincts', implying responses that are genetically based, include foetal and birth experiences.

THE BIRTH DRAMA

Birth – for most of us – is the closest we come to the fear of death for the rest of our lives. And the conditions of our birth – whether it was short and smooth or unduly prolonged, whether it was 'natural', premature, artificially induced or involved a caesarian delivery – cast a shadow forward across the years. The quality of the experience, along with our impressions of foetal life, become imprinted in the very core of our being. The effects can be relieved or reinforced by later experiences, but the first impressions remain, forming a central framework or armature around which later experience accumulates.

Time runs out
As your mother's pregnancy reaches its final stages, you come to occupy all the available space in the womb and find it increasingly difficult to move freely. The placenta may become less efficient and you may suffer a shortage of oxygen. However, if life has been good up until then, you probably continue to feel at peace in the cramped surroundings, although held very tightly. Your mother's emotions may briefly disrupt the sense of feeling good, but the previous pattern soon re-establishes itself. At about the time that your head reaches the ultimate size of the exit, the mother-child system crosses a crucial threshold, a point of no return, and the birth process is triggered.

The crisis begins
As your head connects with the cervix, the exit at the base of the womb, the first contractions start to press in. Your soft, pliable, tender, vulnerable body is kneaded and squeezed by the overwhelming force of the immensely strong muscle on all sides. This is new, different. You try to kick, to struggle, but can't move. The pressure is unbearable, there seems to be no way out. Except for the continuing 'thump, bump' sound of your mother's heart, the old world has gone. The pressure relaxes for a bit. That feels better. Then the force comes back. It is hell, agony, torment. It's endless, hopeless PAIN. The contractions continue, the cervix begins to open and the passage through the birth canal begins. It's a fight for survival against the threat of annihilation. It's a battle of the titans, an epic duel against a crushing, grinding monster. It hurts like hell – but it's also intensely, painfully pleasurable.

The crisis continues
The ordeal goes on. It's frightening. You struggle. It doesn't feel so hopeless. The force pushes you on. Your head and face are being crushed. You're stuck. Now there's a twist. Stuck again. This is too much. You're so tired. Can't do it. Give up. Crush. Pause. Crush. Pause. Crush. Suddenly bright lights hurt your eyes. Your ears hurt. There's noise. The 'thump, bump' has gone. It's all gone. Everything's strange. Strangers clutch, probe, pull, hold you upside down. This is the outside world.

Birth and later life

The upheavals we all experience in the process of being born – the distress, delays, distortions, interruptions, pressures, challenges and paradoxical pleasures – are built into the grain of us. They add an overlay of memories on to those already embedded in the bodymind by the experience of life in the womb. Birth teaches us a wide array of lessons that we unconsciously apply to similar challenges in later life, although the distress laid down at this time may be either alleviated by later events or reinforced by them. The experience includes feeling hurt or in pain through being crushed, squeezed and compressed, feeling threatened with physical annihilation and feeling angry, frustrated and confused. It may also include the experience of extreme physical pleasure, vigorous stroking and massage by the contractions, and of pleasure and pain occurring together. Some of us learn from these experiences that bad feelings and pain can be endured and survived and that effort brings results. But if the bad feelings and pain are intolerable we give up under pressure. Other lessons include learning that struggle, hurt and feeling bad can lead to uncomfortable, frightening new experiences; learning what it feels like to be in perfect bliss, to lose it and to yearn for it again; learning that bad feelings inside continue in the outside world; and learning that change, pleasure, pain, struggle and excitement can culminate in an exciting new beginning.

Memories within our culture

The foetal and birth drama lives on in all of us, but is kept quiet through an infinite variety of defences. It remains a sleeping monster, not only in our personal lives but in the whole of our culture. British psychologist David Wasdell has shown that the whole of Christianity makes sense as a collective group fantasy for sealing off foetal and birth memories from consciousness. Heaven and Paradise, for example, represent the memory of oceanic bliss of life in the womb for which God is seen to be responsible. The memory of deep contentment is projected out, in the form of wishful thinking, into an imaginary 'next world'. At the same time Hell – a threatening world below – is a metaphor for the forgotten agony of birth and unmet needs for food, oxygen and love in the womb, for which the Devil or Evil is seen to be responsible. Christianity is not the only religion to embrace these metaphors. Buddhists, Moslems and Hindus, all share the notion of an idyllic or unpleasant other life. And it is interesting to note that for Hindus the equivalent of Heaven is freedom from the cycle of re-birth. American psychohistorian Lloyd de Mause has paralleled this by showing that the group fantasies of politics follow similar patterns. Political leaders, for example, are often portrayed as all good or all evil and seen as responsible for all our suffering or good fortune. And when this extends into a national projection of our disowned feelings on to the enemy, the seeds of war are sown.

THE EARLY YEARS
Stages of development

In the weeks and months following birth, the child's mind is a window on the world. If the foetal and birth experience was 'good enough', the window is likely to remain wide open, but if life in the womb and at birth were difficult, the window may be only partly open or even tightly shut. As development proceeds through weaning, teething, crawling, walking, talking and toilet-training, each stage poses a challenge for the baby, giving the mind the opportunity to grow and strengthen. As each new ability is discovered, the child usually becomes more confident, gaining the strength to face a broader challenge – to become an individual with a distinct identity and increasingly independent of parental influence. According to observational research, this 'psychological birth' has five stages. For more information about early development, see pp. 120–1.

5 Consolidating
From 3 years

From this point on, the task facing the young child is to consolidate her distinctive individuality. This is closely paralleled by a deepening emotional stability, which allows the child to maintain a sense of self during periods of brief separation from her parents. As talking and play become more purposeful, observations about the world become more accurate and consistent and a sense of time emerges. Gradually the toddler comes to see herself as 'me' and later as 'I', as distinct from 'you' or 'they', paving the way for an adult sense of identity. Eventually this grows into the adult experience of the self as both fully in the world and separate from it, with the ability to move at will between the inner and outer.

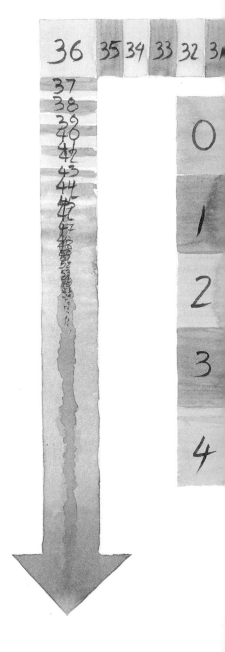

4 Reconnecting
15 months to 3 years

Where before, the toddler might have been worried about losing her mother, now she is more afraid of losing her love and attention. Somewhere around 15 months, the mother, who has ceased to be home base, becomes the person with whom the toddler wishes to share all her discoveries. Exploration reaches a peak as the child tests her autonomy. She also begins to appreciate that there are obstacles in the way of her bid to take over the whole world. Her insistence on her right to do what she likes clashes with the limits within which she can safely operate. The way in which these conflicts are resolved establishes more securely within her mind her own personal identity.

1 Fusion
– 9 months to + 3 months

From implantation through the months of gestation, the child's mind is a branch of the mother's. What she feels it feels. While birth causes physical separation, the mind of the newborn continues to be fused with the mother. At around three months, complete dependence loses its hold as the baby realizes the connection between feeling good and the expression on her mother's face. When automatic grimaces grow into responsive smiling it is a confirming sign that bonding between infant and mother has taken place.

2 Breaking away
4 to 9 months

A new, waking alertness indicates that the infant mind is becoming aware of a world outside itself. At around six months, manual, tactile and visual exploration of the mother's face peak. As the child becomes more mobile, these explorations extend into reaching further, then crawling with increased interest away from and back to the mother. This gradual physical separation brings with it the beginnings of a 'mind of its own' – 'me here, mummy there'.

3 Experimenting
10 to 15 months

As the infant progresses from crawling to standing and then walking, the excitement of discovering new sensations and practising new skills runs at full speed. With walking begins the toddler's love affair with the world. Reality is something to be tested and enjoyed to the full. The young child plunges into life and into every cupboard and shelf. Her mind fills with people, places, activities and things, which she perceives as increasingly separate from herself. A rapidly developing sense of independence takes the child further from her mother, more frequently and for longer periods. Out of the experience of playing alone, self-absorbed, intermittently contacting the mother for emotional refuelling, she comes to understand that she herself exists as an individual separate from her mother.

THE EARLY YEARS
A child's experience

The unfolding individual identity of a child is the foundation on which later personal strength is built. Responding accurately and with empathy to a child's needs from birth onwards actively supports the development of this inner strength in the broadest sense. If children's needs are not met, it will not matter as long as they feel confident that eventually help will arrive. But a persistently inaccurate response to their needs, a lack of response or, worse, a denial of needs, impedes the natural development of intelligence by filling the mind with distress. Distress means not only feeling bad but learning to *be* bad, hurt, confused and frightened, because children literally embody these feelings; they are built into the bodymind.

Reading a child's mind

The newborn baby seems to know what she needs and for the early months she embodies these needs and signals them constantly to the alert parent. But although she is intelligent, most parents see her at first as a little stranger.

So how do we know what is going on in a child's mind? What needs are the crucial ones for the formation of the mind? How can we find out what they are? One solution is to follow what the experts say – Dr S, Professor B, Aunt H, Grandma or Grandpa. This is fine if we remember that no knowledge is value-free, still less if it is about what is human and natural. It is coloured by who paid for it or who stands to gain from it and by the expert's need to be 'respectable'. Until very recently, for example, what experts had to say about bringing up children was based on the classical scientific approach. This involved an observer watching children like insects through one-way mirrors, recording their behaviour and building a picture of the regular patterns of what they do – and so what a 'normal' child will be doing. It meant surveying the coastline of the mind. And many experts on child development still ignore the influence of the child's secret life in the womb. That makes about as much sense as trying to insist that American history began with the Declaration of Independence and that the life of the pre-revolutionary Indians, Spanish, French and British had no effect on the republic. Other, psychoanalytic, experts say that the newborn has appallingly destructive instincts that she must learn to control for her own and everyone else's good. And, although it isn't usually apparent, still more research into the mind of the child is based on the study of mental illness (see p. 160).

An alternative approach

If you have children or expect to have them, perhaps you'll be inclined to reject expert advice in favour of a more intuitive approach, because you find yourself distrusting such advice. If so, there is an alternative approach which you may find useful. It is based on the accumulated experiences of people who have learned how to regress to their own very early experience, using a variety of methods, such as trance and hypnosis. Rather than mapping the coastline of someone else's mind, they have explored the interior of their own mind.

Life in the first year

The ways in which parent and child negotiate with each other in the first year are countless, but four of the more important are bonding, communication, stimulation and socialization. In practice, most babies experience a mixture of positive and negative interactions in all four areas.

Bonding

If the parent is reliable, responsive, available and consistent, the baby absorbs a positive view of the world. 'I feel bad from time to time. I make a noise. Help comes.' 'It's all right to feel bad because it's only for a little while.' 'I like my mother, she's good to me.' If the parent is often unreliable, inaccessible, unresponsive and inconsistent, the baby picks up a negative impression of life and learns that if you trust people, you get hurt. 'I feel bad. I make a noise. No one comes.' 'I make a noise 'til I'm tired. My mother comes. She feels bad too. She's rough.' 'I like my mother but she's never here.'

Communication

A parent who regards the baby as intelligent, communicative and eager to learn teaches her that people are a pleasure and that communication brings response. 'I feel good, hungry, sad, hot or cold. I make a sound. My father makes a sound. I move my hand. My father moves his too. He learns what I like. I learn what he likes. It's fun.' If the parent regards the baby as unintelligent, incapable of communication and having little ability to learn, the baby gives up trying to communicate. 'I feel good, hungry, sad, hot or cold. I make a sound. No-one comes. I keep on making a sound. After a while my father comes. He makes a funny sound. I like it. But I still feel good, hungry, sad, hot or cold.' 'I make a sound. My father comes. He makes a loud sound. He's rough with me. I feel bad now. I stop trying. The world is confusing.'

One very good rule of thumb that has come from this 'inside-out' approach is British psychologist John Heron's model of the child's mind (see pp. 22–3). Heron proposes that all infants are born with a unique human potential to love and be loved, to understand and be understood, to choose and be chosen. The adult who has regressed successfully to the child she or he was, is able to let that child speak. What that child says about her or his needs and potential goes something like this.

To love and be loved

'Accept me. Accept my tears. Accept my delight. Accept my exhilaration. Love me as I am. Let me be. I'm OK. I'm complete. I have everything I need. Don't force me to be like you. Don't force me to be different from you. Don't force me at all. Your needs are not my needs. Look after your own needs. Admire me, like me, enjoy me.

You are my everything. I love you always. You are the sunshine of my life. You are mine forever. Slow down. Be with me. Let me see you. Let me be with you. Open up to me, show yourself. Let me see who you are. Trust me. Trust yourself. Love me. Love yourself.'

To understand and be understood

'I want to know about why, and how, and where and when. I want to know about how many, and how far, and how long and why not. I want you to explain because, and different, and up, and down and no. I want you to explain now, and tomorrow, and never and dead.

I want you to understand that I am tender, open and vulnerable, that I am easily hurt, sometimes unhappy, frightened, sad and angry. I want you to know that I am sometimes confused and that I don't understand what your words mean (though I usually understand what your body is saying).'

To choose and be chosen

'I want to do things my own way. I want to do what I like. I want to like what I do. I want to make up my own mind. I want to choose what I eat, what I wear, how long I sleep. I want to choose my friends and to choose when to say yes and no. I want to choose to belong or to opt out. I want to choose what I do with my energy. I want to be free to do what I like with my own body.

I want to be liked, to be popular, to matter, to be needed. I want to be noticed, recognized and heard. I want to be picked for the team. I want to be asked to contribute, to support, to help, to be responsible.'

These represent the core priorities of all children, and if they are interfered with, denied or interrupted, distress memories that correspond to the denied potential are stored in the bodymind. Denial of love stores grief. Denial of understanding stores fear. Denial of choice stores anger. This distorts the developmental process outlined on the previous page and dents the fledgling identity. However, the inside-out approach also allows us to speculate about what the mind is capable of and how it can be enhanced.

Stimulation

When parents realize that providing the baby with appropriate stimulation can significantly contribute to the quality and speed of their child's development, the baby learns that life is exciting. 'People make funny sounds. I smile. They smile. Look. Moving things, pretty colours.' 'I cuddle with my mother. We are soft and warm. I like my mother. I feel good.' If the parent regards the baby as unintelligent, and the family keep quiet to avoid upsetting the baby, she learns to 'switch off'. 'No mother. Feel bad. Very tired. Feel bad. Sleep now.'

Socialization

If the parents believe their baby to be capable of communicating her needs or feelings, and if they respond with empathy and intuition, the child learns through both encouragement and example. 'I feel good. I smile. They like that. They smile too. When I feel bad, I cry. They like that too. They cuddle me.' If the parents assume that the baby is engaged in some kind of power struggle or is trying to attract sympathy and attention or to 'get its own way', then to give the child attention amounts to giving in and spoiling her. Crying then comes to mean 'naughty' and the child learns to stop trying to communicate her needs. 'I cry and nobody comes. I feel bad. I cry and cry. My father comes. I feel good. I smile. He makes a bad sound. He puts me down. I cry and cry.'

SCHOOL'S SUBTLE LESSONS

School plays a crucial part in the formation of the mind. Any experience lasting six to seven hours a day, five days a week, forty weeks a year, for at least ten years, is bound to make a lasting impression on the growing mind. The child's experience of school, as with all human encounters, divides into the conscious and the unconscious – into the self-evident organized content of the curriculum and the much deeper effects of the way in which it is delivered. Since children are so open to influence, school shapes their minds both directly – by presenting partial views of history, science and so on – and subliminally – by giving them a model of the way they can expect the world to work. A few may try to resist, but for most children, it quickly becomes both natural and inevitable.

The manufactured mind
Many schools today mimic the industrial processes of the society to which they belong. Minds are mass-produced in much the same way as refrigerators or cars. Children (the raw material) are moved about the school (the factory) from one classroom (workstation) to another, where teachers (workers) drill, fill and process them. Eventually, they are graded in examinations (the quality control department), and from there they are passed to further education or the jobs market (the sales department) or rejected.

The fragmented approach
The child learns subliminally that knowledge is compartmentalized. The clock that breaks the day into different subjects instils the idea that to understand anything, you have to specialize. Knowledge is absorbed in isolated chunks, because learning is divided into rigid segments of an hour or less, and intensity of interest is preset at low. The teacher metes out pieces of information, so the child perceives knowledge as something finite that belongs to experts, as something to be taken in bit by bit, rather than something on-going to discover and develop oneself. In the process, the vital connections between subjects very often get lost. And feeling and emotion are often excluded, since knowledge is equated with intellect.

Success and failure

Examinations condemn some children as 'failures' and reward others as 'successes' – simply on the basis of their intellectual development. But long before they are put forward for the stamp of approval, nearly all have already absorbed a sense of failure. Those who do well, the 'successes' who fit the universities' intellectual profile, learn that to gain access to the world of power and influence, you have to share its beliefs about knowledge, power and authority.

Power and authority

In the traditional classroom scenario, with the teacher in a controlling position, children learn that human interaction involves domination rather than mutual participation. In most schools, the teacher sets the agenda for the class, the term, the year, while children are rarely invited to contribute to decisions about the content, pace or relevance of the work they are doing. There is very little choice and usually a large element of coercion. Co-operation between classmates is usually considered cheating and the child soon learns that you have to compete to survive, that intellect rules, and that it is natural and inevitable to have someone in authority over you. However, the denied emotions and personal relationships often tend to emerge and find expression in sabotage, resistance and disruption. Of course there are many caring teachers – particularly of young children – who put a high value on the child's experience and judgement. But inertia and holding to tradition still prevent innovation that would soften the authoritarian approach of the classroom. Teachers' training colleges have been promoting a child-centred approach to education for decades. However, recent research shows that new teachers tend to teach in the way they themselves were taught.

THE TELEVISION 'I'

Broadcast television exerts a decisive influence on the minds of almost all children in developed countries. The benefits are considerable. Where once only libraries gave access to the world's experience, television now not only informs and entertains but adds a new, inspiring dimension, bringing previously unimaginable glimpses of swimming with whales and dolphins or walking on the moon. But while television's colourful entertainment captivates and dazzles children's minds, it also painlessly amputates whole areas of their potential for creativity, self-direction and play.

Two-way projection

Television creates and recreates a galaxy of stars, supermen, superwomen, underdogs, bullies, anti-heroes and heroines and stories, on to which viewers can project their own inner feelings and concerns. In many homes it has taken on this role from the church, whose saints, martyrs, gods and goddesses once helped to keep personal distress quiet by embodying unacknowledged aspects of the personality. Children learn to depend on someone out there in the television to provide inner peace and to keep quiet what they might otherwise be feeling. And this pacifier soon becomes addictive. Wellbeing is seen to be dependent on fame, possessions and wealth, while developing inner resources becomes associated with feeling bad and is neglected. Television offers a reliable way of blocking out uncomfortable feelings, such as boredom, loneliness and unfulfilled ambitions.

The third parent

A high proportion of television programmes presents people who appear to be articulate, persuasive, cheerful and entertaining all the time. Combined with the music and action that come with them, television has become a formidable competitor to any parent. And though even a young child can easily distinguish between a real person and a television image of one, real people can begin to seem very flat and dull compared with the sparkling third parent. This is particularly so when children can share their experiences of the third parent with each other. Perhaps even more dangerous than this is that a child transfixed by the television is also highly susceptible to the messages it conveys – about, for example, wealth, glamour, violence, domination and submission. For as long as the child's gaze is transfixed by the shimmering images on the screen, the space between the ears becomes an occupied territory, controlled by the voice in the box.

Wall-to-wall extraversion
Decisions about programming are based on viewing figures, so the more popular programmes tend to breed more of the same. As this continues down the years, television becomes increasingly extraverted, producing more and more of what research shows viewers like. The danger is that, with few exceptions, TV continually repeats a narrow range of attitudes so that the child sees more and more of less and less, and comes to believe that this is the way things are. Programme-makers may simply be selecting the most acceptable subjects available to them, but to the child addicted to TV, it's reality.

Turned to stone
The first priority of television is to keep people watching. Action, colour, music, emotional tension and violence are skilfully juxtaposed. Yet this frantic activity on screen contrasts with the total inactivity of the viewer. The child soon learns that entertainment comes by simply watching, and that passivity can be delightful – the only price of admission is attention. Taken a stage further, the child comes to believe that knowledge, creativity and imagination belong only to other people. Constant exposure to emotionally charged images also desensitizes children to drama, disaster, wonder and excitement in the real world.

Children of our time
The dominant ideas and activities of the time give the mind shape and meaning. The teeming profusion of broadcast television and the way it has shared out previously inaccessible information and expertise is beyond question the dominant influence in the culture of the late 20th century. This makes it all the sadder that it should be so decisively giving an authoritarian shape to many children's minds.

THE 'GOOD ENOUGH' PARENT

We are all children of our time. We cannot escape the epoch in which we live, any more than we can escape the facts of our own childhood. As parents, it is all too easy to bring the losses, disappointments and hurts from our own lives to bear on our children, and at the same time to reinforce unconsciously the prevailing assumptions, prejudices and expectations of our culture. But it doesn't have to be like that. By becoming more aware of our own personal and social conditioning, we can begin to free ourselves and future generations.

The greatest gift

Confidence, self-esteem, energy and spontaneity are qualities many adults yearn for and long to develop. Children who are actively encouraged to be themselves, to be angry, sad, disappointed, excited, enthusiastic, tearful, hurt, delighted or bored when they feel it, have little trouble with these qualities. Likewise, children who do not feel obliged to confer status, security, pride or respect on their parents will also develop confidence in themselves, their responses and their abilities. But children who, from the beginning, were conceived to give others love, to look after their parents, to be the pet they always wanted, will have a hole in the heart where self-esteem, energy and love should be. The first and perhaps most crucial gift parents can give their children is to accept them as they are.

Cultural and emotional legacies

No child is independent of the society she or he grows up in. Capitalist or communist; industrial, technological or agricultural; first, second, third or fourth world; patriarchal or matriarchal; introverted or extraverted – any of these basic attitudes inherent in the social system will become ingrained in the minds of parents and their children. The way industrial organizations work, for example, is perpetuated in schools (see pp. 122–3). Capitalism is internalized through an emphasis on earning, acquiring possessions, competition and economic growth. Patriarchy – the supposed natural dominance of men – is mirrored in religious teachings, hierarchical career structures, exploiting natural resources and building up offensive weapons. Education, the media, companies, organizations, state institutions, scientific research – all tend to reflect the current bias. But as a parent, you can help your children to a more open choice. By exploring the ways in which cultural tendencies have become woven into your own attitudes, opinions and expectations, you can consciously exclude them from your attitudes to your children. This will mean that they, in turn, can be freer from unconscious conditioning and make their own decisions about which aspects of society to accept or reject.

In every childhood some needs are satisfied and others are denied, ignored or simply not noticed. When needs are not satisfied, children register distress in one form or another. And they soon learn, with greater or lesser success, to survive feelings of distress by some kind of self-defence. But the distress remains behind the overlay of defence, and often emerges in adult life – in, for example, irritation with our children, in selfishness or short-temperedness. So what can we as parents do with this legacy of distress? There are two alternatives: to leave it simmering and allow it to damage our children; or to face the distress, realize that it belongs to ourselves and deal with it.

Perpetuating pain

If the distress remains unconsciously below the surface, it can become an integral part of our relationship with our children. Failing to see our children as separate from ourselves, they become part of our way of dealing with our distress. If we have children to keep a failing relationship together, to bring us the love we never had as children, because we are lonely or bored, or because we want someone to care for us, the relationship will depend on *them* meeting *our* needs. If they fail, we may consider them 'bad', 'wrong', 'difficult', 'ungrateful', 'selfish' or 'greedy' – when in fact they are distressed because their own needs have not been acknowledged and met. Babies learn very early on that approval comes from pleasing their parents – but if this means constantly demonstrating love, respect, care or amusement, then they will not be free to develop their own natural responses. Separation is also likely to pose problems. Children's increasing independence will seem threatening to their parents, and their habit of being there to help and please others may be transferred into adult relationships.

Preventing inherited distress

A more helpful option is to get to know the old hurts that may be threaded through our own personal history by patiently identifying them, so that the pain does not become embroiled in the relationship we have with our children. In this way, we can learn to empathize with the child, while at the same time maintaining enough distance to keep her or his needs separate from our own. As any parent will appreciate, it is not easy to empathize with the continuous stream of demands for attention, understanding and creativity all the time. But it is honourable to try to meet them as often as possible.

Accepting responsibility

One of our cultural legacies in the West is the emphasis on external causes and solutions in preference to inner knowledge – a situation well illustrated by the following story. There was once a community of people who lived on the bank of a great river. The lives of these people were constantly interrupted by the need to rescue people coming down the river who were drowning. The local people found their role as rescuers very inconvenient, since none of them ever fell in the river and the rescuing was absorbing more and more of their resources. So they started to penalize the people who had been so stupid as to find themselves at risk in the river. But they never looked upstream to see who was throwing the people in, in the first place.

The point of the story is that we tend to blame people who are in danger or distress. Yet there are signs that we are beginning to look upstream. These include greater sensitivity concerning childbirth and techniques to help prospective parents to regress to their own early experiences and to re-evaluate their reasons for having a child.

PATTERNS OF PARENTING

Living very close to a young child can be both intensely pleasurable and extremely challenging. Being a parent brings us face to face with our own unresolved personal history, by re-stimulating early hurts (see pp. 144–5) and laying us open to projection. The way in which we deal with these anxieties – how well or how ineffectively – becomes built into the minds of the next generation as a model of how the world works. But, as Lloyd de Mause has shown, if a more caring approach to bringing up children is gradually adopted, it is reflected in less distressed behaviour in the next generation. He claims that much of our social progress towards democracy and social justice has arisen from gradual changes in the way we look after our children. All the historical patterns of childcare appear to be still in existence. See if you can identify your parents' style or the one you would tend to follow on the map opposite.

Infanticide
From antiquity to 4th century

Parents saw children as existing to meet their needs and convenience and, if defective, as responsible for their own misfortune. Unwanted children, including girls or deformed babies, were commonly disposed of by exposure to the weather or wild animals. Right up to the 19th century, illegitimate children were regularly killed. And today, legal abortions continue to allow parents to dispose of children if they are inconvenient.

Abandonment
From 4th to 13th century

Following the spread of Christianity, children were thought to have a soul, so they could not be killed. But since they were held to be full of evil, they were beaten and kept at an emotional distance from their parents. Parents faced with children they did not want usually passed them over to wet nurses and then disposed of them to other families for fostering or as servants. Alternatively, they were sold as slaves. As late as the 7th century, the Archbishop of Canterbury ruled that a man could not sell his child into slavery after the age of seven. Abandonment in a modified form still survives today in foster homes, children's homes and orphanages.

Ambivalence
From 14th to 17th century

During this period parents became more emotionally attached to their children, but still feared they were on the brink of total evil. The ritual of baptism included exorcism of the devil, and parents saw their task as moulding their children, containing them in swaddling for as long as possible, and beating them into shape. When children outgrew swaddling, parents and teachers used threats of ghosts, demons and hell-fire to establish obedience.

Intrusion
18th century

Children were now held to pose less of a threat. The evil had receded and empathy between parent and child became possible. Parents now saw it as their duty to conquer children's minds, to break their will and so control behaviour, through threats and guilt as well as punishments. The child was to be 'prayed with but not played with'.

Socialization
19th to mid-20th century

Parenting moved to become more a matter of guidance, training and teaching manners, good habits, correct public behaviour and how to conform to other's expectations. Beatings continued – but to punish misbehaviour, not intrinsic evil. This form of childcare is the most common one today.

Helping
Mid-20th century onward

This style of parenting is still emerging. Children are seen as knowing what they need better than anyone else. The joint task of parents is to empathize with children and so respond accurately to their needs at each stage of development. This demands that the parents have made considerable progress in resolving their own distress or 'frozen' history. There is no punishment, no discipline, just the belief that if children's potential is fulfilled at each stage, they will grow up to be authentic, gentle, cheerful, resourceful, creative and unafraid of authority.

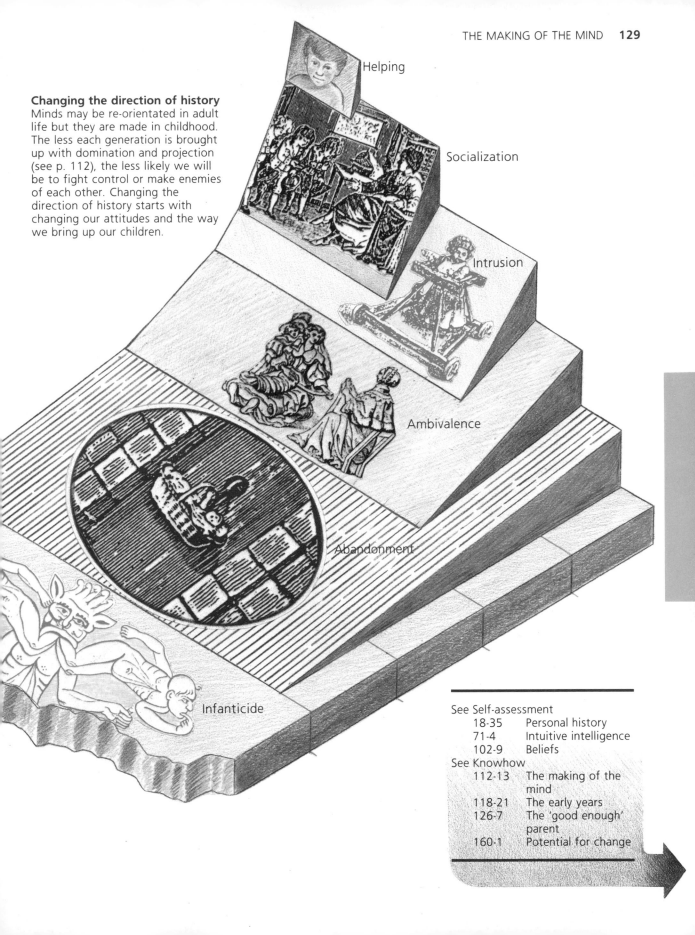

Helping

Socialization

Intrusion

Ambivalence

Abandonment

Infanticide

Changing the direction of history
Minds may be re-orientated in adult
life but they are made in childhood.
The less each generation is brought
up with domination and projection
(see p. 112), the less likely we will
be to fight control or make enemies
of each other. Changing the
direction of history starts with
changing our attitudes and the way
we bring up our children.

THE MIND IN ACTION

What is the mind? Where is the mind? How does it relate to the brain and the rest of the body? As we have seen earlier, the mind is a fiction, a convenient label for a whole range of human experience. In a similar way, a company or business may be a convenient label for the collective activities of several hundred or thousand people. The mind, like a company, has a history, and consequently an identity.

Mapping the mind

To begin to appreciate how extraordinary the human mind is, and to understand it in action, involves drawing together the disparate strands into a 'map'. This allows us to look at its incredible range of activities, skills and capacities all in one piece. There have been innumerable attempts at this – a current text book lists no less than ten different schemes, and in his book, *Maps of the Mind*, British writer Charles Hampden-Turner lists another sixty. After describing a few of the best known models of the mind, I have chosen to present a map that I find particularly useful.

The geography of the mind

The test of a map is whether it helps you to navigate through life with a little more certainty. In this part of Knowhow we begin by using the map to get our bearings. Equipped with a scheme of the geography of the mind, we can then move on to look at 'attention', both out on to the world of people and objects, and within – to the ideas, thoughts, dreams and fantasies of the inner universe of the mind. This provides a useful platform from which to examine the light and shade of the mind – fatigue, arousal, imagination and intuition.

The effects of personal history

How does the mind respond to being challenged or threatened? Why do some people some of the time seem more intelligent or responsive than others? How do we defend ourselves against being hurt? Why do we defend ourselves against being hurt? Why do we sometimes over-react and sometimes under-react? These questions find an answer in this section in the concept of 're-stimulation', which demystifies why and how we become upset.

The limits of science

If this section seems short on science, it is because, in my view, the explosive growth of information in recent years about the human mind has tended to obscure as well as illuminate the subject. Scientific knowledge about the mind is very patchy. Although there has been considerable progress in researching some areas, such as the brain hemispheres, science still finds it difficult to answer questions about memory and recall, for example. Since scientists depend on working methods that separate the subject and the observer, and since their approach is often very technical, fragmented and framed in exotic language – lobes, chiasmas, somites, neurones, dendrites or receptors, for instance – it is often difficult to relate their findings to the richness and diversity of our actual experience. But this richness is accessible.

'Future research . . . will be concerned with breaking through the veil of ignorance that still conceals how developments in human brain tissue of the years of childhood relate to psychological maturation.'
Prof. Colwyn Trevarthen

'How connecting up regions of the cortex actually brings memory into consciousness or allows us to imagine an event that has never occurred we really do not know . . . why we are unable to put all of this together is that our methods of research are apt for analysis but very poor at synthesis.'
P. J. Laird

Business provides two useful metaphors for the human mind.
1 Just as our minds are shaped by how we and our parents earn a living, so there is a 'late capitalist industrial' mind preoccupied with producing, consuming, marketing its skills, exploiting its assets and controlling its environment.
2 Organizations like the BBC or NASA represent the collective identity of thousands of relatively autonomous individuals who join together for tasks, occupy premises, use resources and have a history and an identity. Similarly, the mind is a convenient label for the intelligent purposes, appetites, resources, history and bodies of human beings.

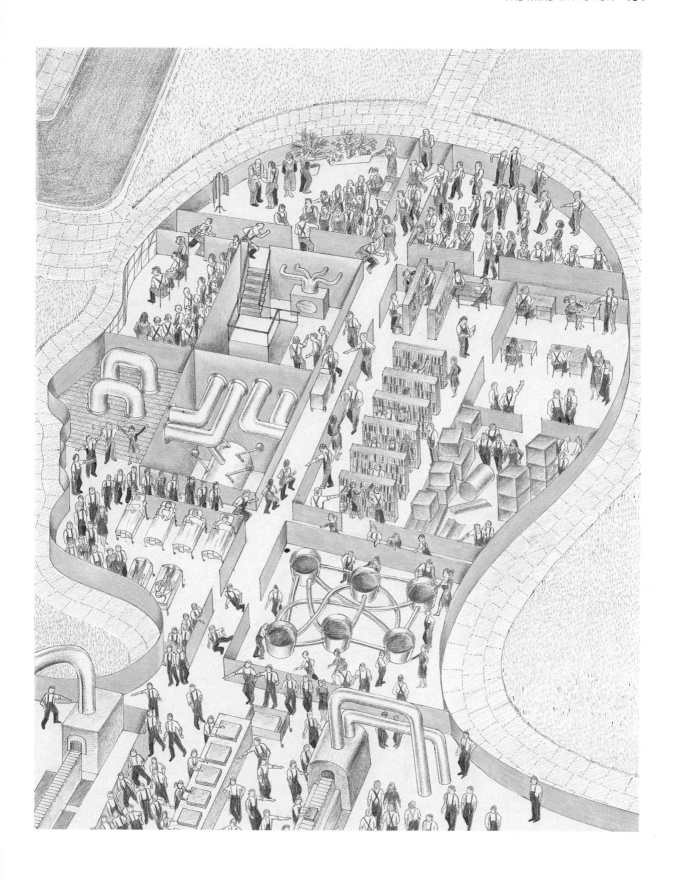

MIND METAPHORS

Work concerned with understanding the human mind involves communicating new discoveries to other people. A shared language, vocabulary and working methods are essential. Perhaps because of this, in the last few hundred years the central metaphor or map for the mind or brain has tended to come from the most advanced contemporary technology.

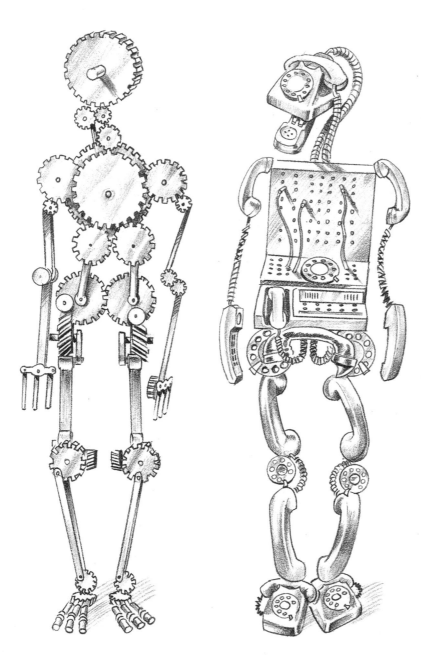

Clockwork

In the 17th century, Descartes and, later, Newton saw God as the clockmaker who had set creation in motion. The universal 'machine' included nature and human beings who were both at the mercy of events outside their control – 'nothing but the motions of certain parts of the organic body'. The human mind was a mere ghost in the machine, insignificant in the grand scheme of things.

Telephone exchange

Telecommunications, information technology and the science on which they are based have made a huge contribution to the way we think of the human mind. Many of the concepts and terms they introduced have worked their way into the science of the mind – including systems, data, feedback, channels, information, transmitters, receivers, signals, codes, networks and processing.

Holograms

Holograms are three-dimensional images made with light, but without a camera. The light, which has to be 'coherent', or unscattered, usually comes from a laser, although simple holograms – found, for example, on some bank cheque cards and greetings cards – use other light sources. A hologram is made by bouncing light off a subject – perhaps a face. When this light combines with a beam of unreflected light, interference patterns are set up that can be recorded on a piece of photographic film. When the film is illuminated by a laser, the whole face comes into view in 3D.

According to the American scientist Karl Pribram of Stamford University, many brain functions are analagous to holograms. He found, for example, that the interference patterns set up between stored memory and incoming vision result in visual learning. Patterns of stored memories emerge from the visual centre of the brain and coincide with the visual signals coming in through the eye. The resulting interference patterns are then added to our existing store of visual memories. Just as one part of a hologram contains the whole image, so the brain registers a single memory in many sites.

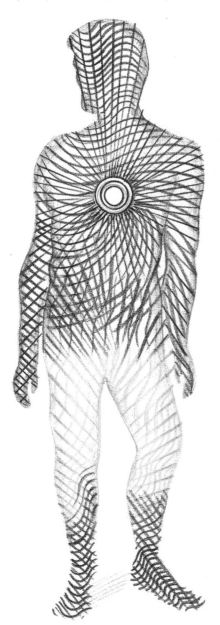

Computers

The digital computer, with its input and output, programming, processors, data, operating systems and units of hardware and programming, remains a strong popular image of the brain and mind. The brain is seen as the hardware, the computer, while the mind acts as the software, the programming input, which influences its output. 'The contents of consciousness appear to be the values of the parameters that serve as the input and output to the operating system.'

Computer models of the mind, however, have been severely limited by the 'one step at a time' approach of present computers. They are very good at logical thinking, but not at imagination, for example, or at creativity. Recently, however, the advent of parallel processing, where computer processors run independently but simultaneously, has provided a more promising metaphor (see pp. 134–5).

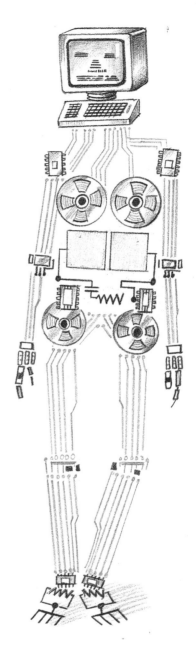

See Self-assessment
    66-81   Intelligence
    102-9   Beliefs
See Knowhow
    130-1   The mind in action
    134-5   Map of the mind

MAP OF THE MIND

Michael Gazzaniga – an American research scientist working with people who have had the two halves of their brain surgically separated to ease epileptic seizures – has put forward a radical new model of how the mind works. He sees the brain as organized into hundreds, maybe thousands, of independent 'mind modules' that continuously absorb and silently respond to what is happening within us. They have no language and can express themselves only through behaviour. One single module interprets this behaviour, makes sense of what is happening and informs another single module, the 'talker', the language centre, which then expresses the interpretation verbally. One of the most interesting features of this theory is that while all the non-verbal mind modules work simultaneously, the 'interpreter' and the 'talker' can only take things one step at a time. This means that much of our spontaneous behaviour happens out of reach of our conscious, verbal selves, and so remains unconscious.

MIND MODULES

TALKER

Mind modules, a cast of thousands

The non-verbal mind modules cover all aspects of perception, memory, sensing and regulatory functions. They absorb new information coming from the outside, they remember experiences, store how we feel about them and trigger a response when a similar experience happens. At the same time they initiate, sustain and control complex physical actions – releasing a hormone here or an enzyme there. Each mind module can act autonomously, although several may work in concert, and together they drive all aspects of experience.

The 'talker'

As the situation demands or as the interpreter deems appropriate, the talker draws on the interpreter's sequentially organized observations. It names and catalogues them, moulds them into the logical patterns of language and then initiates speech.

BEHAVIOUR

READING
SITTING
BREATHING
DIGESTING

INTERPRETER

Post-justification

Perhaps most fascinating of all is Gazzaniga's idea that the interpreter works retrospectively. A mind module triggers some form of behaviour, then the interpreter notices what's happened and devises a reason for it. This means, according to Gazzaniga, that we are endowed with an almost limitless capacity to hypothesize – after the event. The interpreter is a beliefs, attitudes and values factory. So much for us being certain that we are in charge of our behaviour! We say 'let's go to lunch' at 1.15, apparently acting from our own free will, when in reality the decision is more likely to be the direct result of our waning energy levels.

Memories from childhood trigger adult behaviour, such as fear of failure, which the interpreter rationalizes by saying that we feel ill. Similarly, an interpreter that has learned to ignore the body may instruct the talker module to say 'yes', while our posture obviously says 'no'. This model of the mind also accounts for compulsive or inhibited behaviour – when, for example, the mind modules panic in a crowd or refuse to travel by air, or have to keep everyone happy at all costs. It also helps to explain how several 'sub-personalities' – the 'critic', the 'hurt child', the 'perfectionist', the 'pleaser' – can all exist in the same person, hijacking behaviour for a minute, an afternoon or half a lifetime. Memories, for example, of a critical parent, are stored in the mind modules and may be re-stimulated by current events (see pp. 146–7).

The rationalizing 'interpreter'

Normally located in the left hemisphere of the brain, the 'interpreter' continuously scans the mind modules for information. It then compares current experiences with previous ones and makes its own interpretations – about events, about what people say, about feelings, about memories, about being cold, hot, hungry, tired and so on. As a reflexive response, the interpreter constantly marshalls the evidence of what is happening in the body, brain and nervous system and comes up with a step-by-step explanation. It reports its observations to the talker – the language centre. Before we speak, we are thinking with the interpreter – hence the pause while we gather our thoughts or try to remember an event. The interpreter is the 'I', the person in here who notices, evaluates and forms an opinion. It is the viewfinder through which we view the world.

See Knowhow
  136-7   Going into your mind
  140-1   Paying attention
  144-5   Feelings are physical
See Mind gym
  192-3   Attention
  200-2   Identity

GOING INTO YOUR MIND

To see the usefulness of a mind map, let's take a tour of your mind and see what's in there right now. You are breathing and maintaining a temperature to within a fraction of 98.4°F (37°C), like everyone else on this planet. Blood is circulating, and if you've eaten in the last few hours, you may be digesting.

Oxygen balance, temperature, blood circulation and digestion are all being automatically maintained by their associated 'mind modules'.

You are probably sitting down, and holding this book in your hands.

Your mind modules adjust the muscles, maintain balance in your spine, neck, arms and hands as well as in the pressure of your fingertips – again automatically.

You are reading.

Your mind modules continuously scan the page and the printing on it. They recognize patterns of paragraphs, sentences, words and letters and, drawing on these visual clues, connect them with information stored in your memory.

Ah, an opinion.

Your 'interpreter' (see p. 135) is assessing what you are reading – considering whether it is useful, interesting, familiar or relevant.

Now try taking this a step further. Note this page number 136. Then close the book and open it at page 137.

What's going on?

The purpose of this request is to highlight the question of free will. Did you choose to close the book? Did you just automatically follow instructions? Or did you choose to ignore the request? And who, or what, made the decision? Do you make other bigger choices in the same way?

Now try something else. See if you can reach a conclusion about these statements: **1** Babies are illogical. **2** Never despise the man who can stand at arm's length from a crocodile. **3** Illogical people are despised. Watch what's happening in your mind while you struggle with this.

The interpreter is working overtime!

The words make sense one at a time and as phrases, but is there a conclusion?

A highly developed interpreter will have set to work on unpicking the logic of the riddle. What do you feel about this task? Does it strike you as an intriguing problem that demands a solution?

Feelings of fascination.

Or does it remind you of school perhaps?

Feelings of inadequacy.

Sit back and consider for a moment. Has this been a good week? Bring to mind a happy event when you personally felt good.

You have just accessed a memory module.

Did you have difficulty thinking of anything good? Did the awkward, upsetting moments keep pushing out the good times? Did your mind 'wander'? The interpreter is constantly looking for consistency and continuity as it tries to 'make sense' of experience.

Going out of your mind

If, like some people, you feel that giving this much attention to the workings of the mind is indulgent 'navel-gazing' or that it might be dangerous, hang on a minute. When people have 'trouble with their nerves', or become 'mentally ill' or 'disturbed' or have a 'nervous breakdown', it's because their non-verbal mind modules have gone out of control. Perhaps the interpreter has been overwhelmed by an unexpected tide of body signals, or perhaps it has ignored the body for too long. This is something that can happen to anyone. If you know what is in your inner universe and know what your mind can cope with, however, you are less likely to be taken by surprise.

Oh good, you are still with me. Now look back to the previous page, to 'What's going on?'.

What does this tell us?

This light-hearted visit to inner space illustrates the usefulness of the mind map (see p. 134). It also begins to answer some central questions.

Why do thoughts come one after the other?	The interpreter works in a step-by-step way.
Why is thinking straight sometimes so difficult?	If there is a high level of arousal to cope with a challenge or threat, then the non-verbal 'mind modules' may be so active that they overwhelm the interpreter.
Why do images, feelings and memories seem to come to mind as a whole?	If the interpreter is relaxed, through meditation or therapy, for example, it allows the content of the non-verbal mind modules to come through whole.
Why do words sometimes fail us when we try to describe an event or an experience?	In its step-by-step approach, the interpreter condenses a huge range of sensations, memories and feelings to form the logical sentences that underlie language. Sometimes it fails.
How do we sometimes know that we know what we are doing?	This is when one mind module, the interpreter, knows what the others are doing.
How can we be so confident that there are cut-and-dried answers to complex questions?	The interpreter relies on logic and analysis to make judgments. It's easy to be overconfident.
Why are feelings sometimes so overwhelming?	The mind modules responsible for feelings act autonomously and overwhelm the interpreter.
What is intuition?	It seems to be a developed capacity to turn down the interpreter so that more of the activities of the non-verbal mind modules come through.
What is it about questions that make them so intriguing?	They stimulate the interpreter to scan our memory stores for forgotten information and to search out new connections between familiar ideas.

THE SHIFTING SPOTLIGHT

Attention is an inner spotlight that illuminates the many different aspects of our experience. It's through attention that our 'interpreter' keeps in touch with what our non-verbal mind modules are experiencing (see pp. 134–5). Attention constantly shifts between the different functions of our minds, bringing first one, then the other into the light. One moment we may be *thinking* how to find a new job. Then, as the cool evening air comes in through the open door, our attention shifts to *feeling* cold. After we've closed the door and sat down again, we find ourselves *imagining* what we are going to have for dinner. Although we may think we are giving or paying attention, usually we have little or no direct control over where our attention is focussed.

The unconscious

Contrary to popular misconception, there is no such thing as 'the unconscious', although there are mind processes of which we remain unconscious. These 'out of sight, out of mind' activities usually come to our attention only through the filter of the interpreter. But when we sleep, the interpreter is turned off, leaving us open to a universe of inner activities in the form of dreams, which are usually out of reach when we are awake.

Aspects of experience

Sight
Our eyes tell us about colour, size, shape, pattern, speed, distance, perspective, facial expressions, pictures and the written word.

Hearing
Our ears tell us about language, harmony, volume, frequency, distance and tones of voice.

Thoughts
Fragments of recent perceptions and memories are rearranged by the 'interpreter' to produce thoughts.

Memories
These consist of stored information from the past – images, people, places and events.

Ideas
These are the programmes from which the interpreter produces beliefs and opinions.

Beliefs/attitudes
These are habits, inclinations and aims which fuel the interpreter's decisions.

Attention out

Outer attention, our experience of the five senses and perceptions of the external world, is what we normally think of as attention. But although the focus of attention in this case concerns what is outside us, it is still an internal process. As the light of our shifting attention picks up information from each of the senses, via some of the non-verbal mind modules, it supplies the interpreter with perceptions from which it can form an opinion about what is happening in the world.

The collective unconscious

Almost identical images and myths have arisen in the minds of human beings down the centuries and across the world in widely separated cultures. The archetypal symbols that appear again and again echo the non-verbal, automatic aspects of the mind of which we are 'collectively unconscious'. These include two characteristics which we all share. The first is that we all have a human genetic programme that drives our development from a single cell to a complex adult being. And, secondly, we all share the fundamental experiences of life in the womb, birth from a mother, the need for nourishment, learning to feed ourselves, to walk, talk and eventually cope with separation from our parents and later from home. It would be surprising if this common heritage was not reflected in art and culture.

Touch
Our skin and especially our fingertips tell us about texture, pressure, shape, size and temperature.

Smell/taste
Our nose and mouth tell us about edibility and chemical composition.

Distress memories
These are reactions to distressing levels of challenge stored in the bodymind.

Feelings
These are signals from the body which announce automatic reactions to threat, challenge, pleasure or pain.

Daydreams
Random scanning of memories and the senses, without much interpretation, produce daydreams.

Dreams
The result of simultaneous access to non-verbal mind modules. They recall recent events and the earlier memories they echo, with no 'interpreter's' explanations.

Attention in

Shifting our attention in means closing the shutters to exclude the information coming in from the outer world. This involves bringing into the foreground not only the 'interpreter', as it forms opinions and draws conclusions, but also the signals arising from within the body, including memories of stored feelings, breathing, digestion, muscular aches and heartbeat, as well as those non-verbal mind modules concerned with feelings and imagination (see pp. 134–6). Attention centred on the interpreter includes thinking and analysis, and it tends to follow the step-by-step sequences of logic and language.

PAYING ATTENTION

Attention is the process through which we construct the world we experience. There is a world of real events and flesh and blood people, of course, but what we make of them is largely determined by the quality and flexibility of our attention. While it is usually outside our conscious control, we can deliberately shift our focus of attention, if we choose to.

Shifting attention in and out

The eyes play a significant part in where we direct our attention, not least because they are, in effect, a part of the brain. When your eyes are open and active, the rest of the senses tend to take a back seat and your attention tends to focus outwards. If you close your eyes, and keep them closed, your attention will tend to turn inwards. Open them again, and it will turn outwards.

If you find yourself feeling very upset or sunk into a mood, you can choose to help yourself out of it by shifting your attention out on to the senses. Try opening your eyes and, keeping them open, stand up, walk to the window and look out. Then, as your attention comes out, count the books on your shelves or walk around your home and touch twenty red objects. This pulls in the left part of the brain and the 'interpreter' (see p. 135).

If you are someone whose attention is most frequently out, then you may find that most decisions involving emotional responses and commitment tend to be difficult. When this happens, close your eyes, go inside and notice what your body is saying. You may find that it is sad, afraid, or perhaps excited. You don't have to agree, but you'd be wise to take what your body says into account. Bodies have been known to rebel against absentee landlords!

Concentration, imagination and intuition

Concentrating – watching very intently what you are doing – does not, as is often supposed, mean building up an intense 'beam' of attention. You can always concentrate your attention out by turning down the volume of all the mind modules except your sense organs. This will increase the intensity of your sight, touch, smell, taste, hearing and smell. Concentrating your attention fully in, by contrast, means turning down the sense organs – closing your eyes if necessary – so that the other mind modules are turned up.

Using your imagination means teaching your interpreter two skills – to call upon the multiple facets of memory, for the purposes of play, and at the same time to keep an eye out for unusual, surprising, interesting or useful combinations of old memory fragments that arise.

Intuition is associated with the right side of the brain, whose mind modules deal with spatial perception and global concepts, such as myths, maps and the future. Using your intuition means keeping your interpreter on 'low' while your attention is broadly focussed inward, so that your interpreter can pick up messages from a wide range of non-verbal mind modules. With its analytical faculty turned down,

Arousal

Your level of arousal is a measure of how activated your body is – and how alert you are, as a result. You can significantly influence the quality of your attention by taking charge of your level of arousal. Meditation and deep relaxation, for example, which induce very low levels of arousal, close to sleep, shift the balance of attention in. And this can greatly increase the chances of an intuitive leap in understanding that leads to a new creative synthesis. To maintain the optimum level of alertness that you need to work effectively, you may find yourself having another cup of coffee or tea or walking around to stretch your legs. But if you try to sustain very high levels of arousal, before long attention begins to disintegrate, it becomes increasingly difficult to focus attention, and your attention shifts inwards. Since this means getting more in touch with the body's messages – with headaches, hunger or tired muscles – it does not usually seem very pleasant. But if you are tired, you need to know it. Ignoring it for too long can and very often does lead to psychosomatic ailments.

the interpreter can absorb an overview, a general impression, just as it is possible to gauge the mood of a meeting through the general hubbub, without focussing on specifics.

The here and now

A useful reminder is that attention, whether it is in or out, is always happening now. Present time is all there is. Every thought, memory and image, every vision of the future, is a present-time event in the mind. It is difficult to live fully in the present because our accumulated experiences, which usually include some distress from our early history, tend to pull us away into the past or into the future. . . Learning to move our attention persistently back into the present from its excursions into the past or the future is a reliable way of enhancing our intelligence (see pp. 142–3).

Finding your 'self'

The human ability to 'know that you know' has excited a great deal of speculation across the centuries. Our brainmind model suggests that it may be the function of one mind module, the interpreter, watching what all the others are doing (see p. 135). If you want to explore the idea for yourself, try this. Close your eyes. Give attention to the pressure of your body on the chair, to the weight of the book between your fingers, the texture of the page. Now move your attention inward off the book so that you become aware of your breathing. Now back again, off your breathing, on to just you, yourself. Very elusive, aren't you? But even though you may not be able to locate yourself, perhaps there was a fleeting glimpse of the 'who' or 'what' that knows you are reading these words.

Is inner space dangerous?

Given that there is an intrinsically inner dimension to all outer experience, how do you feel about it? If you tend to be easily overwhelmed by your inner world and would love to be able to think straight and be more alert to what is around you, that probably involves building up your interpreter. Setting goals and building up your strengths are a good way to begin (see pp. 203–9). If you fear or disregard the inner universe of your mind, it is worth bearing in mind that the hidden inner contents of your mind will continue to exert a powerful influence on your behaviour for as long as you ignore them. If you have come to believe that the outer world is all there is, then the inner universe of your mind will be a vast area for exploration. Meditation and visualization are good starting points for this process (see pp. 226–7).

Deep exploration of your inner space requires an ability to keep a balance between inner and outer attention, so that, no matter how deep you go, the interpreter is in touch with what you are doing. Co-counselling is a safe way of doing this (see pp. 178–9). But even if attention is not balanced, you can rely on returning to the stable state you are normally in after your self-exploration.

Caution
Drug use of any kind and extreme physical manipulation that involves the use of force, including deep massage, sensory deprivation, and hyperventilation, can swamp the interpreter so that balanced attention is no longer possible and you cannot rely on returning to a stable state.

See Self-assessment
56-7   Body signals
71-4   Intuitive intelligence
See Knowhow
124-5   The television 'I'
134-5   Map of the mind
136-7   Going into your mind
138-9   The shifting spotlight
142-3   Intelligence
See Mind gym
192-3   Attention
195-6   Healing and distress
218-22   Emotional intelligence

INTELLIGENCE

Intelligence is the natural ability to make the right guesses often enough to, at the very least, ensure survival, and, at best, to meet our full personal potential. This definition allows us to adopt our four dimensions of intelligence (see pp. 68–81) – intellectual, emotional, intuitive and physical – as the need arises, without the risk of over-emphasizing any one of them.

How do we make decisions?

What prevents us from behaving intelligently? Let's see what happens when a situation arises where we need to be intelligent. When someone makes a request, a demand or a remark, our brain calls on layer upon layer of stored experience. All of these memory traces are biased by the context of our past experience and so influence our response. If, for example, a similar request or remark aroused guilt, pain, pleasure, annoyance or embarrassment at the time, these same feelings are likely to colour our present-day response. In addition, the mind's 'interpreter' (see p. 135) which assesses our various possible reactions, is itself formed out of an accumulation of previous experiences. So, by the time the 'talker' part of the mind finally makes a response to the current situation, a very complex process has taken place that has inevitably been shaped by the past.

'Will you lend me some money?'

Suppose I, a stranger, come into the room where you are sitting reading and ask to borrow some money – say, the equivalent of a week's wages. I need to make an urgent trip and I can't get any money from the bank. How do you respond? Let's look at your responses in slow motion.

How you feel about money; how much, if any, you have saved; your attitude to me; what you know of my needs and whether you like me, all come into focus in your mind. Trust, for example, involves calling upon numerous memories and feelings from the past. And if they conflict, you may even become a little agitated. Eventually, your interpreter, having analysed your inner responses, makes a decision and passes it on to the talker. It might be 'yes', 'no' or perhaps 'I'll let you know'. Responding intelligently to a request of this kind involves guessing correctly about the terms, conditions and reasons for the request and having a clear view of your own rights and obligations, as well as being able to guess right about the best long-term outcome of the situation. This may involve intellectual analysis of my arguments, and emotional insight into how trustworthy I am. But there is usually another, often overriding, factor in guessing right, which tends to obscure our guesses. And that is how much distress from your personal history is re-activated by the request.

Blocks to intelligence

Hurtful early experiences, which are stored in the form of bodymind memories (see p. 144), are sometimes sufficiently highly charged to re-emerge when similar situations recur later in life – so sabotaging your more intelligent impulses. Acting intelligently in the present means having a minimum of distress of this kind in play in your dealings with the world. Continuing our example. . . if, as a child, you were rejected or deprived because of too much or too little money, or if you were made to feel guilty about being wealthy, humiliated about being poor or critical of people with or without money, this is likely to colour your response and to compromise significantly your intelligence. The more that the space between your ears, and between your elbows and your knees, is occupied by unresolved distress from childhood, the less intelligent you are going to be.

An intelligent, distress-free response might be to tell me that you appreciate the difficulty I'm in, but that unless I have something negotiable, such as travellers' cheques or a camera, as collateral, you don't know me well enough to make the loan I'm asking for. Or another might be to tell me that you are happy to let me use your phone to contact anyone I know – a friend, a relation, solicitor or personal bank manager who could arrange for a rapid transfer of funds, but in the circumstances do not feel you are in a position to lend me the money.

An unintelligent, distressed response on the other hand might be to explode in fury at being thought stupid enough to be taken in by such an old ploy. Another might be to feel so sorry for me in my awful predicament that not only do you lend me the money, but you insist on loaning me your car to drive to the airport to catch the plane. Yet another could be to tell me how stupid I am for failing to manage my financial affairs and that I'm wrong to make the trip anyway, and that you refuse to lend me the money.

How to become more intelligent

There is a great deal of unnecessary confusion about the nature of intelligence (see p. 66) and how it can be enhanced. The surest way to to become more intelligent, to gain free access to our natural abilities is to learn to untie the knots of distress that we carry with us from the past. This approach does require a certain amount of skilful guidance and a great deal of personal commitment. But it is a considerably more powerful and more realistic strategy for enhancing intelligence than memory training, mnemonics, positive thinking and other methods of 'improving our brain power' or 'gaining mental mastery'. All these approaches and techniques are based on the old view that intelligence is synonymous with intellect and that blocks to intelligence can be broken down through mental exercises and practice. Until we know how much the distress of our past history is compulsively driving or inhibiting our current behaviour and limiting our performance and productivity, we won't know whether the skills we need are really missing or just temporarily out of reach. And unless we begin to unearth and resolve our distress, it will continue to interfere with our abilities and take up the space that could be filled with intelligence.

See Self-assessment
26-35   Life events
47-9   Self-esteem
54-5   Coping with change
66-81   Intelligence
84-6   Self-presentation
87-8   Communication
94-5   Conflict and
          commitment
104-6   Personal beliefs
See Knowhow
114-15   Life before birth
116-17   The birth drama
118-21   The early years
134-5   Maps of the mind
144-5   Feelings are physical
146-55   Self-defence
166-71   Humanistic
          psychology
186-7   Resolving conflicts
See Mind gym
195-6   Healing and distress
197   Keeping a journal
198-9   Life review
203-9   Self esteem
214-17   Transformation
218-22   Emotional intelligence
223-5   Physical intelligence
226-7   Intuitive intelligence
228-9   Intellectual
          intelligence

FEELINGS ARE PHYSICAL

There is often a great deal of uncertainty about emotions and feelings. How do I know what is the 'right' emotional reaction? If I am emotional, is it a sign of weakness? Why do I tend to overreact with certain people? How can some people be so cold and thick-skinned? Feelings have two related origins, the body and its history. **Feelings are physical**. They are body signals, arising from the body's built-in response to threat, pleasure or pain. They are felt internally as, for example, anger, fear, happiness or grief, and expressed externally in shouting, shaking, laughter or tears, with many subtle variations in between. Many present-day feelings are relics from the past. When we encounter threat, pleasure or pain in the present, old feelings of distress, coupled with patterns of survival strategies, may be re-stimulated (see pp. 26–35).

We are *not* responsible for our feelings

Whenever we encounter a painful threat or a pleasurable challenge, our non-verbal mind modules (see p. 134) absorb the information and act autonomously. Someone close to us is hurt – we feel a lump in the throat, tears. A baby is born – our eyes glow, we smile. The feelings happen – anxiety, annoyance, elation, sadness. But we only become aware of them retrospectively, through our interpreter (see p. 135).

Pain from the past re-stimulated

Events in the present that echo a painful earlier experience re-stimulate the old distress recorded in the bodymind and the corresponding defensive strategy. If, for example, we experience a painful separation from a parent as a young child and respond by forgetting the pain, then in adult life parting from someone close to us is likely to re-activate the forgotton memory, so that the adult separation may become an emotional disaster. The bigger the array of early painful memories, the greater will be the number of events in the present that are likely to trigger them. Not surprisingly, we all tend to go to some trouble to avoid potentially re-activating events.

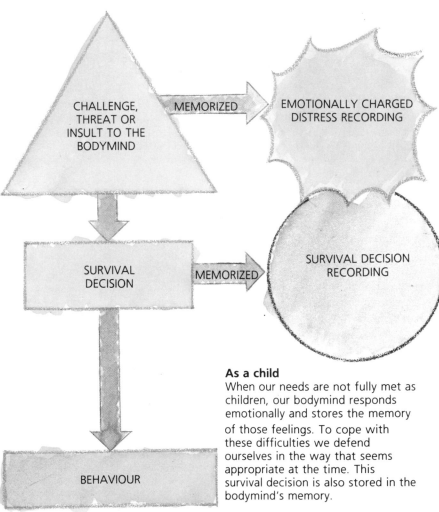

As a child

When our needs are not fully met as children, our bodymind responds emotionally and stores the memory of those feelings. To cope with these difficulties we defend ourselves in the way that seems appropriate at the time. This survival decision is also stored in the bodymind's memory.

We *are* responsible for what we *do* about our feelings

We have no choice about our spontaneous feelings. But because we have an interpreter, we can choose how to act on them. A friend arrives unexpectedly and is clearly upset. We have urgent work to finish and feel irritated and anxious about the neglected work and sad about the friend's predicament. We are not responsible for these feelings. They happen. But we have a choice. We can act on the sadness and help our friend, we can tell her we are too busy, or we can tell her that we are annoyed that she arrived without phoning first.

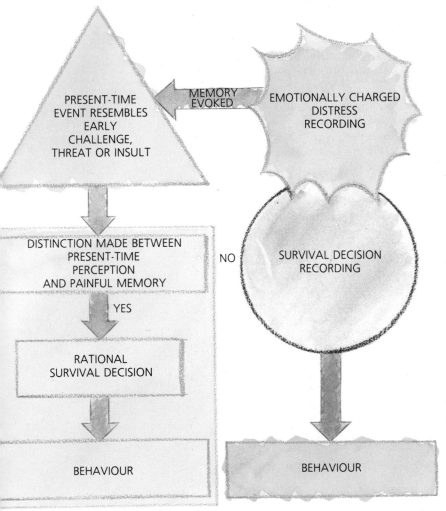

As an adult

When an event occurs which reminds us of the earlier difficulties, it evokes the original feelings of distress that are stored in the bodymind. We then have a choice. We can decide to respond appropriately, and reject the influence of the earlier survival decision, or we can allow the earlier survival decision to recur automatically so that we continue to behave inappropriately.

SELF-DEFENCE
Storing the pain

How do we make the world? We construct it out of our own experience, in the light of our personal history. The whole style of our behaviour – our reactions, our inclinations and many of our disabilities – is shaped by how we learned to survive when we were babies and young children, and later how we learned to survive the process of socialization. This history lives on in us always. There's no easy escape from it. But we can reduce its powers over us.

The need for self-defence

As a foetus, a baby, and later as a child, growth always pushes our development from within. There is a tension between our inner needs and the outer world and we learn to accumulate strategies for coping with the times when our needs are not met. If our needs are met in a timely and sensitive way, then we remain open and welcoming to the expanding universe of mother and family and we learn to feel good. But if a number of our fundamental needs remain unmet, then a great deal of our energy goes into survival strategies that take away the pain of 'feeling bad' (see pp. 26–35).

The strategist within

The 'interpreter' has a key role in devising our defence strategies (see p. 135). From our very earliest days, when something difficult happens, it decides how we can best get over it, forget it, put it behind us or switch off. It has a prodigious capacity for fielding the pain, limiting our experience so that feeling bad is minimized. And the strategies that work well, that successfully shut out the pain, it uses over and over again. From the very beginning, through life in the womb, birth, infancy, childhood, adolescence and throughout our adult lives, the interpreter is making sense of what happens to us, silencing the painful, negative or unacceptable aspects of life, and devising logical explanations for our feelings and behaviour. We learn to edit the news that crosses the boundary from 'out there' to 'in here'.

Conscious and unconscious

Experiences that we like and that we regard as acceptable to others, we admit into our consciousness. Those that hurt or worry us, the interpreter disowns or censors and, along with a huge amount that is just mundane, they slip into unconsciousness. But they remain stored in the non-verbal areas of our minds (see p. 134). And because they are non-verbal, we may experience them, intermittently, as feelings, sensations, physical pain, discomfort or restlessness. Since these disowned experiences have no verbal language, they express themselves in more subtle and insidious ways, driving, compelling, inhibiting and distorting our behaviour, and influencing our tone of voice, body language, posture, self-esteem, attitudes and beliefs – even our choice of partner. (For examples of many of the most pervasive and deeply affecting experiences that we learn to 'forget', see Personal history pp. 18–35).

Recognizing the pain

The intensity and depth of past hurt can vary enormously. It's easy to imagine the pain that is being kept quiet in the mind of a child growing up in Ethiopia, Northern Ireland or Beirut in the late 20th century, or in Vietnam in the 1960s or 1970s. The behaviour arising from our own more civilized deprivations is usually more difficult to identify. For most of us, our painful past history is made up of foetal distress, birth material and a variety of hurts involved in the process of growing up. If you doubt whether your past distorts your present-day behaviour, then consider the times when you overreacted and felt very over-emotional about an apparently minor event, or when you under-reacted and went blank when something very important happened. This is how the early hurt takes over. If you have no sense of this pain at all, it is likely that you are investing a lot of energy in keeping it locked up. This can result in lethargy and inertia, often called low-level depression.

Painful or difficult experiences early in life may also be perpetuated in the body as psychosomatic ailments and these distress signals recorded in the bodymind can distort the health of the respiratory, digestive, nervous, endocrine or circulatory systems, and even the limbs, muscles, brain, skin or eyes. Asthma, diarrhoea, colitis, muscular tension and eczema are common examples. Additionally, defending against early overwhelming pain may seriously distort the personality, leading to self-destructiveness, self-absorption, withdrawal, avoidance of intimacy or close relationships, inability to express feelings, or a persistent sense of worthlessness, guilt or unreality.

Social defences

Our personal defence systems interlock with powerful social pressures which stop us from expressing the extremes of positive and negative feelings. Laws against incest, rape, murder, theft, extortion, damage to property and betraying state secrets serve to back up personal defences. They also provide a defensive backdrop in groups and crowds where personal defences easily evaporate. If the defences of one or two people collapse, a domino effect can immediately demolish the defences of those around them. People who are very contained can become frightened or hostile in a crowd, regressing to infantile behaviour.

The silver lining

Although at first sight it may seem otherwise, all this is good news. How? Because you are here, you survived. At every point where you needed a safety net you were able to devise one. However, all defensive styles are potentially damaging and many of them lead to personalities that are rigid or stagnant. But the impetus to resolve the inner struggles can be a constant spur to creativity, when it compels people to express the experience of living with the pain. Most, if not all, of the greatest music, singing, stories, acting, art and poetry appeals to us because it echoes our own inner struggle and the possibility of release from it. But more than this, along with the hurt and pain, the defences may have bottled up pockets of delight.

SELF-DEFENCE
The dragon in the cellar

The image of the dragon, the demon or the devil in myths and fairy stories, has long unwittingly symbolized the pain of birth and hurtful childhood experiences. A more modern version, which reflects the view taken by humanistic psychology, sees the psyche or individual identity as a house with a dragon walled up in the cellar. The dragon embodies our accumulated pain, while the cellar walls represent the natural defence strategy that allows us to forget the pain that was too overwhelming to be accepted. During periods of stress, burnout or overwork the walls of the cellar can weaken, allowing part or all of the dragon to get out.

The dragon paradox
The dragon, or 'unfinished business' from childhood, is usually well walled up in the basement of our minds. But when we're under pressure, the dragon may begin to break out, or the walls may weaken, allowing the earlier hurt to spill over into the present (below, left). This is how we start overreacting to situations. The energy we spend on maintaining and rebuilding the cellar walls may leave us feeling lethargic, depressed or blocked.

The dragon can take many forms. When it starts to join in a row or dispute, it can seem huge, ferocious and terrifying, poisonously vicious, smilingly obsequious or frustratingly compliant. But if we can make friends with it, we may find it is sad, fearful and far more terrified than terrifying. And it may guard a hidden treasure (right).

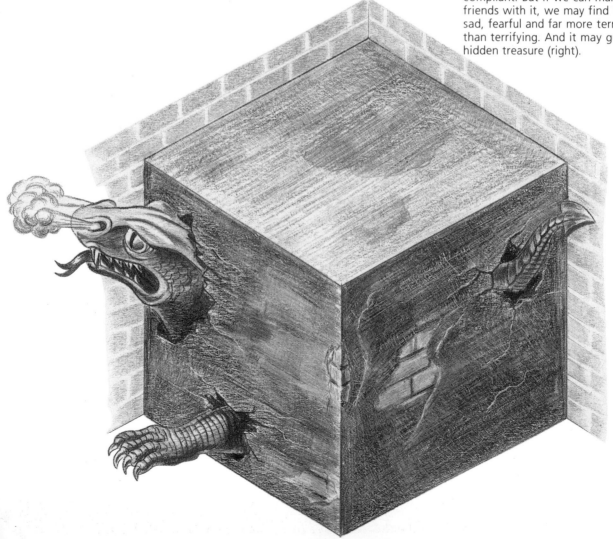

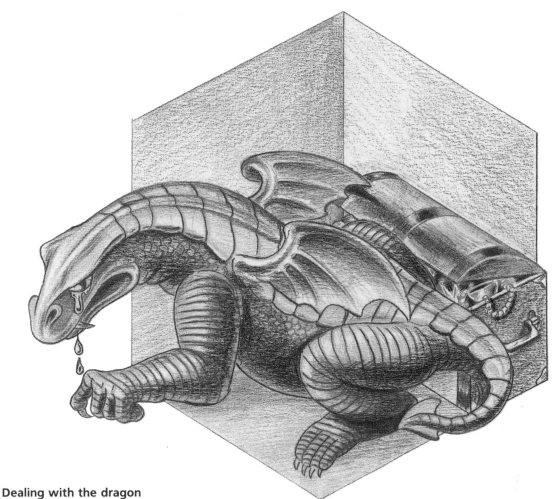

Dealing with the dragon
Since Freud, many psychologists,
including Otto Rank, Wilhelm Reich,
Arthur Janov, Stanislav Grof, William
Emerson and Frank Lake, have
uncovered ways of working with
the dragon through encouraging
people to re-experience early pain –
a role once fulfilled by shamans,
exorcists and other traditional
practitioners, who confronted the
dragon in attempting to deal with
demonic possession. Gradually
becoming familiar with the dragon
through hypnotic regression, for
example, co-counselling (see pp.
178–9), primal therapy or Reichian
bodywork, can lead to new energy,
insight and creativity.

LF-DEFENCE
Diverting the pain

There are five clear strategies we use in adult life to shield ourselves from the memory of past pain, five ways of 'making the best of a bad job'. Of them all, projection is perhaps the most widespread, but it is not unusual to resort to several or even all of these defence strategies. The images presented here are intended to be aids to personal exploration – not facts.

This is a person who in some way echoes the part of me that I dislike, fear, or find I can't accept.

This is a part of myself that I fear, dislike or can't accept.

Projection

When we find in another person, an institution or an object some echo of a part of ourselves that we lack, hate or refuse to accept, we escape the inner discomfort by attaching our disowned faults or qualities to them. We can then convince ourselves that they don't belong to us. If we feel bad, we may believe other people are bad; if we lack good feelings, we may think others are wonderful. Another familiar form of projection is scapegoating – where one member of a family or one particular group becomes the dump for the personal hostility and hate of the rest. In Europe, several generations of 'spiritual leaders' projected their personal history on to millions of innocent victims through witch hunts and the Inquisition. Other examples of scapegoating include Joe McCarthy and his 'reds under the bed', and Hitler and the Nazis against the Jews. In the 'heroic' counterpart of projection, a group elects a charismatic leader, guru or chosen one who is considered infallible, even when leading the group to disaster, as in the mass suicide in the 1970s at Jonesville, S. America.

Christianity too can be regarded as a massive screen for projection (see p. 154).

The unacceptable side of me is activated. I feel uncomfortable or upset.

I project my uncomfortable feelings on to the other person.

From now on the other person is seen as causing the feelings that I don't accept as belonging to me.

Introjection

When someone important to us voices opinions, judgements or criticism, we may introject them, embrace them as our own, and accept their projections on to us as true. So if we have a father who has doubts about his intelligence and who projects it on to us, repeatedly telling us that 'we are stupid' , we may introject this view and come to believe it. Or if, following a painful experience of life in the womb and at birth, we become difficult as a baby, we may come to think we are 'no good', because we make our mother cross. If she is afraid of her hostility and compensates by projecting her desire to be pleasant on to us through flattery, we may introject this and come to believe that we are 'good', 'brilliant' or 'intelligent'. In later life, we may find it difficult to live up to this idealized image.

A person whose opinion I value criticizes me.

The criticism activates a part of me that I dislike, fear or can't accept.

I feel uncomfortable.

I embrace (introject) the other person's criticism as being true and act accordingly.

Denial

When feelings from the past or in the present are too painful or unacceptable, we may block them out and deny them. If, for example, our fundamental capacity for fun, creativity, humour or anger appears to be unacceptable to the people around us, we may deny it. If a situation is too difficult, we may forget it, cut it out or switch off, or conceal our pain behind a facade of cheerfulness. With denial, our public face belies our private thoughts.

Displacement

If we fail to 'own' what we feel as belonging to us, we may displace it on the environment or on other people by 'taking it out on them'. Alternatively, our unacceptable feelings may insist that people are bad; or we may displace our distress through abuse, swearing or violence to other people or, if we feel lonely, through harassing other people.

Something happens that activates a part of me that I fear, dislike or can't accept.

Something happens that activates a part of me that I fear, dislike or can't accept.

I feel uncomfortable or upset.

I feel uncomfortable but I smile to avoid revealing how I really feel.

I act out my uncomfortable feelings by 'taking it out' on someone else.

Splitting

When an experience is so hurtful that it drives the emergency reactions of increased heart rate and temperature to life-threatening levels, we may survive it through splitting it off from consciousness – forgetting it. The split-off experience is kept at bay by physical 'armouring' – layers of muscle and tissue more or less permanently in tension. We become tight lipped, thick set and overweight or barrel-chested. The forgotten feelings may remain out of mind, if not out of sight, for a lifetime, but they can predispose us toward psychosomatic ailments and to using the intellect as a way of walling off old feelings. At times of extreme stress, fatigue or ill-health, these feelings may break through into consciousness.

This fire flares up and almost destroys me.

My body deals with it by splitting off the experience from consciousness and building body armour to protect me from the memory.

Experiences that echo my split-off memories may be inexplicably intolerable.

SELF-DEFENCE
Dealing with the pain

Difficulties in adult life that re-stimulate the past tend to provoke inappropriate responses. If we or others behave in a bizarre way, it is likely to be an acute defensive reaction, which looks 'crazy' because we only see the present event and the emotional reaction, but cannot see the defence strategy involved nor the past hurt.

The scale of our defences

The intensity and extent of the original pain or deprivation define the degree to which they influence adult behaviour. If, for example, our experience of life in the womb and at birth was relatively pain free and all our needs were met, we are likely to respond to problems openly and constructively. If our early life was not ideal, but 'good enough', so that it was not too difficult to cope with occasional shortfalls, then we are well placed to persevere stubbornly in the face of later difficulties, despite feeling bad from time to time. If the pain was so severe that we had to split ourselves off from the memory, in adult life we will find it hard to cope with certain situations. We will be likely to project the bad feelings out on to other people or the world and find it difficult to be open and trusting. If the original pain was intolerable, if the experience felt like torture, if pain and pleasure became interchangeable and nothing mattered, our adult mind is likely to turn in on itself, willing its own destruction and wanting to die. The mind may retreat from the body altogether, to take refuge in the head. The more pain we have suffered, the more defensive we are likely to be in later life, and the more the defence will come to occupy all our available intelligence.

Individual styles

Our response to present challenges not only depends on the scale of our early pain, but also on our individual defensive style. There is a huge variation in the way each of us responds to the same situation. Suppose, for example, we find ourselves assigned to a workspace in the same small room as a man who has a bullying manner and a harsh tone of voice. We begin to feel agitated, embarrassed, unsure, humiliated and powerless to object. Away from the room, we know he means us no harm, that it's just his manner, but as soon as we return to the room, bad feelings well up again. In this situation, our own individual survival strategies will come into play. Here is a range of possible responses:

I am to blame. I should control my feelings. I deserve to be punished. He is to blame. He is making me feel bad.

I am going to make sure nobody knows how I feel. I'm thick-skinned, invulnerable. I can take it. I always come through smiling.

I am going to make sure everybody knows how I feel. I'm spontaneous, instinctive, impulsive, wilful.

I am going to spread my feelings around. He's awful, this place is awful, they're all awful. I'm in a bad mood. Poor me. Why should I put up with this?

Christianity as a defence

One of the benefits of unpicking projection in our personal lives is that it reveals how it operates at a social level. Christianity, for example, may be a massive screen for our projections – an effective way of keeping painful history quiet. Here are some speculations from research into foetal experience (see p. 112).

Evil, Hell and the Devil are projections driven by foetal and birth distress.

Demonic possession is the resurfacing of submerged early pain.

Heaven, angels and the promise of everlasting peace are projections of forgotten foetal bliss.

Generations of people have projected their personal history on to Jesus, the Palestinian radical. The whole sequence of events in his life closely mirrors the agonies of foetal experience and the eventual release at birth.

Rituals invite the faithful to project their early experience on to the suffering Christ.

God, the Father Almighty, is a projection of our own father.

Clear communication

Admitting to ourselves and others when old hurts are interfering in the present helps to clean up communication with other people. By deliberately re-stimulating memories of old hurts, we can explore our defence strategies and learn to use new, constructive strategies, instead of defensive, coping ones. The more thoroughly we are able to pursue this, the less we will be living under the tyranny of our own history.

I've got to escape. I think I'm going to be ill.

I'm weak. I'll collapse under the strain.

They did this to annoy me. I'll make them pay for this.

If anyone cared about me, they'd know I hate being here with this man.

I don't have to take this from anyone. Take that!

I must get away somehow.

He's a wicked, evil man.

Something like this always goes wrong for me.

I'm sure I must be ill.

I knew I'd been enjoying myself too much.

The radio has been beaming poison at me again.

I'll find something to distract my attention, so I don't notice.

He's out to get me.

I have no right to be here. I shouldn't exist really.

He's cross with me. It must be because I did this or that. I mustn't do it again, it obviously makes him cross.

I am wicked and sinful.

I'll be all right one day, when I'm married, have a baby, have a new kitchen, move house.

Responsibility, compassion and oppression

Once we realize that we can attribute a proportion of our present behaviour to the past, it can be tempting to use it as an excuse to evade responsibility. This is merely another defence strategy. Just because we have powerful reactions that are rooted in our personal history, that does not mean we are absolved from taking responsibility for what we do about them. Taking responsibility means moving to constructive instead of defensive strategies.

Compassion for ourselves is equally important. If as an adult we feel unhappy about our semi-automatic behaviour, it's important to accept that our original survival decision was honourable and necessary.

It is also essential to appreciate that, while our history of being persecuted, harassed, maligned and bullied affects how we relate to others, there are also people who, in turn, bully, injure, undermine and sabotage others because of their history. When they do this, most or all of what we feel is going to be the result of their actions. When we find ourselves in conflict, the contribution of our own personal history may be considerable. But this does not mean that we should get the idea that oppression should be appeased or should not be resisted.

For most of us some level of distress is unavoidable. Happily, one of the greatest contributions of the 20th century has been the exploration of ways in which past hurt can be surfaced and dealt with by the bodymind. Growing more aware of the distorted perceptions, attitudes and behaviour that we constantly enact to keep our personal history quiet is the first step to freeing ourselves from them. This, in my view, is the only thing that makes talk of a 'new age' at all acceptable.

Constructive strategies

As we become aware that our personal universe is an idiosyncratic place that intimately reflects our personal history, more helpful, non-defensive coping strategies open up. These include:

Acknowledgement – identifying and admitting to the elements in our personal history that are colouring our behaviour.

Celebration – identifying and valuing the areas of our mind that are clear and strong.

Contradiction – finding ways of actively interrupting old distress when it emerges by contradicting or reversing what it directs us to do. 'I must' then becomes 'I can choose'.

Self-management – actively and consistently treating our life as a project, rather than as an incipient disaster.

Regression – learning to trust that reconnection to childhood distress can result in the reframing of our original survival decisions.

Assertiveness – finding distress-free ways of ensuring that our rights are respected and that we are free to fulfil our obligations, without allowing others to exploit us.

OTHER CONNECTIONS

For some people, the model of the human mind I have outlined in this part of Knowhow may seem too materialistic, too technologically inspired, too rooted in the physical aspects of life. Doesn't this exclude spirituality? Doesn't it put too much emphasis on history? What about politics? No, it doesn't exclude spirituality. No, I don't believe it puts too much emphasis on history. Yes, it is very political.

History

I hope I've shown that any approach to the mind that does not fully acknowledge its personal and social history will be of dubious value. We are children not only of our parents but of our epoch. There is a late-twentieth-century capitalist, consumer mind that has virtues and blindspots as have all other minds across history. From this point of view, we are all 'inside history' and the more we ignore it, the more we will be destined to relive or trip over our own bit of it. This makes it all the more extraordinary that general education does not include any study of the way in which the mind's personal history affects careers, choice of partners, health and creativity. More important, it forms no part of the education of most psychiatrists, doctors, lawyers or teachers, who are all called upon to judge people's state of mind. Making decisions about other people's personal and social problems without first looking at our own, so that we are aware of what we may be projecting on to them, is a scandal.

Politics

Just as we often deny our personal history, so we also tend to ignore the political dimension of the mind. But we can't escape that either. Babies learning to bite back the tears of disappointment because their mothers are too poor to provide more than one meal a day, are learning how personal politics can be. And so are children in the classroom who are learning to be obedient employees and good citizens, and the homeless sleeping in cardboard boxes. The rich profiteer with a private jet, three houses and a stone where his heart should be has also internalized a political approach to life. It may enable him to close down people's lives without a qualm but it's unlikely to bring him peace of mind.

   Politics worthy of the name never loses sight of wonder at the astonishing phenomenon of flesh and blood. No-one who is fully in touch with it will want to harm or exploit other people, or be able to. People who explore their own history of personal distress will have a political face, because they learn to resolve internalized oppression both in themselves and in others. Politics that is truly personal is also likely to be spiritually awake.

Spirituality

But surely *real* spirituality is still excluded? Isn't it too exquisitely subtle to be brought into such a worldly view? For me, the infinitely subtle complexities of the inner space of bodily experience *are* the spiritual domain that throughout history has always been a part of human reality. Ignorance of this leads to constant suffering as we project our inner needs, desires and aversions out on to others. Spirituality is the business of releasing ourselves and others from this suffering. It means freeing ourselves from the idea that the world and other people can be separated from our perceptions of them, and progressively letting go of the parts of our personal history that maintain this illusion. So far as we can do this, we have the possibility of being united with other people in a single, connected existence. It may be inexpressible, but it is liveable. And ways of entering and experiencing this spiritual domain are constantly being rediscovered.

The limitations of language

A continuing difficulty that tends to mystify the spiritual realm of experience is that it is too subtle to be more than hinted at in words. The left brain's logical interpretation of experience and its expression in language, maps reality – but it can do no more than suggest the depth and scale of the actual inner territory of intuition, sensation, thoughts and feelings. Language is useful as long as we don't forget its limitations and as long as it stays rooted in our own experience. We often find that when we try to communicate our experience to others, it becomes distorted in the translation into the step-by-step nature of words and sentences, and the richness and complexity are lost. Processes tend to become things and people become objects. The spiritual dimension of the mind slips out of reach. For this reason, we constantly seek it, even though it is within us all the time.

Non–defensive spirituality

One of the ways we can avoid spiritual sterility is to reappraise accurately which of our notions of spirituality are rooted in some form of projection of our inner personal history on to outer events. Once we have a clear base from which to move, we can begin to reach towards our full human potential, which may well yet include telepathy, clairvoyance and many forms of magic. But the ground-clearing, a recurring historical task, I suspect, seems only recently to have got underway. A practical, workable spirituality that does not involve projecting inner history on to some ethereal other world is likely to be a considerable threat to conventional politics, because eventually it will replace it. But such a spirituality is within reach. It is becoming increasingly accessible to hundreds of thousands of people through meditation, group work, stress-release programmes, psychotherapy, hallucinogenic drug experiences, non-violent direct action and green politics. But it first requires us to free ourselves from projection, introjection, denial, splitting and displacement. Powerful though this inner dimension is, how we experience it is a matter of culture and educational creation. Look for it through a capitalist or a communist microscope and you won't see it. But it is there just the same in both observer and observed. In the 1960s it leaked out in the 'flower power' effusions of music and LSD, and from those beginnings a range of 'new age' activities continues to emerge.

The spiritual cul-de-sac

Keeping experiences of the spirit grounded in bodily experience helps to avoid the spiritual wasteland of mood-making. Many so-called spiritual activities tend to keep the spirit divorced from the body, so blocking both personal and political change. The magic of a light, sweet, high mood of devotion, peace and bliss can become an effective way to avoid the difficulty and inconvenience of our personal history – until, one day, we step in it. According to the Tibetan teacher Chogyam Trungpa, spirituality can be, unhappily, a very successful global defence that surreptitiously aims to keep life manageable, safe, predictable and pleasurable, excluding doubt, confusion and surprise. This is no reason to neglect spirituality. But it is advisable to review constantly the conditions necessary for developing a non-defensive spirituality.

CARING FOR YOUR MIND

In every age the question arises of how the human mind can best be enhanced and cared for. One choice is to re-affirm traditional values and beliefs about the mind. But where will this lead us? If we maintain a world view that is based on projection and denial, with the rate of change running as fast as it is, there is every chance that it will lead us to global disaster.

Possibilities for change

Is there then any cause for optimism? The answer is, not a lot, but some. White, male dominance isn't going to go away tomorrow nor the day after. But at least we know it isn't natural or inevitable. Just as the idea of 'nature' is a human creation, so too is 'human nature'. And because we have made it, we can unmake it. Similarly, projection, denial, forgetting and other ways of defending ourselves against the hurts of childhood will, if our model of the mind is accurate, always be with us until we learn more constructive strategies. But the role of belief and attitude in making the world what it seems to be, need no longer be a mystery.

The paradigm shift

Caring for our minds against this background involves, as we shall see in the following pages, a simple choice. It means switching from the idea that others should care for our minds to the newer concept that it is our own responsibility. This change, or paradigm (pronounced 'paradime') shift, is at the basis of the insights and energies driving the 'new age'. To paraphrase American science historian and philosopher Thomas Kuhn, who first described paradigm shifts in his book, *The Structure of Scientific Revolutions*: led by a new paradigm, people adopt new methods, look in new places. Even more important, they see new and different things when looking with familiar methods in places they have looked before. It is rather as if the community had been transported to another planet where familiar objects are seen in a different light and are joined by unfamiliar ones as well.

Taking charge of yourself

Moving out of the old paradigm of relying on experts to diagnose and treat any disorders that may emerge in your mind can feel frightening. You may feel that there are parts of yourself that you'd sooner not know about. Maybe there are demons or dragons lurking in the background that might take you over if you gave them half a chance, and you feel more comfortable pretending that they don't exist. If this is where you start from, that's fine. It's an entirely understandable reaction. Be reassured – the old choice of assigning responsibility to others for what you think and feel hasn't disappeared. But it is no longer the only choice available. Slowly but surely you can now begin to take charge of what you think, feel and believe so that you are no longer a slave to your reactions. Where you draw the line between how much of it belongs to you and how much to other people is your decision.

Unity in opposites
A sudden paradigm shift in human attitudes after a period of gradual social change can be represented very precisely by modern mathematics. The three-dimensional folded surface of a Catastrophe Theory map when used to represent human behaviour, can show how apparently opposing opinions and beliefs are actually united. Change may be smooth and gradual at the back of the map and abrupt as we approach the near, curved edge of the map. This folded surface exactly echoes the Taoist yin-yang symbol, which likewise embodies the way that the opposite poles we see in the world may appear separate but are in fact intrinsically interdependent.

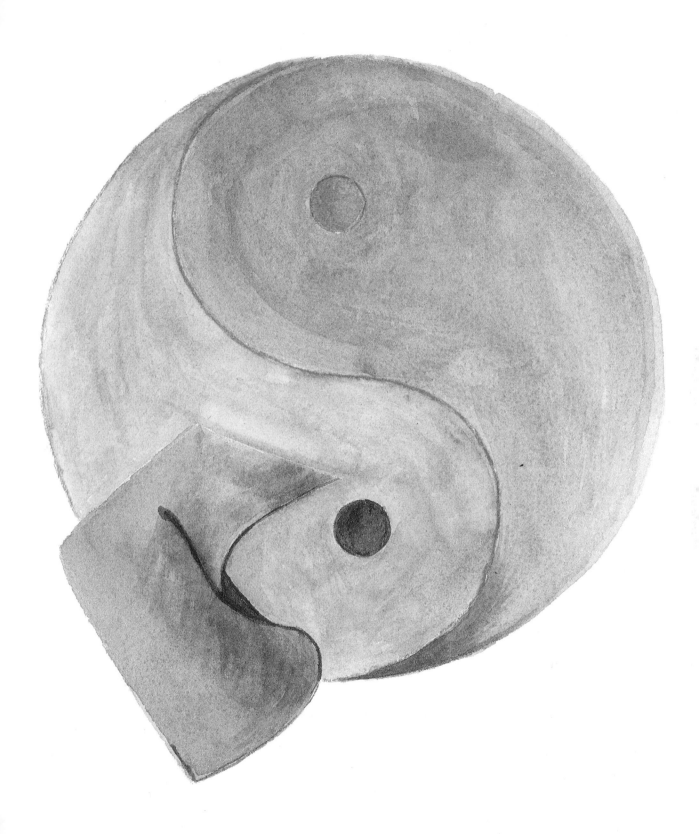

POTENTIAL FOR CHANGE

When considering the possibilities for changing our own minds, it is useful to see where we stand and how our position varies. The graph (right), based on the work of the British psychologist David Wasdell, shows how at any one time a small minority of any adult population is likely to be relatively free from distress (A). A similar number are likely to be severely distressed because so many of their childhood needs were left unmet (D). But most of us fall between these two extremes (B-C) and carry around a moderate amount of pain from the past. Our position on the human map does not remain static, however. Most of us oscillate (E) between less distress (B) on our best days and more distress (C) on our worst. Where we stand on the graph is influenced both by how much distress we have and by how successful we are at keeping it quiet. When life gets difficult and we are tired and pressurized, hidden distress tends to surface, pulling us back from B toward C. But by finding effective ways of working with our underlying distress we can begin to remain permanently at B, or even move towards A.

Limits to change
Wherever we stand on the graph, changing our minds involves identifying the origins of our distress and taking steps to resolve them. How much we can change depends to a large extent on our upbringing. And different starting points on the graph demand different strategies. Those who begin at position A seem exceptionally clear of early pain. The only personal work needed is to consolidate what you have learned – and to convey to other people starting a family how you were brought up! Those who begin at B are in a strong position to change their mind and will find working with distress easier to sustain. If we start at C, we may need to work harder to reduce the distress from our childhood but the benefits will be considerable. If we begin at D, we may need to start by learning to survive more efficiently from day to day, before we can create enough space in which to work on the underlying distress.

The 'mental illness' barrier
The concept of mental illness draws a clear dividing line between the 'mentally ill' and the 'healthy' – somewhere around F on the graph. Until recently, this made it impossible for the so-called 'healthy' majority to acknowledge their own distress. It is now clear that almost everyone carries an underlying spectrum of distress, not least those who decide who is mentally sick and who is healthy – the doctors, psychiatrists, clinical psychologists and social workers.

The means to change
Professional approaches to the mind – psychiatry, psychoanalysis, behaviour modification and medical research – developed almost exclusively from work with very distressed people, in the D segment of the graph. All tended to ignore the broad spread of the rest of the population. Fortunately, humanistic psychology (see pp. 166–71), which focuses on the experiences of the whole range of people, has emerged in the last forty years or so. It gives us the means to understand our individual difficulties, to learn to resolve our distress and to move toward greater wellbeing.

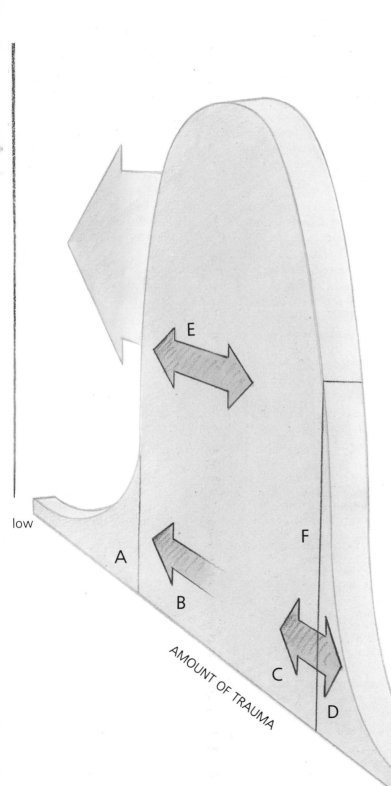

A

B

C

D

E

F

AMOUNT OF TRAUMA

high

Change on a large scale

Looking at the graph as a whole, it's easy to see that there is a clear priority for the whole population to move toward greater health. And this involves minimizing the amount of early distress that gives rise to difficulties in adult life. This can be done through increased sensitivity to mother and baby during pregnancy, as proposed by the Canadian psychologist Thomas Verny, among others, through reducing the traumas caused by birth difficulties, as proposed by several people, including Frederick Leboyer, and through a wider understanding that newborn babies are intelligent, know what they need, and can communicate these needs from birth on. The general trend, according to the American psychologist Lloyd de Mause, seems to be towards lower distress levels caused by upbringing. Whether he's right or not, we need to support this already accelerating process. Everyone can contribute by learning to resolve their own distress – the less we have, the less we pass on. It's not hard to imagine a time when our insensitive attitudes to bringing up children and our surprise at resulting adult distress will seem as curious as not seeing the link between sexual activity and childbirth.

THE OLD PARADIGM

At our point in history, as at any other, there is a world view, a paradigm, a list of assumptions about what seems to be natural and inevitable. From time to time there is a revolution in these attitudes and some abruptly become obsolete, or 'old paradigm'. Slavery once seemed natural and inevitable until the paradigm shifted and slavery was abolished. Until recently, domination seemed natural and inevitable. But we now know that it is a basic strategy that human minds have used to defend themselves against memories of personal distress. Painful experiences carried forward from childhood have been denied, crushed, repressed or projected out on to heroes or enemies. Dominating others is very often a way of acting out past hurt while keeping things under control.

Domination within society
Since domination has been woven into our individual minds, it is also built into the structure of the institutions we live through – the family, the church, education, medicine and politics. And they in turn operate through denial, crushing, repression, exploitation, blame and idealization. Through these institutions, domination is legalized, and since it is usually covert and subliminal, it appears all the more natural and inevitable – part of human nature. Some of the key elements that are prevalent in society and have slipped into the old paradigm include:

Hierarchical structures: where control is transmitted primarily one way, from the top down.

Authoritarian communication styles: where giving orders, issuing instructions, confronting others and making unilateral assessments always predominate over consultation, co-operation and negotiation.

Idealization: relying on a prominent public figure to embody a population's yearnings and aspirations.

Scapegoating: using an enemy to carry a population's hates and anxiety. Common elements of a population's personal distress, such as fear, are projected out on to another group of people or another nation.

Stratification: dividing populations or organizations into horizontal layers according to status, power, influence, class, qualifications or 'maturity'. 'A place for everyone and everyone in their place.'

Seniority: using age or family background as a basis for status, or promotion rather than merit.

Specialization: breaking down complex tasks into smaller tasks so people are encouraged to know more and more about less and less.

Discrimination: favouring some people and denying others on the basis of sex, age, sexual orientation, class or race.

Expertise: confining generally useful knowledge unnecessarily to a profession as a way of maintaining its power and status.

Reversal: making a belief or system the reverse of what it claims to be. National defence, for example, constantly involves aggression.

Secrecy: where whole populations are deemed too irresponsible or too immature to know what is being done in their name, or where disclosure and discussion would undermine the policy being pursued. On a smaller scale, the same mechanism is at work in the family, where child abuse and violence are concealed.

The legacy of distress

The legacy of pain from our own childhood and from the generations of people before us is threaded through our social and political institutions. Part of the function of the family, the church, the presidency and the government is to keep our collective and our individual distress quiet. That is why social change and the collapse of these symbols of stability can seem so threatening. But just as repressing our own distressing memories is never completely satisfactory, so institutions that put the lid on collective distress and add a heavy weight to keep it in place cannot always rely on repression. Eruptions in the form of wars, rebellions, revolutions and criminal behaviour have always broken out.

An end to fantasy and violence

Following Freud and his associates early this century, ways of minimizing the distress of personal history have been developed, so that force, coercion and projection can be withdrawn. As the experience of resolving distress has begun to spread and weave itself into our culture, the seeds of a new personal and political paradigm have been sown. This has given us a new perspective on the old strategy of domination. Increasingly, more and more people are now recognizing the fruits of domination in terms of irreversible ecological damage, non-sustainable economic growth, the devaluing of people according to colour or sex, the technical plans for thermo-nuclear suicide and the economic distortions caused by communist and capitalist aggression. The more we have discovered what we are doing to ourselves, the more the institutions driven by the old paradigm have come to appear not only out of touch with reality but also insanely dangerous – a threat to the survival of the planet and the whole human race.

In apparent response to the devastating effects of the old paradigm, a 'new age', with a new paradigm, seems to be emerging. But, in reality, what is a new paradigm? Is the 'new age' a mirage, a flight to some new paradigm leafy suburb, leaving the old paradigm inner city to rot? Can the grip of the old age ever be broken? It can – but only gradually, because we all literally 'embody' the old paradigm. To know what it takes to get out of the old and into the new requires a clear overview of the old paradigm and an assessment of how much we are possessed by it. Otherwise the 'new age' will be no more than the old, filled in with new colours. The mind can switch attitudes very quickly, but the moment we feel anxious and our non-verbal, unconscious memories are triggered, the old paradigm defensive strategy will reappear. There is no evolution of the mind without evolution of the body. If they are not coupled with bodily changes, mental changes are likely to be no more than 'mood-making'.

Dominance and education

Dominance is covertly built into the social fabric through the educational system, including higher education. Students are controlled and assessed according to the unilateral, authoritarian judgements of the staff. Given a predetermined syllabus, encouraged to learn in ways dictated by others and taught by people who make the final assessment, what do students do? They conform to the attitudes and preferences of those who decide their futures. The inner dialogue tends to run something like this: 'to survive, I must go along with the system and guess what is expected of me. I must accept the fact that I am here so that other people can tell me what to do and tell me whether I have made it or not. If I subscribe to this with sufficient intellectual application, I may, if I'm lucky, arrive at the point where I can dictate the system that other people have to conform to.' An authoritarian system distorts education, not least because it ignores personal development, interpersonal skills and the ability to work with feelings. It is only able to focus on students' intellectual and technical competence, and so represses the autonomy needed for emotional competence.

See Self-assessment

26-35	Life events
52-3	Bodymind
66-81	Intelligence
82-101	Relating
102-9	Beliefs

THE NEW PARADIGM

The old paradigm of the mind as a command capsule steering the human spaceship through alien social space has served its purpose. It's worn out. The old programme cannot adjust to a new environment and meanwhile it's destroying many of the people who base their lives on it.

But, we hear that a 'new age', a new paradigm is just around the corner. What does this mean for our minds? How can we be sure that the 'new age' is not just some projection of our disappointment with the struggles of making our way in this world on to yet another promised land? We can't be sure. Some people will use the notion of a new age, even of a post-nuclear armageddon as a blank screen for their projections. But what we do know is that there is an urgent need for a change of mind, a new paradigm or a new age. Personal and planetary survival depend on it.

Signs of a new age?

But is there any tangible evidence that we are moving towards a new age, that a whole new philosophy is beginning to take root? Here's how it looks to me. Over the last fifty years or so, several genies have got out of the bottle and are never going back. They include:

The Freudian developments in psychology

The exploration of how the mind creates the world through projection and denial, signals the beginning of the end of the 'medieval' mind – of witch hunts, Heaven, Hell and Evil as a way of explaining our own and other people's offensive behaviour.

The explosive growth of science

Technical innovation after World War II, driven by massive defence spending, has fuelled information theory, cybernetics, computers and artificial intelligence. Work on models of the mind still proliferates and the science of the mind has become an industry.

The breakthrough in subatomic physics

The 'uncertainty principle' demonstrates that the act of observation changes what is observed. Mass, space and time are shown to be intrinsic to each other.

The Bomb

The poisonous fruit of unlimited scientific progress based on male supremacy, signals the possibility of the end of civilization. It also signals the beginning of the end of uncritical acceptance of the value of male-dominated science.

The earth as a globe from space

Planet earth is seen and experienced as a single entity for the first time, through photographs and television. The ecology movement is born, and concern for the environment begins to grow. Gaia, the concept of the earth as a living organism, is proposed.

The women's movement

Enough women now have enough economic power to take a look at themselves without the aid of men. What they see is exploitation, oppression, degradation, inequality and discrimination. Some women who share this view are too committed to their roles in the status quo

---

Are you moving into a new age? How do you tell if you are making progress toward a new paradigm of mind? You could begin by looking at yourself and those around you to see how many of the following new paradigm attitudes of mind you have already adopted. Are you able to:

Explore your own distress memories from childhood?

Recognize authoritarian structures within organizations?

Recognize authoritarian communication styles?

Respond to people without using power or manipulation?

Identify when you are projecting on to others and when others are projecting on to you?

Realize when you are denying your own experience – saying yes when you mean no – and when others do the same?

Detect authoritarian knowledge – when an expert tells you to do something without explaining why?

Spot inauthentic behaviour in others – when body language contradicts verbal statements?

Recognize discrimination against sex, race, age or disability and confront it?

Make choices about what you do in conjunction with others, without being dependent on them as a result of past distress?

See when a supposedly equal relationship is not reciprocal?

Willingly contribute personal resources and skills on a reciprocal basis?

Understand that appropriate self-disclosure is an important way of cementing relationships with other people?

Discern the difficulties and rewards of mutual help?

Appreciate that a transpersonal version of spirituality, can avoid projections on to magical worlds; that it does not have to deny the body and that it is entirely compatible with political action?

Recognize emotional competence in others?

to leave it. Many others refuse to tolerate sexist domination and begin to create a world where being a woman counts.

Hallucinogenic drugs

Millions of people take the risk of exploring their own inner space. Experiencing their own personal heavens, hells, purgatories and paradises changes a lot of people's minds about the value of their lives. Daily life begins to look technocratic, competitive, linear, one-dimensional and violent. Some researchers, using LSD25 to explore hallucinogenic experiences discover that in many acid trips birth and foetal memories appear to be re-activated. The implications of this birth and foetal research still await integration into the medical and psychological establishments.

The stress concept

The US psychologist Hans Selye's development of the concept of stress makes it increasingly feasible to admit to having emotional difficulties without being diagnosed as 'mentally ill'. Feelings and emotions become more respectable since stress is accepted as a response to challenge and threat.

Green politics

Non-violent direct action is increasingly used against some of the more obviously oppressive institutions. Demands for accountability and greater openness about policy-making are constantly reiterated.

The route into the 'new age'

These developments are giving us an opportunity. The door is open. Will we walk through it? Will enough of us walk through it? We would all find it easier if the old age could just be put out with the garbage. But moving into the new age necessarily involves gradually ridding ourselves of our patterns of oppression, blame and idealization (see pp. 104–5). It means letting go of our habit of relating to others through power, patronage, control and manipulation and learning to co-operate and share resources and opportunities. From within the old paradigm, this is likely to feel wishy washy. That's what a paradigm shift means. From the old, the new is invisible or looks wrong. From within the old, it is difficult to see the rigour, intensity, effectiveness and sheer efficiency of the new. In practice, our minds are already being reshaped by the new paradigm regardless of our intentions, but we can also learn to participate, and take charge of the process. An excellent way of approaching this is through humanistic psychology, which emerged as a result of dissatisfaction with the Freudian psychoanalytic and behaviourist approach to people. Humanistic psychology takes a more optimistic view, regarding human beings as fundamentally good and as having been born with a huge potential that is distorted when personal and social needs are not met. It works with the emotional, intellectual, physical, transpersonal (see pp. 188–9), creative and political aspects of human potential. A selection of its principles and techniques are elaborated in the following pages and in the Mind gym chapter (see pp. 190–245).

Express positive and negative emotions?

Tolerate others expressing positive and negative emotions?

Delay expressing emotions until an appropriate moment?

Recognize the importance of the ability to direct your own life?

Respond creatively to conflicts of interest or resources of your own making?

Respond creatively to conflicts of time or interest when other people make demands?

Understand the interpersonal dynamics of people in groups?

Enhance the capacities of people in groups or teams to co-operate and collaborate in a variety of ways?

Understand the dynamics of conflict?

Call on a variety of methods to resolve conflict?

Keep your feelings in balance, so that you can interpret their origins?

Keep your observations of your own and others' behaviour distinct from what you imagine or feel.

HUMANISTIC PSYCHOLOGY
Central ideas

Existentialism

This concept is based on the existential movement in philosophy. Sartre's saying: 'Man is nothing else but what he makes of himself' fits very well with humanistic psychology, with its emphasis on authenticity and the real self. Existential philosophers, such as Sartre, Heidegger and Binswanger, influenced humanistic psychologists Rollo May, Alvin Mahrer and Ronald Laing, and they in turn influenced many others within the human potential movement. Fritz Perls has been called the existential therapist *par excellence*.

Self-actualization

The concept of self-realization is essential to humanistic psychology. It has ancient roots in Eastern philosophy but was taken up by the 19th-century philosopher Hegel and was later modified in the US by Ralph Waldo Emerson and others. The basic idea is that personal development and evolution is a naturally occurring process, but that we can help or hinder it through conscious action. If we help it, we are consciously moving with what, in nature, is an unconscious process of evolution.

The person-centred approach

Through early 20th-century psychoanalysts such as Otto Rank and Alfred Adler came the idea that people are naturally healthy and to be trusted – and if we can just open the shutters, oil the doors and let the sun shine in, all will be well. This approach to therapy has been very consistently applied by the American psychologist Carl Rogers, and all the recent theory on this subject owes a great deal to him. He applied it not only to one-to-one therapy, but also to small groups, organizations, whole communities and even entire nations.

Zen Buddhism

There is a fascinating compatibility between the peak experiences obtained within humanistic psychology and the enlightenment experiences dealt with in Zen. The way the world looks to a Zen master or mistress seems to be very similar to what Maslow talked about as 'Being perception'. Anyone involved in humanistic psychology who reads the Zen classics will feel on familiar territory.

Since World War II, an increasing number of people have become disenchanted with domination as a way of life. The desolation and despair of the old paradigm have led to a new paradigm of mind, now endorsed by millions of individuals and thousands of organizations. This collective reaction to the danger and damage of the old paradigm is variously known as the 'growth movement' or the 'human potential movement'. It

Emphasis on the body

Another central theme – the importance of working with the body – came mainly through the German psychologist Wilhelm Reich, who made his major contribution in the early 1930s. But bodywork has grown so far that Reich would hardly recognize much of it. In the US, the schools of Alexander Lowen, Stanley Keleman, Ron Kurtz and Charles Kelley are important, and in the UK, David Boadella is a prominent exponent. Other humanistic therapies, such as primal integration and encounter, also place much emphasis on the body.

Mind-expanding drugs

Though psychedelic drugs like LSD came on to the scene quite briefly in the 1960s, they arrived at a time when humanistic psychology was in its fastest period of growth. Peak experiences gained through LSD, mescalin and psilocybin gave people such as writer Aldous Huxley a glimpse of what is possible in transcending ordinary states of consciousness. The doors of perception were opened, and the vision remains.

Group dynamics

In the late 1940s, Kurt Lewin, a mainstream, yet innovative American social psychologist, developed a way of working in groups, called the T-group. This centres on group participants giving each other honest feedback on their actions. It grew out of his work on democratic leadership and became the basis of the National Training Laboratories at Bethel, Maine, USA. Since then, a great deal of early work in humanistic psychology has developed out of the T-group method, including the first open encounter groups.

Peak experiences

The American psychologist Abraham Maslow talks at length about peak experiences as pointers toward what the real self is all about. In a peak experience, we get a sense of the infinite, not as an abstract concept of the intellect, but as something real and important. In a peak experience we may go beyond apparently logical opposites and arrive at a state of consciousness that can accept the paradoxes of life. Many people have had peak experiences, but few have really done justice to their experiences when they try to express them.

The Freudian legacy

In humanistic psychology, we often find words such as projection, repression and resistance still used in their Freudian senses. Freud is now a part of our cultural heritage and it is impossible not to be influenced by him, just as it is impossible not to be influenced by the ideas of Einstein or Darwin. And because Freud was working in the same field as the psychotherapists and counsellors within humanistic psychology, much of what he discovered is of direct relevance to their work. Freud, however, is not referred to as an authority by humanistic practitioners.

consists of a broad range of disciplines and developments, including bodywork, meditation, the occult, social change, counselling and traditional therapy. At the core of this exploration is a loose affiliation of people, groups and organizations that has become known as 'humanistic psychology', which encompasses the following basic principles and ideas.

Self-direction

One of the key ideas in humanistic psychology is that we can arrive at a position of owning our own power and running our own lives. We can achieve self-direction or 'autonomy' by coming to know and understand ourselves and by healing the splits and conflicts within our personalities. This concept includes 'spontaneity', an idea introduced by Jacob Moreno, in which the whole person acts as one.

Tantra

The emphasis on the body as a source of energy and wisdom which we find in Tantra fits very well with the similar emphasis in humanistic psychology. Tantra also has a very good attitude to the relationship between female power and male activity, which humanistic psychology would do well to pay more attention to. In Tantra we find an experiential approach to religion – to try something, rather than to believe it – and this is very much shared by the exponents of humanistic psychology.

Taoism

The essence of this Eastern philosophy is the idea of 'not-doing', of letting things do themselves, of not pushing the river, because it will flow by itself. This approach goes very well with the emphasis on spontaneity in humanistic group work and psychotherapy and there is even a book by the American psychologist John Heider on Taoism in industrial psychology. The work of American physicist Fritjof Capra, which include such books as *The Turning Point* and *The Tao of Physics*, is relatively well known, but what is less well known is that he is also a committee member of the Association for Humanistic Psychology.

HUMANISTIC PSYCHOLOGY
Key people

Alexander Lowen
One of the main schools deriving from Wilhelm Reich is bioenergetics – a system devised by American psychologist Alexander Lowen. Bioenergetics lays great emphasis on the body as the repository of past experiences and in particular on the ways in which defences against past experiences are laid down in the body as 'character armour'. The client undresses for the session and the therapist works directly with the body, identifying and watching areas of tension. The client is encouraged to adopt stress positions that bring out internal conflicts and enable blocked energy to flow again.

Walt Anderson
People in the field of humanistic psychology often become interested in how it applies to the political scene. What are the political implications of an emphasis on spontaneity, authenticity and autonomy? The American psychologist Walt Anderson, one of the best writers on these matters, makes it clear that a very powerful critique of the present social system emerges from humanistic psychology. He was actively behind the anti-nuclear resolution adopted by the Association for Humanistic Psychology.

Charles Hampden Turner
A British writer educated at Harvard, Charles Hampden Turner has applied the theory of humanistic psychology to a number of different fields – personal development, community development, politics and philosophy. He makes it clear that if two qualities are in opposition, any attempt to stick to one of them and steer clear of the other perpetrates evil. This is a profoundly dialectical vision, since it accepts paradox and contradiction without wanting to eliminate them. Many people within humanistic psychology, however, find this a difficult concept.

Fritz Perls
American psychologist Fritz Perls moved from sophistication to simplicity. As his work in gestalt therapy (see p. 170) progressed, it became less theoretical and conceptual and increasingly based on personal experience. He was so concerned with the truth of a person, and helping him or her to reach it, that he tended to ignore the nurturing and nourishing aspects of therapy. His approach was perhaps the most direct and straightforward of any of the therapies.

Alvin Mahrer
Perhaps the most important original thinker to come out of humanistic psychology is Alvin Mahrer, who practises and teaches at the University of Ottawa. He has written a complete humanistic psychodynamics – an account of what is going on beneath the surface in a person. He has also developed an original and very exciting form of therapy, which embodies a strong critique of much that passes for psychotherapy today. If people ever ask who the theorists are within humanistic psychology, refer them to Mahrer.

Rollo May
If you are looking for someone to represent the existential stream within the theory of humanistic psychology, Rollo May is the person to choose. He is influenced by all the great existential thinkers, but adds his own personal touch to all of them, and is a very important influence in his own right. A writer as well as an academic, he was responsible for putting existentialism on the map in the United States.

The humanistic psychology network spans the world, but it tends to have a low profile – perhaps because of its rejection of the old paradigm and perhaps because, like any innovation, it looks unfamiliar at first sight. It has no central organization and though the various national associations co-ordinate, communicate and publish, they do not have a controlling role. Through its

Chris Argyris
One of the key areas in which humanistic psychology has been used very successfully is in management and organizational consultancy. A leading practitioner in this field, American psychologist Chris Argyris has been influential in revising the vocabulary around which organizational consultancy operates. He advocates, for example, looking at what management says it is trying to do, and comparing it with what it actually does. This is to treat an organization in much the same way as a therapist deals with a client.

Roberto Assagioli

Most of the Jungian influence within humanistic psychology came through Roberto Assagioli, who opened his Psychosynthesis Institute in Italy in 1926. During the 1960's, his ideas became very popular within the growth movement, and today almost all group work in humanistic psychology uses material derived from psychosynthesis. Later the work which he had pioneered became more generally known as Transpersonal psychology, and this became so big that it broke away from humanistic psychology to form its own organization and journal.

Bill Swartley

Another great integrator was Bill Swartley, one of the originators of primal integration. This is an approach to psychotherapy that uses all four of the Jungian functions (sensing, feeling, thinking and intuiting) and puts great emphasis on the whole person. It is a well worked out theory that looks at the entire life of a person from conception to the future, and simply tries to go wherever that person seems to need to go, using a wide variety of methods.

David Boadella

One of the few eminent British people in the field of humanistic psychology is David Boadella. His work is based on Reich, but departs from it in a number of respects, particularly in giving more respect to the spiritual dimension of the work. He is in demand internationally as a teacher and practitioner of his own school of bodywork, which he calls Biosynthesis.

Will Schutz

The person who did most to integrate all the strands of humanistic psychology was the American psychologist Will Schutz. He integrated the academic, the experiential, the industrial and the philosophical with great panache and style. He developed the open encounter group, and showed that a group leader could be endlessly resourceful and wise.

Harvey Jackins

There are some anomalous cases within humanistic psychology where a person is quite clearly a part of the tradition, but denies any connection with it. One example of this is Harvey Jackins, the inventor of Re-evaluation counselling, and its derivative, Co-counselling.

range of contributions, humanistic psychologists may be the only group with the breadth of experience, depth of rigorous enquiry and creativity of theory and practice that are essential for a new paradigm of mind. Here is a selection of some of the key contributors to the development of humanistic psychology.

Carl Rogers

Of all the people within humanistic psychology, American psychologist Rogers has perhaps the greatest claim to represent all the many aspects of it. In his work, he embraced the evolutionary (or Hegelian) approach in his feel for natural development and his indefatigable optimism; he supported the existential approach in his concern for the present moment and his refusal to theorize; he reflected the academic approach in his massive research work; and he used the experiential approach in his development of person-centred therapy.

Abraham Maslow

There are two important tendencies within humanistic psychology – the evolutionary (or Hegelian) and the existential. An American psychologist, Maslow, represents the more evolutionary approach, with its emphasis on growth as an inevitable process. Maslow was enormously influential in getting humanistic psychology as a movement off the ground. He was an academic, and did not get much involved in the more experiential aspects of the movement. But if you want to understand humanistic psychology you must read Maslow.

Jacob Moreno

One of the greatest innovators in humanistic psychology was Jacob Moreno, who started working in Vienna in the 1920s, and later came to New York. His method of psychodrama (see p. 170) is possibly the most significant in the whole field of humanistic group work. It offers a rich profusion of techniques, covering virtually the whole gamut of what it is possible to do within a group.

HUMANISTIC PSYCHOLOGY
Styles in practice

Out of the core theories and principles within humanistic psychology, a broad range of innovative practices has developed. You will probably find some aspects more appealing than others. This is because, assuming there are four styles of intelligence (see p. 66), some parts of humanistic psychology favour one particular mode. Some, including gestalt and psychodrama, put great emphasis on feeling, while some, such as bioenergetics, concentrate on what a person does rather than thinks, feels or intuits. Psychosynthesis and transpersonal psychotherapy on the other hand work with the more intuitive aspects of experience, and others go to great lengths to balance all four. The range of alternatives is wide. It's left to you to find your own preferred style.

Psychosynthesis

Psychosynthesis is very close to the heart of humanistic psychology, in its emphasis on trying practical exercises and activities, instead of making verbal interpretations. It also concentrates on getting in touch with your 'higher self', the 'transpersonal self'. Through considerable emphasis on 'guided fantasy' – a way of intentionally generating dream material – you are encouraged to explore patiently the whole of your inner universe. This approach leads to the discovery of one or several sub-personalities, corresponding to aspects of your personality that may be in need of more, or less, attention.

Psychodrama

In psychodrama you explore your mind through enacting the conflicts, difficulties or choices that you face in life. Psychodrama is usually found in a group setting, and as a member of the group you can elect to have a personal issue re-enacted by everyone present. After you have given a detailed enough account of what you want to explore, the group leader engages the talent and creativity of the others in the group to play the characters and generally recreate the situations you are interested in working through. You can choose to have people to support you and to speak for you or to voice what, in your situation, they might be thinking and the director will make time for you to clarify what you are learning.

Gestalt therapy

This therapy is very widely available. It is basically a one-to-one method – even in groups the leader will work with only one person at a time. Great emphasis is placed on being in the 'here and now', being in touch with the whole of yourself and learning from your experience of yourself. This is further pursued through looking at *how* you do what you do rather than *why*. You are invited to speak from experience, using the first person, 'I', and to get to know the parts of your mind that constantly tell you what you 'should' do or who you 'ought' to be.

Co-counselling

A minimum 40-hour training in basic skills teaches you the fundamental co-counselling methods of how to work on yourself as a client, and also how to listen with 'free attention'. Following this initial training, co-counselling involves meeting someone else who has done the same basic training. In a co-counselling session time is divided equally between the two participants. Each takes it in turns to work as client, with the other as counsellor. The working methods provide an easily learned and comprehensive way of exploring your mind. They can take you rapidly to the core issues from your early life and, since you are always completely in charge of the exploration, there is little danger of moving too far or too fast.

Person-centred counselling

This method starts from the assumption that when someone needs counselling, their rigid patterns of behaviour have become entangled either with each other or with those of another person. Unlike conventional counselling, the counsellor gives no advice and assumes that you already have the answer to your difficulties, but just need help to discover it. She or he provides a safe, empathic relationship in which you can do what you need to do for yourself. To facilitate this, the counsellor needs to have resolved a significant amount of her or his own personal distress, to prevent any 'inner talk', or personal material, from constantly interfering with what you are doing.

Bodywork

Derived from the German psychologist, Wilhelm Reich, the many types of bodywork are based on the principle that defensive patterns, originally necessary but now inappropriate, are held in the body in the form of tension and stiffness. The way we hold our bodies, breathe and sit, and our tone of voice convey to others what amounts to our 'character'. Since this 'character' can be thought of as armour that defends us against the world, working directly with the parts of the body where most of it has accumulated is effective as a way of releasing the stuck energy and/or memories.

Human nature

Just as the old paradigm was based on an underlying view of 'human nature', humanistic psychology has its own set of proposals about what is 'human' and 'natural'. As you will see from the list below, many of them directly contradict the view of human nature of the male-dominated old paradigm.

Human beings have a built-in desire for personal growth and development.
Human beings are basically self-directing.
Human beings are fundamentally good.
Human beings are responsible for their actions.
Human beings are fundamentally co-operative.
Personal growth and development necessarily involve the body.
Experience is the essential basis of personal knowledge.
Through our upbringing we suffer damage and deficits that limit our potential.
Our survival decisions made during childhood continue to be re-enacted inappropriately, shaping our adult lives.
Personal growth and development require contact and feedback from at least one other and preferably many other people.
The present moment is all there is.
Resolving our frozen history gives access to the underlying unity of all things and all life.

Encounter groups

Basic encounter is relatively gentle and no specific techniques are offered. What the leader does essentially is to create a safe place where whatever the participants need to explore can emerge – the principle being that, given a place of safety, you will automatically attempt to heal any hurts. The leader is nonjudgmental and actively supportive of others and simply shares with the group what she or he feels is happening for her or him, without interpreting. *Open encounter* is more directly concerned with what your body is, or is not, saying. The leader is very active in setting ground rules for what is then a head-long plunge into openness, personal honesty and the release of stuck feelings, often accompanied by explosively energetic actions and very loud sounds. When open encounter is working well, there is a deep sense of caring and healing, and it can be a powerful way of moving forward.

Assertiveness training

This method shows you how to distinguish between aggressive, manipulative and submissive behaviour in yourself and others, and teaches you to adopt assertiveness as an alternative, where appropriate. By looking at these aspects of behaviour, assertiveness training tends to raise all the fundamental issues about how your mind works – why some reactions are too big and some too small, where and how you learned manipulation, who you are really trying to please when you are inappropriately submissive, and so on. Ways in which you can take steps to change your mind, such as improving self-esteem and taking responsibility for what you feel, are outlined and practised. With the mixture of practical, useful recipes it offers for personal growth, assertiveness training has recently become a very widespread point of entry into humanistic psychology as a way of exploring your mind.

THE NEW PARADIGM LEADER

Facilitation is a key concept in the move from the old to the new paradigm. It marks the shift from a primarily authoritarian approach to leadership to a more co-operative one.

A facilitator is anyone who initiates, confronts, guides and supports within the context of a work or training group or in one-to-one counselling or therapy. At the moment, facilitation is found mainly in humanistic psychology and professional training, but this model of supportive leadership can be applied to any situation at work or at home where the appetite for authoritarian control is fading.

Becoming a facilitator

The basic qualification needed to be an effective facilitator is to have made significant progress in working through your own history of personal distress, so that in working with other people you neither impose it nor feel inhibited by it. Learning how to facilitate your own personal development lays a very secure foundation for helping other people to do the the same – in my opinion, it is essential and unavoidable if you want to work with and help people. Good facilitation also involves acknowledging how incomplete this task always is, and admitting when any of your own personal history intrudes in your relations with others, as and when it occurs.

Developing as a facilitator

Facilitators can only safely take other people to a depth of exploration that they have personally experienced. But those in the foothills of their personal exploration can still do useful work with other people provided they take care to stay in their undistressed areas. There is, however, a rigorous form of assessment in humanistic psychology (see pp. 182–3) – an alternative to the authoritarian qualifying examination. Developing as a facilitator means being able to initiate a wide range of activities, from bodywork – arousing and quietening physical energy and loosening muscular controls – to emotional work, involving catharsis – emotional release – and ordering and presenting theory. If the facilitator is to work with groups as well as one-to-one, it also includes continuously assessing and planning time, action and resources, as well as intuitively anticipating the changing needs of the group. In addition, a good facilitator needs to be able to communicate skilfully in a wide variety of ways.

When to use which style

None of the styles, shown right, should be regarded as better than any other. Facilitation is an enabling style of leadership. It presumes that, given the opportunity, people will be responsible, creative and self-directing. However, situations such as emergencies, need a rapid, highly directive leadership response. Others, such as merging two departments of a company or helping a family that is separating, may involve moving through all of them. Whatever the circumstances, facilitation emphasizes two things: matching the style of leadership to the individual's or the group's needs; and persistently drawing attention to the *process* of what is being done, whether it's a family or business situation.

Where to use facilitation

How we get a job done and make decisions tend to drop out of sight when its a strain to finish what we are doing and keep to schedule. Facilitation is based on improving this process, on looking at how we do what we do. It can be used anywhere where creativity, productivity and quality are important, from factory management and small businesses and partnerships, to families.

Facilitation styles

The clock (below) reveals the range of facilitation strategies available to a new paradigm of mind. It is also a useful guide for assessing your own or other people's styles of leadership. If you have a leadership role, which styles do you tend to use and which do you avoid?

Directive
The facilitator takes responsibility for how the group sets about its work.

Interpretive
The facilitator comes up with explanations to account for group behaviour.

Confronting
The facilitator affectionately challenges any distressed behaviour.

Releasing or cathartic
The facilitator works to resolve distress through laughter, tears, sobbing, shaking or storming.

Structuring
The facilitator determines the variety and kinds of group activities.

Disclosing
The facilitator shares her or his feelings about what happens in the group.

Non-disclosing
The facilitator remains silent about her or his feelings about what happens in the group.

Non-structuring
The facilitator does not get involved in deciding the group activities.

Non-cathartic
The facilitator encourages tension release without catharsis.

Non-confronting
The facilitator creates a climate in which members can confront themselves.

Non-interpretive
The facilitator may do no more than point to elements of the group's behaviour.

Non-directive
The facilitator delegates responsibility for devising group work methods.

The skilled facilitator

A good facilitator is someone who can move freely between different working styles and activities. But above all, a facilitator of quality is one who has a new paradigm of mind already installed – someone who, to some extent already embodies the new paradigm. How can you recognize one? A Tibetan Buddhist says that in the teacher of quality, teaching will have the quality of freshly baked bread. In other words, it is baked afresh each day of her or his life.

See Self-assessment
87-8   Communication
92-3   Personal responsibility
94-5   Conflict and commitment
See Knowhow
164-5   The new paradigm
176-7   The workshop
180-1   Communication
186-7   Resolving conflict
See Mind gym
230-1   Conflict
234-5   Projection
236-8   Relationships
238-41   Synergy

STARTING POINTS

The challenge of making the transition to a new paradigm of mind is beginning to be quite well understood. It involves managing our feelings, dealing with dominance and submissiveness in our own behaviour and learning to resolve unfinished business from our past, so that we have less distress to project on to the present. Alongside the old paradigm, humanistic psychologists have gradually been developing powerful new ways of conducting human relationships that are practical, well researched and theoretically sound. Among those that I have personally found well grounded and useful are ways of developing emotional competence, interpersonal skills, conflict resolution, assessment and self-management. All involve personal exploration that encourages self-direction rather than passivity and does not deny the realm of feelings.

Where to start in humanistic psychology

You have already started. This book and the dozens of others about the 'new age', the growth movement and humanistic psychology are one way to gain the information and impetus to go out and find a class, a group, a therapist or a counsellor. Learn to meditate or try a class in intuitive massage, relaxation and stress management, or assertiveness. Any of these will provide a good, non-threatening introduction to working with your mind in a new paradigm way.

Finding a good 'teacher'

Finding a facilitator who is good for you is a major step on the road to changing your mind. There's no guaranteed way of doing this. But patiently attending a range of classes or groups with different teachers will give you experience of the different styles of facilitation. The one where you feel you are making the most progress, where you are most in charge of your own progress and where you are persistently being challenged to pursue your own process of self-enquiry creatively, is likely to be of the most enduring value.

A good facilitator is someone who is well on the way to developing a new paradigm mind for themselves (see pp. 164–5). She or he may invite you to take risks and persistently confront you about chronic patterns of behaviour, but will not take you further and faster than you feel ready for. High-quality facilitation will create a place of safety where it is possible to feel whatever it is you have within you. It may be terror, anxiety, delight or love, but any feeling can be frightening if it has been held out of reach for a long time. But whether you should dip in and out or plunge in should be your choice alone. A good facilitator will also be able to interrupt any tendency of the group to push one member into taking a risk that they do not feel ready for. If you do find that people are hectoring you and dumping their negative feelings on you, don't be afraid to resist this group pressure. Working with feelings has a different quality to dumping. It may be loud or vicious in tone, but it is always done with full adult awareness.

'I'm in business. What will people think?'

If you think of yourself as a hard man or woman who needs to remain invulnerable in the face of any challenge, then humanistic psychology has great benefits in store for you. While you are young, the macho life – swallowing disappointment, choking back rage, fending off criticism, smiling at bullies, being patient with people who are a 'pain in the neck' – lays down patterns of health-damaging distress. Luckily, there are lots of professional self-development courses in the field of staff training which could help. Staff development is, however, often a euphemism for productivity or for selecting people for promotion. But if you search for them, there are many courses (see pp. 246–7) that offer professional development at the same time. Two examples of the professional/personal link appear in conflict resolution in interpersonal skills training.

One of the bridges between the old paradigm and the new has been the recognition of the harm that excessive stress and challenge do to people in management. Increasingly, good management includes conservation of its human assets, along with profit, forecasts and market share.

Is it dangerous?

In my experience, danger will only arise if a facilitator has a significant amount of unworked early material and fails to notice coercion creeping in. Only such a person would be likely to lead people into doing more than they are ready for. Another possible danger comes from being compulsively ambitious – wanting to make a lot of progress very fast. This is inner coercion.

If you have been unaware that you were carrying around a lot of painful early distress, you may feel very uncomfortable when it first surfaces. If this happens, it's helpful to remember that though it may feel dangerous, the defences that kept you feeling all right before are always ready to come back up and shift your attention away from any distressed feelings if they are too overwhelming. If at the moment you feel constantly upset, however, you will need to build up your strength before vigorously attempting to explore your early history. Wait a while before going farther. If you feel so wobbly that your attention is poor, you won't be able to learn much.

What is reasonable progress?

I'm inclined to say, slow. But this may not be true for you. People who have come to a personal crisis and are well prepared through reading or other experience may, for example, be ready to plunge in to working on themselves immediately. But a more reasonable expectation of progress is that within a few months of actively exploring your mind, you will have uncovered a number of aspects of your personality that leave you feeling much more comfortable with yourself. There are also likely to be less comfortable findings, that may be painful or embarrassing at first, but become transformed by the sense of relief when you discover the origins of problems that have been bugging you for years. 'Oh, that's what it is! That's why I've always . . . or couldn't . . . or never dared to.' Other benefits might include learning to trust your feelings, being able to express them more freely, growing more in tune with your body, and generally becoming more accepting of all sides of yourself.

Is it self-indulgent?

Some people may feel that giving attention to your inner life is 'navel-gazing' and, in some way, selfish or indulgent. If, after reading this, you still feel that you shouldn't be giving this much attention to yourself or to your inner life, then you probably learned at some point not to think of yourself, and found that it was much more acceptable to care for other people. But does the attention you give them perhaps help to keep your own disquiet under lock and key? Is it keeping you from making decisions and being creative? Exploring your mind might confirm that giving your attention to others rather than yourself has always been your conscious personal choice and that it is in your own best interests, as well as other people's. But unless you examine your assumptions, there's no way of being sure. This is the point of the exploration that humanistic psychology makes possible.

'How do I know if it's right for me?'
If you are in doubt about the value of a class, workshop or technique, ask what the aims of the course or session are before you enrol. If, when you start, you find the organization is run in an authoritarian style, ask yourself if it is for them or for you. If you have doubts about the competence of the facilitator, refer to pp. 172–3. But whatever you are doing, your intuition is the best guide. If it seems to be working for you, if you can see real benefits in day-to-day life, then you are probably successfully beginning to explore your mind, to resolve old difficulties and move toward the new paradigm.

THE WORKSHOP

One of the major innovations of the growth movement has been the development of the workshop. A workshop does not distinguish between education, counselling or therapy. Those people attending are there primarily to learn about themselves, and deep knowledge of yourself generally turns out to include a deepening knowledge of other people too. The emphasis is on learning through experience – trying something, noticing what happened or what you learned, then moving on to try something new. If any theory is given, it will be to provide a framework or to help you make sense of yourself, or to encourage further exploration.

The circle

A common feature of workshops is that everyone sits in a circle while sharing experiences or discussing the exercises. This builds power-sharing and personal responsibility into the life of the group. At a casual glance, it is usually difficult to spot who is acting as the group leader, or 'facilitator'. The circle also allows everyone to see and hear more or less equally, what is being said both verbally and visually through body language.

Ground rules

In many workshops the first priority is to agree on a set of ground rules for the session or series of sessions. These may include time-keeping, the limits of permissible behaviour and the fairly universal rule of complete confidentiality. If you can be sure that others will not gossip about what you did or said, then you're more likely to risk digging into the dark corners of your experience. Other essential conditions include speaking only from 'I', from 'my experience', and agreeing that only one person speaks at a time. Once agreed, these rules may be pinned on a wall and anyone can challenge a breach of them.

Working together

Many workshops begin with energizing exercises to liven everyone up and to 'break the ice'. At other times the whole group may work together or divide into small units of three or more, or work in pairs. The group then returns to the circle so that members can share their experiences. Often each person speaks in turn to counteract the competitiveness and submissiveness that people may bring into the group.

The benefits of workshops
Within the general workshop format, a wide range of experiences can be explored, but whatever the specific focus, people usually find the following benefits emerge.

Self-understanding
Exploring aspects of your mind in a workshop usually leads to increased self-awareness: 'How am I doing this?' 'What is my contribution to this difficulty?'

Autonomy
Being persistently invited to take charge of your own development, to set your own goals, methods and learning programmes, greatly increases your capacity to behave autonomously.

Self-esteem
As you develop your capacity to act and choose without distress-related constraints or compulsiveness, you learn to value your inner strengths and come to be less at the mercy of your weaknesses.

Creativity
At the beginning, learning to be personally creative and not to rely on a leader to do it all for you can be a bit of a shock. But as the old constraints are lifted, creativity becomes a source of delight.

Spontaneity
Because the workshop is a safe and encouraging environment, it is easier to step through fears of failure and insecurities about personal worth and to say what you want to say. Imperceptibly, inner fears begin to lose their power, and ideas and experiences become more directly connected to what we say and how we behave.

Openness
In a well-run workshop where what you say and do is confidential and where attacks and criticism will be challenged and worked on, you are less likely to feel the need to defend yourself. The workshop setting gives you permission to explore the kinds of feelings and behaviour you usually have to keep quiet.

Risk-taking
The relative safety and the full confidentiality of the workshop create a climate for exploring the limits of our mind and behaviour. It gives you the opportunity to try yourself out and to take risks. And since success and failure mean nothing in the workshop context, you can try out new ways of behaving without feeling threatened or at risk.

Personal responsibility
If some deep material comes to light, someone may elect to explore it further, with the support of the group and the guidance of the 'facilitator'. The essential point is that people are all in charge of their own personal development. This can be difficult for many people at the beginning, because the old paradigm habits of being told what to do run deep. The role of the 'facilitator' is primarily to ease the exploratory process, although she or he will probably set the objectives of the workshop and devise its format.

CO-COUNSELLING

In co-counselling, following a short basic-training course of a minimum of 40 hours, individuals are equipped to engage in their own 'change of mind'. For me, co-counselling is one of the most striking innovations in humanistic psychology. In the depth of enquiry it makes possible, in the directness of its methods, in the way it contradicts authoritarian structures of learning, and the means it provides of developing emotional competence rapidly, it represents a microcosm of the best of the humanistic psychology tradition.

Basic principles

Co-counselling is based on the view that people are fundamentally intelligent, responsible, able to co-operate and find a balance between their own and other's interests. It maintains that our capacity to be intelligent is compromised by the hurts and lacks we suffered as a child, but that as adults we can reconnect to these early experiences, re-evaluate the solution that we adopted then, and choose to behave differently. Re-connection is not an intellectual task but involves emotionally and physically re-experiencing the early event in which a pattern of distress was laid down. At the point of re-connection there is both a physical transformation and a rush of insight into what needs to be done and how to do it, as the blocked intelligence is restored. Other fundamental ideas are that, to be valid, learning about ourselves has to be based on personal experience, that our learning has to be self-directed, and also that only we can come to know ourselves – no-one can do the work for us. Co-counselling is available internationally (see p. 247).

Self-direction

The essence of co-counselling is that the client is always in charge. The training teaches participants to be self-directing and their counselling skills are founded on their experience as clients. The 'counsellor' learns to make no judgements or interpretations, and to abstain from giving advice and from sharing personal experiences. Above all, there is absolute confidentiality between both people involved about what is revealed during the session.

Co-counselling aims at dismantling patterns of distressed behaviour. This involves contradicting those patterns to enable blocked memories of past distress to come through. Sometimes this can mean first celebrating and reinforcing personal strengths for a considerable period before the client is ready to look at the patterns of distress. Since the client is always fully in charge, she or he can choose how far and how fast to proceed.

Training

Co-counselling training follows the workshop format and it takes a minimum of 40 hours to achieve competence in the basic skills. It is not recommended for people who are distressed to the point of being unable to listen to other people. During the training, each person learns to use a collection of powerful, practical techniques, including role play, celebration, free attention, contradiction, repetition and intensification. In later co-counselling sessions, she or he can then apply them to any current concerns. All these techniques, with the exception of the listening skills, are intended for use only with other co-counsellors, not in daily life. During the training, the participants learn how to make a co-counselling session into a formal ritual and so create a situation in which they can both deal with patterns of distresss. This may involve, for example, identifying past or present oppression, or working through the early origins of a stubborn psychosomatic ailment.

A typical session

Two people who have satisfactorily completed the formal co-counselling training meet at one of their homes or, perhaps, at work. They decide how much time they have, and divide it equally between them. One person elects to work first as 'client', with the other person as 'counsellor', and the roles are reversed for the second half of the session. The client takes a little time to scan the mind for some current personal issue. Then, using the working techniques learned in the training course, she or he plunges in and explores it with the support of the counsellor. The style of the session depends entirely on the needs and inclinations of the client. It may be cognitive – seeking to understand and draw conclusions from earlier sessions or from current experience – or it may involve returning to some distressing episode in the past that continues to cast a shadow over the client's life. At the end of the session, the client will clarify what she or he has learned and perhaps at the prompting of the counsellor, sum it up in a pithy phrase that will make it easy to take out into everyday life. The two people then reverse roles and the process is repeated for the 'counsellor', who now becomes the 'client'.

The client and the counsellor

The co-counselling client's working methods include celebrating her or his strengths, contradicting weaknesses and the shoulds and oughts of past obligations, and exploring distress patterns arising from present oppression or early formative experiences. She or he aims to re-live these experiences directly, to discharge the distress emotions that remain attached to the memories and afterwards, to re-evaluate and replace the early survival decision with one more appropriate for adult life.

The counsellor's principal strategy is lovingly to interrupt the client's distress patterns, by reminding her or him of the repertoire of working methods they have both learned. Throughout the session, the counsellor's main role is to give high-quality attention to whatever the client is doing, without advising, interpreting, judging or discussing what is happening.

COMMUNICATION

Humanistic psychology takes an optimistic view of humanity and of our mind's capacity for self-direction and co-operation. It sees people as creative, intelligent and responsible and acknowledges the emotional dimension of communication. Coupled with its strong emphasis on learning through experience, these fundamental principles have led to a wide range of methods for teaching interpersonal skills. One such method involves looking at the range of communication styles you use. When other people are talking can you choose to be silent? Can you move freely from challenging someone to being supportive? Can you switch easily from giving advice or instructions to eliciting information? One of humanistic psychology's main achievements has been to draw attention to the ways that our personal history may be limiting our choices, especially in the way we interact with other people. The first step in seeing whether our choice of responses is limited is to look at the range of options that is available to us.

Informative
Aim: to impart information.
You give your basic viewpoint, your perception, your opinion, your own experience or other people's opinions. You make predictions, suggest plans, explain a context or background, give feedback, describe images, give handouts or references or demonstrate.

Result: other people have a more intelligent appraisal of their situation.

Directing (or prescriptive)
Aim: to guide other people's behaviour.
You order, command, direct, insist, instruct, tell, rule, exhort, advise, recommend or, less strongly, commend, suggest, invite, request, ask, express a wish or a hope.

Result: greater choice for other people.

Confronting
Aim: to challenge other people's automatism, to awaken them to aspects of their behaviour that may not be working in their best interest. You challenge them with facts about their unconscious 'frozen needs', unaware, oppressive or collusive behaviour, unnoticed group behaviour and sexist or racist discrimination.

Result: other people become more aware of the way they behave.

Supportive
Aim: to affirm other people's worth through giving them good attention, expressing loving feelings, care or concern and appreciating or affirming their strengths. The supportive style includes loving touch, giving things, sharing and self-disclosure, as well encouraging others to celebrate themselves.

Result: the other person is able to think and act more positively.

Releasing (or cathartic)
Aim: to help other people to deal with painful or difficult emotions, such as grief, that may be distorting their behaviour. You enable them to shift from analysis to experience, to move into the present, to re-enact a previous experience, to relax, or to express positive or negative feelings.

Result: other people become more competent to deal with their feelings.

Eliciting (or catalytic)
Aim: to provoke self-discovery in other people.
You help other people to map out their options and to discover the unconscious patterns in their behaviour by echoing back what they seem to be saying and asking them to elucidate it further.

Result: other people are encouraged to be more self-directing.

Six styles of response

Over the last 15 years, the Human Potential Research Project at the University of Surrey, UK, has developed a penetrating analysis of interpersonal behaviour based on the initiatives of John Heron, their first director. It identifies six basic ways of responding or intervening in situations with other people. Known as the Six Category Intervention Analysis, this takes the form of a workshop (see pp. 176–7) which you are invited to recognize the six different styles in yourself and others, to identify which you use frequently, which occasionally, and which not at all, and to work on the neglected ones. While none is better than the others, attention is given to the ways in which some styles may be missing or over-used, due to old distress. Initially, as with any training, there may be some surprises, but with practice, a considerable increase in empathy, flexibility, spontaneity and authenticity results. This technique is a powerful tool for personal and professional change, and is especially relevant to those whose work involves a lot of interviewing. Here is a résumé of the six types of intervention.

These three communication styles are essentially *authoritative*. They take the basic form of 'I tell you . . .' Of them all, confronting is usually the most difficult, because it tends to re-activate old distress in both people involved.

These three communication styles are basically *facilitative*. They take the form of 'you tell me . . .' Of them all, the releasing, or cathartic, style seems to give the most difficulty because it may involve the re-activation of old distress in both people. The supportive style, which implies being loving and caring, is an essential precondition for all the other styles of intervention.

SHARED ASSESSMENT

The way we are assessed at school, in higher education and in professional training reflects the attitudes of the old paradigm. It is one of the ways in which authoritarian frames of mind are most securely kept in place. Experts set standards which we are not allowed to see. Other anonymous experts judge whether the standards have been reached. We have no say in the matter. Such a one-sided evaluation encourages unbalanced development. Intellect is emphasized at the cost of interpersonal skills and emotional competence, distorting the quality and integrity of the minds of everyone involved. This form of assessment is not only unfair, however, it is also profoundly contradictory – because it encourages students and employees to be responsible, intelligent and capable of initiative, while at the same time denying them the opportunity to take responsibility for their own personal development.

The new paradigm approach

Education in the new paradigm (see pp. 164–5), whether in formal learning, professional training or self-development, sees students as responsible people, with a capacity for self-direction. Given a supportive climate, students are perfectly capable of assessing their own level of attainment, according to a set of learning objectives. However, because none of us exists in isolation, and because we are social beings who exist in relation to each other, we also need some input and feedback from other people who are going through the same training or self-development process. It's not that others have the right to impose their views on us, but rather that we, as self-directing, responsible people, wish to draw on their views in accurately refining our own opinions. The opinions of our peers ensure that the assessment is rigorous, and that we neither devalue nor overvalue ourselves.

This approach to assessment can transform our attitudes toward learning. *How* we learn becomes more important than *what* we learn. One of the most useful side-effects of concentrating on the process of learning how to learn, is that it teaches us a method of reaching a whole range of goals, instead of just one.

The assessment process

The first stage in assessment is to decide what to assess – a skill, a level of experience or competence, a product, or a combination of these. The next step is for everyone involved to agree on the assessment criteria – the optimum levels of competence, awareness, skills, judgement or experience – and to agree what form the final assessment should take (pass/fail, credits, grades or qualifications). Different areas may, of course, be given more weight than others. The procedure from then on involves a self-assessment statement, then questions, then peer-assessment statements, then possibly a revised self-assessment.

1 Self-assessment statement First you make a full self-assessment, detailing your strengths, weaknesses, areas of uncertainty, any lack of resources or unforeseen difficulties plus areas that need more work, and what you plan to do about them. Your assessment should include explicit references to the agreed assessment criteria and, if required, a suggested grade or credit.

2 Questions A short period of questions may follow, limited to points arising from your statement that need clarifying.

3 Peer assessment Other members of the group now have an opportunity to contribute to the assessment process. There is, essentially, only one issue for them to address – whether or not they agree with your self-assessment. If they accept your evaluation, they say so, adding any qualifications they feel are pertinent. If they accept your self-assessment as a whole, but disagree with some of the details, they specify where and why they disagree. In an alternative version how you use other people's feedback is no more than a contribution to your own self-assessment.

4 Revised assessment By the time everyone has spoken, it is usually obvious whether or not everyone accepts your statement. If they do, then the group can move on. If there is some disagreement, then you may want to revise your assessment until everyone is satisfied. If there is still disagreement, you may want to repeat the process until an agreement is reached or you decide to re-think completely your assessment. In an alternative version, how you use other people's feedback is entirely up to you, provided this is agreed at the start.

Applying self-assessment

Attempting to change the way you and others around you are assessed will quickly reveal attitudes toward power – a fervent rejection of the idea, for example, points to an old paradigm devoted to authority. Since this assessment process demands only time with a minimum of resources, it can be introduced independently and informally into non-controversial areas. It can also run alongside formal examinations where participants feel oppressed by the usual system, and be used in any situation in which people realize that only those who know them well can realistically contribute to their assessment.

As with other new paradigm approaches to living and working together, self- and peer-assessment requires a certain amount of interpersonal and emotional competence (see p. 186). If we are to risk disclosing honestly our deepest insights into ourselves and confronting others with any discrepancy between their claimed performance and our personal perception of it, while keeping clear of projection (see p. 150), then we need more than the usual intellectual competence.

Shared assessment may initially feel a bit risky for 'senior' people if their own competence is open to consideration. But the self-disclosure it entails can dramatically enhance the trust and cohesion of a team or work group. Paradoxically, peer- and self-assessment is one of the best routes to achieve the free and open co-operation so sought after in management and other teams. It may make sense to start with a diluted version of the peer assessment initially. Perhaps begin the process with sympathetic friends and colleagues, then invite the people who normally assess you to join in a shared assessment.

WORK WITHOUT EXPERTS

Taking steps to change our minds involves breaking away from needing to have the old paradigm of 'experts', 'bosses', 'gurus', 'leaders', 'controllers', 'directors' or 'senior people', to interpret reality for us. What we do then and how we do it comes sharply into focus. If we don't have an expert on hand to advise, adjudicate or diagnose, how do any of us know whether what we are doing is valid or not? This question applies to decision-making in any group or individual situation – in the human, social and physical sciences, in business, and in self-management. It applies to all areas of research in which people want to move away from the old paradigm of dominance.

A new basis for validating projects

From within the social sciences, a developing strand of 'new paradigm research' or 'co-operative enquiry' has shown that we can both learn about ourselves and organize ourselves without resorting to experts, coercion or deception. Although it began as a research method that acknowledges individual intelligence, creativity and responsibility, the working methods of new paradigm research can be used to structure almost any kind of project.

Under new paradigm working methods, everyone who is to be involved contributes to the choice of project or the topic of research. Everyone internalizes the ground rules of the project and is expected to contribute to its development. Unlike conventional research where a published report is usually the aim, the outcomes of new paradigm research are likely to result in a change of mind, new skills or improved effectiveness for all concerned. This is why new paradigm research methods can be of such value in any situation where a group wants to develop skills, organize work or learn about themselves.

Is what we are doing valid?

Here are some guidelines for people-based projects that replace expert opinion, control groups and double-blind testing of the old paradigm, which I have personally found to work extremely well. They begin with three basic layers of question that may affect your whole approach – ethical, theoretical and practical (see right).

Parallel with these queries is one that asks: How do we distinguish between truth and illusion? The new paradigm research answer to this question is a set of procedures that constantly reviews the project's process, so that accuracy, validity, relevance and coherence are always under scrutiny. These procedures are still under development, but those that have proved very useful include the following:

The research cycle

This involves setting up a sequence in which we propose a course of action, plunge into the action, review the action, then go round the cycle several times. The research cycle has numerous virtues. We can start with just the germ of an idea and elaborate on it or we can begin with a grand concept that we then simplify and modify through repeated actions and reviews. The whole point of the cycle is that it encourages a progressive movement toward greater accuracy and

Three central lines of enquiry
Before you start, and throughout your work, it is helpful to consider three broad areas as guidelines.

Ethical
Does what we are doing:
Really matter to us and/or other people?
Contribute to improving the quality of human life?
Contribute to personal or social change or liberation?
Involve manipulating, deceiving or oppressing other people?
Result either directly or indirectly in the denial of other people's rights?

Theoretical
Are the ideas and concepts we are using helping to organize and make sense of what we are doing? Are they:
Logically coherent?
Relevant to our needs?
Comprehensive enough?
Well enough grounded in existing knowledge?
Imaginative enough?
Broad enough in scope?
Sufficiently self-critical?

Practical
Do the conclusions of the research or development:
Match our own experience and actions?
Reflect everybody's views about the findings?
Accurately reflect the information from findings?

validity. If it drifts away from its original aims, the direction of the whole project can be simplified or corrected, and confused first intuitions can be clarified. The cycle also allows for a deeper, closer or more extensive view of the aims of the project.

Is there a constant balance between experience and reflection?

Constant vigilance is needed to keep the action phase and the reviewing phase in balance. The right proportion depends on the project, but it is important that one does not swamp the other.

Is the work distorted by emotional distress?

The validity of any work is most likely to be undermined by projection (see p. 150) – caused by unresolved distress from the past. Typical ways in which unconscious projection can distort the process might include: picking situations or behaviour to pieces, so as to 'understand' them; pursuing trivial topics; treating people as objects; manipulation; breaches of confidentiality; and obstinately drawing conclusions that ignore others' wishes or findings.

Have we all internalized the procedure?

If we are working at changing our minds using a new paradigm approach, the value of what we do will depend on sharing the work of constantly questioning and reviewing equally between us. If some people are 'carrying' others, the enquiry is likely to have a lifeless quality, because some people are surreptitiously following the others. It's essential that everyone fully internalizes the whole procedure.

Is there enough variety in our approach?

Have we tried enough different activities or enough different explanations to account for what we are doing, and enough different ways of recording, recalling or collating our methods of doing it.

Has there been enough chaos?

The project and the enquiry will be greatly influenced by the extent to which imagination, creativity, exploration and innovation are pushed to their limits. In my experience, this means tolerating occasional peaks of chaos, confusion and ambiguity. If this disorder is shut off due to past distress, creativity will be truncated, because new discoveries often lie on the other side of chaos.

What are we avoiding?

New paradigm methods of enquiry put every idea and process to the test of experience. But 'my experience' risks inviting 'my history' to participate. As a group we are likely to ignore information that contradicts our pet assumptions. It is useful to challenge the enquiry process by playing devil's advocate and taking a detached view.

Are we beginning to make sense or reach a conclusion?

There is a danger that once we reach the final stage of making sense of what has been done, our conclusions may be too painful to accept or may point to action none dares take. The devil's advocate approach is once again useful to ensure that we are moving toward simplicity, understanding and effectiveness, not simply to a palatable result.

Can the procedure be repeated or continued?

If the project makes public statements about what should or should not be done, they need to be well documented for future use.

Do-it-yourself science
For several hundred years, the old paradigm scientific ways of learning about our minds seemed indispensable. This is no longer so. The new paradigm approach to organizing how we live and work together provides a rigorous basis for any project, whether it's changing your mind or changing your life. It is growing and spreading. If you belong to a group or an organization that is moving away from authoritarian management, it could work for you too. Why not try it?

RESOLVING CONFLICT

Conflict, it is often said, brings out the worst in us. There is some truth in this, but it is much more likely to bring out the *past* in us. When challenging or threatening conflicts arise, they tend to echo similar situations in the past, provoking a variety of defensive reactions (see pp. 146–55). This seriously limits the choices we have in the present and, when it happens to several people at the same time, it can temporarily extinguish choice altogether. A useful way of looking at how we respond to conflict is to look at how much energy, zeal and commitment we put into what we do and at the way we balance our own interests with those of other people. When we draw a map showing these two influences based on modern mathematics we find that the surface is curved and folded over on itself (see p. 158). As you pursue your own and other people's interests with greater or lesser energy, you can trace your progress on the surface of the map. With low energy, your rapport, the vertical dimension, changes smoothly. With high energy, zeal and commitment, there are catastrophic jumps in your rapport with other people.

Five zones of conflict behaviour
Any point on the map represents the behaviour that arises from a combination of energy, zeal and commitment levels, and the degree of self-interest. There are five distinct zones.

Withdraw
When you retreat and avoid conflict, you are looking after your own interests but without putting much energy into it. Your rapport with others is quite low.

Emotional competence
A dramatic improvement in levels of co-operation can be achieved through taking steps to develop emotional competence in everyone in a team, working or living group. Emotionally competent people who, on their own initiative, can recognize and deal effectively with unaware projections both on to and from other members of a team, or the distress arising from the task in hand, are able to balance their own and other people's interests very much farther up the scale of energy, zeal and commitment than other people. Such a group composed of emotionally competent individuals can achieve a remarkably high level of creative synergy.

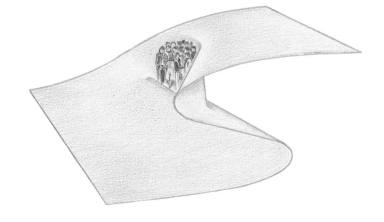

Accommodate
When you are obliging to others you are looking after their interests rather than your own, but not putting much energy into it. Your rapport with others is high.

Smooth
When you appease others, you are looking after their interests with a great deal of energy and zeal. Your rapport with others is very high.

Demand
When you resist and confront others, you are looking after your own interests with a tremendous amount of zeal and energy. Your rapport with others is very low.

Compromise
With conciliation, you put a moderate amount of energy into balancing your own and others' needs. Your rapport with others is average. Although this is preferable to other zones, there is a more desirable position (see opposite).

Middle ground
The middle ground of compromise disappears if we pursue either our own or other people's interests very energetically. This is why reaching a compromise often means 'backing down', 'backing off' or a 'cooling off' period.

Making up
If we have fallen out with someone, we have to go a long way across to meet their interests before we can 'make up' with them in a reconciliation.

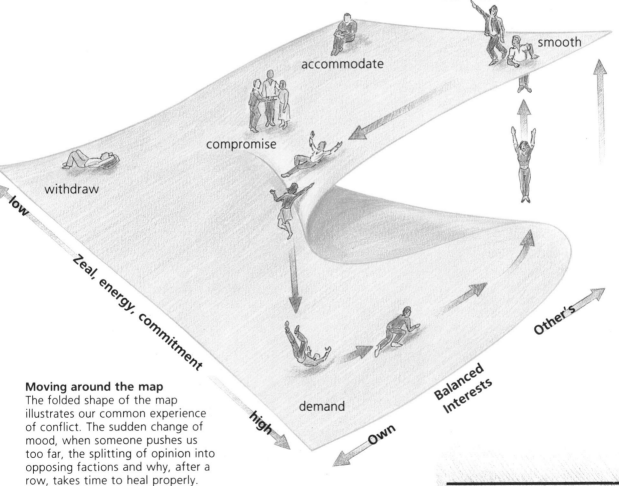

Moving around the map
The folded shape of the map illustrates our common experience of conflict. The sudden change of mood, when someone pushes us too far, the splitting of opinion into opposing factions and why, after a row, takes time to heal properly.

Falling out
If we usually smooth over conflicts, when we do start to insist on our rights, we may feel edgy or on the slippery slope. Eventually we may 'fall out' with someone or be dropped from the team.

See Self-assessment
    94-5   Conflict and commitment
See Mind gym
    230-1   Conflict

TRANSPERSONAL PSYCHOLOGY

Despite all the evidence about the mind and its workings, it still flickers in many of us as the experience of something elusive, delightful, sometimes infuriatingly insistent and seemingly completely intangible. This illusion is echoed in a whole range of 'new age' interests from ESP, channelling, crystal healing and astrology to telekinesis, synchronicity, clairvoyance and altered states of consciousness. Unless they are well grounded in our bodily history, they may be disappointing vehicles for personal change. As humanistic psychology and other research have shown, projection, denial and other defensive manoeuvres (see pp. 146–55) tend to underlie many of our cherished beliefs. But the notions of transpersonal psychology, fortified by this and other research, has stepped over the emptying shells of religions – which have yet to recognize these defences in themselves – and has proposed a variety of do-it-yourself ways of approaching the spiritual dimensions of the mind.

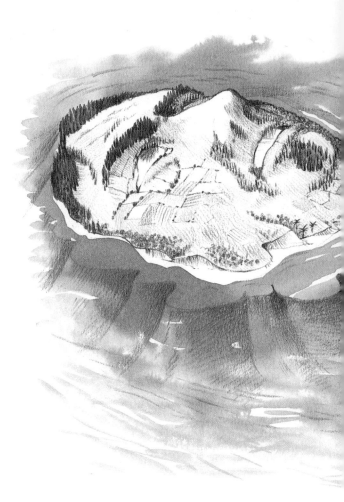

Just as the ocean conceals the reality that two separate islands belong to one land mass, so the bodily independence of human beings, reinforced by cultural beliefs, such as competitiveness and dominance, tends to mask our psychological and planetary interdependence.

Toward a new culture

Transpersonal psychology supports the idea that, in any epoch, it is possible to generate a new culture. In our present time, this is already under way in a variety of different forms. Transpersonal psychology supports the idea that it is possible to generate a culture in which:

We can create afresh for ourselves a sense of wonder at both the cosmic patterns in the universe and the complex bodily reality which give us substance.
We hold life, in all its forms, as sacred – infinitely more important than national boundaries, ideology, power or money.
We generate new rituals that respect the passages of life, birth, loss, ageing, dying and death.
We acknowledge love as a more potent evolutionary quality than force.
We see political action that eradicates oppression as a central part of a fully formed spirituality.
We regard spirituality and politics as something that can be lived every day in the real world.
We become aware of unconscious projections and so recognize the unity beneath the luxuriant diversity of life and culture.

The great escape

Unfortunately, transpersonal psychology, like conventional religion, can be used to provide an escape route from the burdens of our materialistic, competitive way of life. A mood of cosmic abundance can be a seductive alternative. Also transpersonal spirituality can seem to provide a way of side-stepping domination. The trouble with this is that, for as long as we carry it around in us, it will tend to pop out somewhere, no matter how spiritually refined we become.

The future

Thermonuclear annihilation is a practical possibility. Ecological and economic disaster loom. Yet from within the shadow cast by this dark umbrella, we all yearn, on our best days, for clarity, coherence and compassion, for a deeper, broader more comprehensive and richer experience of ourselves and others. However distressed we are, we long to have more meaning in our lives and to mean more to other people. And yet, for me, veins of caution are threaded through this optimism. Human nature, and the human mind as we have constructed it in the late twentieth century, is stubbornly wedded to their history – as perhaps minds always have been and perhaps always will be. The pressure to seek the light, the spring shoot of a new age pushing through the earth to meet tomorrow, can only grow as fast as those around us will let it grow. There is no quantum leap in consciousness to be had unless we all bring our friends and they bring their friends and their friends' friends too.

A viable spirituality

How can we create a workable spirituality that discards escapism, that is fully alive and includes rather than retreats from knowledge and experience of the modern world? Here are some suggestions:

By appreciating that the best way to make spiritual progress is through self-directed exploration, in free association with others.
By exploring current ideas about the way the mind works and making sure that they do not exclude other possibilities.
By trying to ensure that the ways we approach the transpersonal do not lead to idealization.
By maintaining a profound scepticism of people who claim to have found 'The Way'.
By moving towards living in the present – appreciating that all thoughts, ideas, fantasies, wishes or regrets of the past or future are events in the here and now. Not only is there no time *like* the present – there is no time *but* the present.
By appreciating that the interconnectedness of all things and all life is a physical fact, according to the best contemporary knowledge.
By realizing that experiencing this interconnectedness means fusing the personal and the political. This involves being able and willing to bear the pain of both your own and other people's suffering and despair, as well as your own and their delight.

MIND GYM

Is it really possible to change? Can we really change the way we see and feel about ourselves and the way we relate to other people? The answer is yes, but it takes time, effort and commitment. Ensuring that the change will be real and lasting means trying things out for ourselves, to find out directly from personal experience what seems to work best for us. The exercises in this chapter present a practical way in, an introductory taste of what is possible and available. They are offered in the spirit of personal exploration and enquiry, and they presume that you are intelligent and self-directing – able to choose your own pace and direction and able to find out, through trial and error, what is good for you.

Meeting your own needs

You may want to start by looking through the exercises for those that meet a present need. If this isn't what you are looking for, you could try again or move on to something else. If you begin to feel a little overwhelmed during any of the exercises, stop and try something a little lighter. There is no need to go further than you want at any stage. You may find that some exercises bring to the surface memories, feelings, reactions and thoughts that point you to specific topics within the chapter. If so, follow your own inclinations – you know better than anyone which areas of your mind you would like to clarify and change. Not all the exercises will be useful or appropriate for everyone and some will be more effective at some times than others. Feel free to adapt any exercises to suit your own needs – you may, for example, like to interrupt an exercise to explore an issue a little further. But, if you do decide to change a sequence, ask yourself, 'what might I be avoiding by doing this?'

Essential conditions

The first priority in self-exploration is privacy. This means setting aside some time when you know you will not be disturbed and where you can feel free to release whatever emotions come up. If you are working with other people, you may want everyone to agree to absolute confidentiality and equal time. While you are engaged in an exercise, avoid judging yourself and others; complete it, then review it to see what you learned. To keep sterile speculation at bay, it is usually a good idea to speak directly from your own experience, from your own feelings and discoveries. Before you begin the exercises, do read 'First things first'. It contains essential information for all the exercises.

Where to go from here

While you can do most of the exercises on your own, don't let that fool you into thinking that as you take steps to change your mind you have to do it all alone. Sure, start on your own, but as soon as you can confidently move through the basic exercises, reach out for support – either to go deeper or to share the excitement of your discoveries. A book like this can set you on the road to self-discovery, but when journeying deep into your mind, it can be a great help to seek a guide, someone who knows from their own experience where the tripwires are and where the treasure might be buried. It's true that you have to do the work for yourself – no-one can do it for you – but there's no need to reinvent the wheel. Consult the Resources on pp. 246-7 for pointers to workshops, counselling, therapy and training.

Remember, whatever you find, it was already there when you started. Plunge in. Go at your own pace and when you feel ready, take a modest risk. You have nothing to lose but your illusions.

How to use this chapter

All the exercises in this chapter can be used on their own or in conjunction with the SELF-ASSESSMENT and KNOWHOW chapters. Be active in using the cross references to clear up any doubts you may have about the purpose or background of an exercise. If you have already worked through some of the self-assessments, it is good idea to review any notes you made. If you haven't looked at that part of the book yet, you may want to refer to it from time to time to identify your strengths and weaknesses.

This chapter consists of four main parts: 'First things first' – which outlines some essential basic exercises and information; 'You and yourself' – which looks into individual identity, emotions, intelligence and self-esteem; 'You and others' – which looks at your interactions with others; 'You and the planet' – which branches out into global awareness.

Tape recordings

For several exercises, you will find it helpful to record the sequences. You may want to experiment with the sound until you get a tone and volume that you like. Use a slow, calm, steady voice without too much emphasis.

FIRST THINGS FIRST

ATTENTION

Exploring your mind involves learning how to shift your attention between inside and outside and learning how to raise and lower your level of arousal. Both are equally important skills when you are working on yourself.

If shifting your attention is new to you, then I strongly suggest that before trying the following exercises you experiment with alternating your attention – going in for a couple of minutes or a few seconds and coming out again, then repeating the process. It takes a little practice, but it's quite easy.

Goal: to get used to shifting your attention inwards.
Number of people: alone or with others.
Resources: a quiet room.
Time: 30 seconds to 2 minutes.
Points to remember: time tends to drift when your attention is focussed inwards. Keep this exercise to 5 minutes maximum.

Going in

Shifting your attention in means reducing sensory signals coming from outside. You need a quiet, fairly dark room where you can be comfortable and confident that you will not be disturbed by other people or the phone.

Step 1 Sit or lie down somewhere where your body is supported.
Step 2 Close your eyes.
Step 3 Notice what's happening in your body. If any part of you wants to twitch or fidget, let it.
Step 4 If any thoughts or images come into your mind just notice them and let them drift away. And if there are any sounds either in the room or coming from outside, note their existence and just let them go.

Goal: to get used to shifting your attention outwards.
Number of people: alone or with others.
Resources: anywhere.
Time: anytime.
Points to remember: use as often as you like.

Coming out

Moving your attention outwards involves giving attention to what your senses are telling you, especially your eyes, which have a high input into the brain.

Step 1 Open your eyes.
Step 2 Look around the room and notice what is there.
Step 3 To bring your attention further out, try one or several of the following:

Hold eye contact with someone, or with yourself in a mirror.
Stand up and walk around.
Count the number of books on a shelf.
Count the number of red objects in the room or the number of pieces of cutlery in a drawer.
Sort the cutlery.
Describe out loud and in great detail the scene outside the window.
If none of these seems to work well, try the following:
Spell several words backwards.
Name twenty rivers or cities.
Do awkward mental arithmetic, such as 19 x 27 or 31 x 17.

Attention in and out
Going in means gaining access
to the inner universe of your
memories, thoughts, ideas,
teaching and sensations.
Coming out means bringing
your attention out on to your
perceptions of the outer world
of colour, texture, shape and
people.

Balancing attention

Once you have gained some experience of shifting your attention in
and out, a further skill is to learn to balance your attention. This
means being able to keep your attention out without excluding the
inner sensations and feelings from your body. It also means being able
to let your attention go in while keeping a fraction of your attention
out. Maintaining this small degree of outer attention is what makes it
possible to explore your inner world consciously and intentionally. It
allows you to choose to go in deeper or to come out at will.

AROUSAL

The level of arousal of your body – how activated or relaxed it is – affects your mind at all levels. Fluctuating arousal is a normal part of life but sometimes you may fail to notice that it is running very high or very low so that you are either agitated or sluggish. For this reason it is useful to be able to raise or lower your level of arousal at will.

Energizing

Raising or increasing arousal means physical exercise. Try any of the following:

Walking, running, singing, shouting or dancing.
Vigorously shaking each foot and leg, then each hand and arm in turn.
Vigorously massaging your head as if shampooing your hair.
Showering followed by vigorous towelling.
Vacuuming or other forms of housework.

Goal: to gain experience of raising your level of arousal.
Number of people: alone or with others.
Resources: anywhere.
Time: as little as a minute of vigorous exercise will raise your arousal level.
Points to remember: if you are unfit or have a heart condition take it very easy and stop at the slightest sign of discomfort.

Relaxing

Lowering your level of arousal means relaxing, reducing your bodily activity, and it is central to some of the exercises that follow. To be able to relax you need a quiet, fairly dark place where you will not be disturbed. For some people, finding this can be the most important step towards lowering arousal. Lean back on a chair with your feet supported, or lie down. Don't be surprised if you go off to sleep, your body will only sleep if it needs to. Try any of these techniques.

Tense then relax

Tense each part of your body in turn. When you can hold the tautness no longer, slowly let your muscles sag. Begin with your left foot, then your right, and work all the way up your body to your face. Let your attention focus on your breathing and try not to hold your breath. Notice the air coming in and going out. If you find yourself drifting into thoughts and feelings, just let go of them and come back to your breath as it moves in and out.

Draining

Imagine your whole body is hollow and filled with a sweet-smelling liquid. At the lowest point, perhaps the back of your heel, there is a small tap. Gently open it and feel the liquid slowly draining out of you, taking all the tension with it.

Massage

Ask your partner to stroke you all over, using a light, loving, rhythmic touch. Let your attention rest on the point of contact between you. If you find yourself drifting off, let your attention return to the point of contact again.

Water and music

Take a long hot bath and arrange to have relaxing music playing.

Goal: to lower your arousal at will.
Number of people: alone or with others.
Resources: a quiet room.
Time: if your arousal level has tended to be very high, it may take days, or weeks of regular practice to bring it down to a low level.
Points to remember: after a heavy meal your body is busy digesting. A low level of arousal won't be accessible for an hour or more.

HEALING AND DISTRESS

The amount of distress from the past that we carry around with us seriously distorts our behaviour and limits our intelligence. But we can learn to release this childhood burden and so become more intelligent. At the same time we can minimize the distress we off-load on to our children and the people we live with. One or two of the exercises that follow may have the effect of releasing some distress in you. You may feel sad, cross or anxious, particularly if you do them thoroughly. Beginning to explore your mind may involve dipping into such feelings, but it's good to remember that delight, creativity and spontaneity are very often locked up with them.

Access to distress

Your own personal history is unique, and at different times and in different places it may be more accessible than at others. How you get in touch with the formative emotional experiences from your past is a matter for you personally to decide. The exercises in this section give a sample of what is available to you, but it's your choice how far and how fast you go.

Healing?

Healing means intentionally supporting your bodymind in doing what it needs to do to be well. Your body can heal cuts and bumps through scarring and bruising and, given the chance, it can do the same with less tangible hurts such as separation and loss. Healing a present-time hurt – crying because someone close to you has died, feeling how much you miss them and expressing it in some way – gives the body the opportunity to do its healing work. Healing an early hurt, however, means intentionally going back in time, re-experiencing the old hurt and then, as an adult, making a new decision about it. For example, you may have decided: 'Yes, the best I could do at that time was to smile, even though I felt desperately lonely and afraid. But now as an adult I don't need to keep on doing it. I can make a new decision. As an adult I can acknowledge my loneliness and anxiety and do something about them.'

Healing the distress fully of both present-time hurts and frozen history may involve a lot of emotion. Laughter, tears, shaking and angry storming movements can contribute to the essential healing of early hurts and deficits through deactivating built-in physical defences such as muscular tension.

Permission to feel

For healing to take place, you need to give yourself permission to feel whatever you need to feel in order to become well. If you criticize yourself (or other people) for being weak or inadequate because you feel upset from time to time, you may inhibit the healing process – for example, by stopping the tears before they have run their course. When your body has done its work the tears will stop of their own accord and you are likely to feel deeply relaxed, clear headed and full of insight about what has been happening to you. Beware of other people caring for you with suggestions that you 'dry your eyes', 'pull yourself together' or 'get a grip on yourself'. Such advice is very often for their benefit, not yours, and by interrupting your bodymind process they will also inhibit the benefits of it. Try giving yourself permission to be upset for as long as it takes to come out of it. If you feel you need to 'come out' a bit before you feel safe enough to really let go, then do so by opening your eyes, standing up and concentrating on your surroundings.

Blocked feelings

If you do not feel very in touch with your feelings, you may think that 'going in' and getting closer to what you feel is frightening or that you might get stuck there in some way. But this is unlikely. If you can focus well enough on the outside world then going in will come to an end whenever you choose because your normal stable state will quickly reassert itself. (See Coming out, p. 192.)

Overcome by feelings

If you are easily upset or frequently feel anxious, then working with your bodymind involves being able to climb out of the feelings of distress long enough to see where you are and what needs to be done. You can then gain a sense of proportion, see who may be oppressing you, build up your strength and increase the amount of choice you have available.

Appropriate settings

Actively exploring your mind is helped by finding an appropriate setting. Of course, to begin with anywhere will do but eventually you'll probably need somewhere that is quiet, where you won't be overlooked, overheard or interrupted.

Oppression

At any time during these exercises it's useful to check out how much of what you feel, or what seems to be an obstacle, is due to some form of oppression. Distress caused by painful early history is often entangled with present-time oppression – either external because others are giving you a hard time, or internal because you are giving yourself a hard time. In a challenging, rapidly changing world it can be only too easy to blame others for our own pain, but there is a danger also in blaming ourselves when in reality we are victims of other people's distress. This can be avoided by giving persistent attention to how what you feel and do is shaped by where and with whom you live, and especially where and with whom you work. Being a fully healthy person requires a healthy society and we don't have that yet.

KEEPING A JOURNAL

Goal: to provide a focus for self-enquiry.
Number of people: alone.
Resources: loose-leaf folder as described and/or use a word-processor.
Time: daily entries as they arise, although there's no need to make daily entries in each section.

A very good way of beginning to work on yourself is to monitor what is going on in your mind by keeping a journal. This is especially useful if, for the moment, you don't have anyone with whom to share your interest in working with your mind. So if you already keep a diary, or you have often felt you'd like to, here is a skeleton structure that you can personalize, adapt and shorten to suit your own needs.

Step 1 Find a loose-leaf file, a supply of the appropriate size sheets, perhaps in several different colours, and some index separators.
Step 2 Use the separators and the different coloured papers to make up a personal journal file with the following sections. Use it daily or as often as possible, to make the kinds of entry indicated:

Period journal – make entries about how your life is in general. Note any feelings, such as well-being, optimism, doubt or confusion.
Daily journal – make daily entries under the following headings:
  People – who you met, for how long and what was said.
  Work – what you did at work, your interests, hobbies and tasks.
  Society – what was going on around you, in the family, the neighbourhood or the nation.
  Events – what happened to you, what you witnessed or perhaps participated in.
  Body experiences – make entries about how you felt in yourself, your emotional state and any moods that were around.
The Well – use this section to make entries of anything that you notice that might have come from outside your conscious awareness, such as extrasensory perception or *déjà-vu* experiences, daydreams, fantasies or unusual coincidences and dreams. The following subheadings are useful:
  Dream log – keep a record of any dreams you remember.
  Dream-work – use this for any exploration or enlargements of dreams that you undertake (see Dream-work, pp. 226-7).
Personal history – use this section to keep a record of any early memories that may be triggered (see Feelings are physical, pp. 144-5) or any other aspect of your physical history that emerges.
Stepping stones – use this section to keep a record of any event or situation that looks as though it may have unusual long-term significance – for example, something that diverts or distracts your attention from your chosen path, or looks as though it might accelerate your progress in some direction.
Crossroads – use this section for choices that you make. List the options and how you made your choice.
Present time – use this section for spontaneous, uncensored out-pourings on any subject.
Explorations – use this section for exploring your reactions, options and discoveries you make during exercises, like the ones in this chapter.

YOU AND YOURSELF

Our individual sense of ourselves is often so submerged in the pressures coming from other people that our range of personal choice about how and with whom we live and work can seem very limited. Opening up a wider range of choices means looking into your mind, seeing what belongs to you and what to other people, and making adult choices about what to keep and what to reject.

LIFE REVIEW

In order to gain a sense of perspective, to see where you stand and where you are going, it is helpful to step back and take a look at your life as a whole.

Life scan

From where you stand today, take a broad look at your life, concentrating on each of the following aspects in turn.

Goal: to clarify what and who is important to you.
Number of people: alone or with a partner.
Resources: pen and paper, or your journal.
Time: as long as it takes.
Points to remember: notice what you may be feeling at each of the steps. Try to avoid judging or blaming yourself or others.

Step 1 What was the high point of last week?
Step 2 Who is the one person who has done most to help make you who you are? How were they significant for you?
Step 3 What was the most risky decision you ever made? What was so risky about it?
Step 4 Write about a missed opportunity in your life.
Step 5 If you could change one thing about yourself, what would it be and why?
Step 6 What do you most like about yourself?
Step 7 What did you want to be when you were young?
Step 8 Who is your heroine or hero and why?
Step 9 If you were told you had 6 months to live, what would you do in that time?

Life as a landscape

Goal: to surface hidden attitudes to yourself.
Number of people: alone or group.
Resources: drawing or painting materials.
Time: as long as you like.
Points to remember: let go of any inner criticism. If it really belongs to you, that's enough.

Draw your life as a landscape and add yourself as a figure within it. If you believe that you can't draw or paint, step over your inhibitions and try it – artistic ability is irrelevant to this exercise. Just draw what seems true using colour, texture or whatever kinds of materials you prefer. Let your imagination run riot to create whatever realistic or fantastic scene you like. Enjoy it. (See also p. 220 for further remarks.)

Life as a book

Goal: to reveal your outlook.
Number of people: alone or with others.
Resources: pen, paper/journal.
Time: as long as it takes.
Points to remember: humour and truth are likely to be intermixed.

Take the time to look at the whole of your life as though it were a book. What would the title be? If a chapter was devoted to each of the significant periods of your life, what would each of the chapters be called? What kind of book is it – a text book, science fiction, travel, non-fiction, horror or romantic fiction?

Goal: to take an overview of your life.
Number of people: alone.
Resources: whatever helps you to write efficiently.
Time: not more than an hour.
Points to remember: beware of censoring or writing what you think others might want to see. It's better to keep the story private than to undermine its usefulness by censoring any parts of it.

Life as a fairy story

Write out your whole life as a fairy story. Give each of the key characters of your life fairy-tale roles – animals, wizards, goblins, fairies, princes, or princesses. Then concisely, but leaving out nothing essential, write your story. When you get to the present day, quickly and directly resolve the story, give it a conclusion. Have fun. Go to wild extremes of imagery and characterization. Let humour, irony and wit run free.

Fairy story

Once upon a time there was a little boy called John who lived in a castle. His friend Murgatroyd lived with him. Murgatroyd knew everything. John was very happy.

One day, Murgatroyd died and John didn't know what to do. He felt sad for many days and then decided to go and see the White Sorceress who lived on the cliffs. She looked in her crystal ball and at last she said. 'If you stay in your castle, it will burn down. You must take the boat at the bottom of the cliff and row across the water 'til you reach an island. Under a rock on the island you will find a comb and a goat's fleece. Comb the fleece and put it on. It will protect you.' John was just on the point of leaving when the witch called him back. 'Bad news, I'm afraid' she said, 'the Thought Police are on to us now. It does sometimes happen with crystal balls.'

'Rubbish!' said John and rushed down to the rowing boat. But when he arrived at the island, the Thought Police were already there. John looked behind him and saw that his castle was already burning down. 'You're stuck with us now because we know all about you. But

we're not really so bad. All you have to do is think the right thoughts and we'll leave you alone'. 'Can I have my comb and my goat's fleece?' asked John politely. 'Well, you can have the comb, if you like. It doesn't look much good to me. I can't give you the goat's fleece because we've taken it away to try and analyze the magic that was in it'.

With that, the Thought Police got into a flying saucer and left the island. John wandered about and saw the island was covered with fig trees and pools full of eels. He found a transparent stone that could be used as a magnifying glass. So he was able to make a fire and keep himself warm and cook the eels. He stayed on the island, living on figs and eels, for several years.

One day, he decided to leave the island because he felt lonely. The moment he thought this, along came a flying saucer. It was the Thought Police. 'You can't leave' they said. John was so frightened that he said 'All right, I'll stay here'. So the Thought Police left.

Then John remembered the magic comb, which he had never used, and was still under the rock where it had been left. He stuck the comb in his hair and decided again to leave the island. The Thought Police didn't come. So he was free to plan what to do next. He wondered whether to go back to the mainland where he had come from. The castle was a ruin and all that lived there now was a colony of vultures. He would have to go to another country to start a new life.

He spent years trying various ways of travelling across the sea, finding different places, each more lonely than the last. At long last he came to a country full of oaks and elms. It felt like home. He met all sorts of people there. One of them said, 'why do you always go about with a comb in your hair?' 'To stop the Thought Police' said John. 'You can do without that now', said the person. 'The Thought Police never existed you know. The White Sorceress wanted you to believe in them for her own reasons. She was the one who killed Murgatroyd and burnt down the castle. She was really a Red Sorceress.' 'How do you know?' asked John, 'I am Murgatroyd' the person said. John saw that it was so. 'We can have a good time now'. They both agreed.

IDENTITY

The sense we have that our identity is a consistent, coherent whole is a powerful, perhaps essential, illusion. A closer look is likely to show that our identity is made up of a collection of more-or-less autonomous sub-personalities who play distinctive roles in our life. Making friends with them and re-balancing the power between them is an important aspect of changing your mind.

Postcard personalities

A good way to explore the different sub-personalities is to give them a chance to attach themselves to evocative images. You can use the images here or choose your own.

Step 1 Look at the array of postcards opposite and pick a pair that represent:

Yourself at work.
Yourself away from work.

Step 2 Take the first card and use it to describe yourself in the present tense: 'I am . . .'. You can speak it out loud or write it down, whichever you prefer. Now do the same with the second card.

Step 3 After both cards have had their say, begin a dialogue between them. What do they want to say to each other? How do they feel about each other?

Step 4 Make a note of what you discover.

Step 5 Repeat this process for:

Yourself as you are.
Yourself as you'd like to be.

How you see yourself.
How others see you.

Goal: to explore the different facets of your identity.
Number of people: alone.
Resources: tape recorder to record statements and dialogue or pen and paper.
Time: as long as it takes.
Points to remember: this kind of exercise helps to free your spontaneity and creativity. If you feel awkward, keep going.

Goal: to explore your identity.
Number of people: alone or with a partner.
Resources: tape recorder if available.
Time: around 30 minutes.
Points to remember: when reading the text either for a partner or onto atape machine leave pauses of say 10-15 seconds between each element of the fantasy. Make a journal entry of who you met and what they said if it seems significant to you.

Inner personalities

This guided fantasy enables you to look at your sub-personalities. Here is a way of getting to know them.

Step 1 Record the text in ***Step 4*** or ask a friend to read it to you.
Step 2 Lie down or make yourself comfortable in your quiet place and try to ensure that you will not be disturbed.
Step 3 Take time to let your breathing settle and your body relax.
Step 4 Now start the tape or ask your friend to begin reading.

You are walking along a path that winds through a meadow . . . The day is warm and still . . . Birds are singing in the trees at the edge of the meadow . . . There are wild flowers in the grass . . . In the distance there is a house . . . As you approach it you hear sounds of a party going on . . . When you reach the house you walk up to a window and look in at the people inside . . . You watch them for a while . . . noticing how people are relating to each other and who is there . . . you may know some of the people there or none of them . . . After you have watched the proceedings for a while you make contact with the people in the house . . .and go in to join them . . . Perhaps someone greets you . . . or you talk to the host . . . or you look for the refreshments . . . Join the party . . . See how you feel as one of the guests . . . After a while you may feel drawn to one of the guests . . . or spend a lot of time either listening to someone or talking to them . . . you may even be drawn to someone and want to stay . . . Now you're going to leave the party . . . You take your leave of the guests and come out of the house . . . In front of you is the pathway down which you came. You walk back along it to . . . the here and now.

Step 5 Lie quietly without speaking and let your mind rest on the images or characters that emerged.
Step 6 Make a journal entry of anything that stands out as interesting or important.
Step 7 Check on p. 206 for suggestions about interpreting this guided fantasy.

SELF-ESTEEM

The general opinion of yourself, accumulated during and after your childhood, has a global effect on how you behave. Seeing how your sense of self-esteem differs from your actual worth and abilities can lead to a helpful self-re-evaluation.

Goal: to enhance your self-esteem.
Number of people: alone.
Resources: pen and paper.
Time: one hour.
Points to remember: you will need to run through the exercise several times, adding to the messages and changing and improving the contradictions each time.

Disarming the inner critic

An inner critic can exercise a powerful hold on our day-to-day behaviour. It pops up to tell us that 'no, that will never work' or 'no, you aren't good enough, strong enough, clever enough or attractive enough'. The inner critic plays safe, it likes things the way they are. Taking risks, changing how you do things, particularly the sense of your own value, often brings out the critic. Reducing the power of an inner critic means patiently dismantling it, choosing what you want to keep, understanding why some of its messages are so compelling and damaging, and finding reliable ways of contradicting its harmful or negative messages.

Step 1 Make a list of inner messages that your critic uses to undermine, distract or sabotage you. List them down the left side of a large piece of paper. This stage may take some time. When you have a representative list of your critic's messages, move on.
Step 2 Take each message one at a time, check it against the following list and make a note of which ones apply.

1 Has your critic made a general rule from one isolated example?
2 Has your critic got into the habit of using exaggerated positive or negative descriptions instead of accurate ones?
3 Does your critic have tunnel vision? Does it insist on paying excessive attention to small parts of your experience?
4 Is your critic an extremist. Does it insist that everything you do has to be brilliant otherwise it regards it as rubbish?
5 Does your critic lead you to take responsibility for events that are actually out of your control?
6 Does your critic assume that the whole world revolves around you and your interests?
7 Does your critic know for sure that other people don't like you, are cross with you, or don't care about you?
8 Does your critic insist that you are either totally responsible for everything that happens around you or that you have no responsibility and are a helpless victim?
9 Is your critic intensely emotional?

Step 3 Now, armed with the list of messages from your critic and some insight into how they may be distorting your self-esteem, see if you can creatively devise a way of contradicting each of the messages. Short pithy phrases work best. See if you can find one for each of your critic's messages, such as 'I may sometimes misunderstand, but that doesn't mean I'm stupid'.
Step 4 Keep the whole list in a safe place. Bring it out whenever you suspect the critic might be getting out of hand and add to it. (See *Self-Esteem*, Matthew Mckay and Patrick Fanning.)

Goal: to reinforce your self-esteem.
Number of people: alone or with a partner.
Resources: quiet room with no interruptions. Strongly recommend tape recording the text for playback.
Time: 10-15 minutes.
Points to remember: this exercise may release some feelings. You may for example feel sad that the critic is going. If feelings do come up, accept them but try not to give them any energy.

Deflating the inner critic

This guided fantasy enhances your self-esteem through reducing the power of any negative, undermining, sabotaging or demeaning memories you may be carrying around with you. If you are unsure about taping this, see p. 191.

Step 1 *Sit or lie down in your quiet place and ensure that you won't be disturbed.*

Step 2 *Close your eyes and count yourself down: Ten . . . nine . . . you are sinking deeper and deeper with every breath you take . . . eight . . . seven . . . very relaxed . . . six . . . five . . . sinking deeper and deeper with every breath . . . four . . . three . . . down . . . down . . . ever more relaxed . . . two . . . one . . . Now open the door or window into your own special, private secret place that you alone can enter. Make yourself comfortable.*

Step 3 *In front of you is a large blackboard . . . On it are listed many of the negative thoughts and evaluations you have of yourself . . . Read through them and add anything that seems to be missing . . . (long pause) . . . At the bottom of the blackboard is a rubber and a piece of chalk. Take the rubber and wipe out the whole of the list, every last mark . . . Now take the piece of chalk and write on the board as many of your strengths as you can bring to mind . . . Take your time, there is no hurry . . . (long pause) . . . Now stand back and look at what you have written . . . In the weeks and months to come you will be able to remember these strengths whenever you choose to . . . Now there is one more thing to attend to in your special private place . . . If you look over in the shadows to the left of you, you'll be able to see your principal critic . . . If you let her, him or it come closer, you'll see that there is a small tap in the top of the critic's head . . . If you open the tap . . . all its power will evaporate . . . Try it . . . open the tap . . . There is a rush of air and the critic begins to deflate, sagging down to the floor, it sinks and disappears . . . Now sink back into knowing that you are a good and valuable person . . . Enjoy feeling good . . . Accept the good feelings as belonging to you . . . Accept that you deserve them . . . bask in them.*

Step 4 *When you are ready to . . . take your leave of this private place to which you know you can return whenever you choose . . . Begin to count yourself back out again . . . one, two . . . slowly and without any hurry . . . three, four . . . up and out . . . five, six . . . coming up and into the present . . . seven, eight . . . almost there . . . nine, ten . . . Open your eyes . . . back to present time . . . here and now.*

Strengths and weaknesses

Goal: to assess your self-worth accurately.
Number of people: alone.
Resources: pen and paper.
Time: as long as it takes.
Points to remember: there's nothing wrong with having faults. Don't use the exercise for self-attack – hiding anger doesn't mean that you are a 'phoney', being aware that you are overweight doesn't imply that you are 'fat'.

This exercise follows on from the SELF-ASSESSMENT exercise on pp. 47-9. If you have read the intervening KNOWHOW chapter, here is an opportunity to look at your strengths and weaknesses from a different perspective. If you have not yet read these other entries, refer back if you like or just carry on.

Step 1 List your strengths and weaknesses in the following areas:

How others see me
Performance at work
Performance of daily tasks of life
Mental functioning
Sexuality
Relationships
Personal manner
Social awareness
Self-awareness
Express each strength and weakness in specific, accurate and non-critical language.

Step 2 For each weakness find an exception or corresponding strength.
Step 3 Note anything you discover or learn from this.

'Shoulds' and 'oughts'

Goal: to deal with inner critics.
Number of people: alone.
Resources: pen and paper.
Time: could take days or weeks to get a comprehensive list.
Points to remember: work from easy to difficult and try to use your phrase every time the inner critic is active. The more you can use humour to divert the 'shoulds' and 'oughts' the better.

Identifying the inner voices that tell you that you should do this and ought to be doing that can greatly increase the range of choices you have in your life. An inner voice that nags you in this way is likely to be an internalized parent or someone who was important to you as a child. Many of the 'shoulds' and 'oughts' are essential of course (see below), but some act to undermine and sabotage the strength and directness of what you think and do.

Step 1 In your daily life, begin to notice whether you have an inner voice that is very insistent about what you should or ought to do.
Step 2 Make a list of the most frequently recurring statements that the voice or voices make.
Step 3 Go through the list and evaluate them. Ask yourself if this is a redundant voice from the past that you no longer need. Or is this something that you choose to listen to?
Step 4 Learn to devise and use a short, pithy phrase to contradict or interrupt 'shoulds' or 'oughts' that you no longer need or wish to respond to. An effective phrase will be related in some way to the original need that now no longer applies. It will also remind you of the negative consequences of following the old pattern – for example, if the inner voice says that what you're doing 'ought to be better, more serious, better paid, more important', your phrase could counter this with 'I'm doing all right' or 'This is enough'.
Step 5 Use the phrase to cut out of your inner chat the 'should' or 'ought' that is sabotaging you.

Essential 'shoulds'

Some of your 'shoulds' will be legitimate rules to live by and these do not undermine or sabotage your self-esteem. If you violate or ignore a sensible 'should' then some harm may arise, either to yourself or to someone else. If you feel that you have violated a legitimate 'should', then it is appropriate to make up for the injury you have caused.

Step 1 Acknowledge the wrong to the person who was hurt and deal directly with her or him.

Step 2 Offer to recompense the harm you have caused. This should be real, not symbolic, and proportional to the harm done.

This procedure will help keep your self-esteem clear of energy-draining guilt feelings.

'Shoulds' versus 'wants'

Goal: to deal with inner critics.
Number of people: alone.
Resources: two chairs or cushions.
Time: 5-20 minutes.
Points to remember: the greatest benefit from this kind of exercise comes from vigorously letting each voice loose in a completely uncensored way. If you get stuck, leave it and come back to the situation later.

This is another way of working with 'shoulds' and contradicting inner critics if you have them. The exercise works by getting the inner voices out into the open so that you can see what they are doing and, sometimes, who they are. You may want to think of a decision you need to make and keep the dialogue specific to that issue, or have a more general discussion.

Step 1 Set up two cushions or two chairs next to each other.

Step 2 Sit on one of the cushions or chairs and let the 'shoulds' inner voice speak out freely and vigorously.

Step 3 When it has had a good run, shift to the other chair or cushion and give voice equally freely to your 'wants', whatever they are.

Step 4 When your 'wants' voice has had its say, or when the 'shoulds' voice interrupts, shift to the other chair or cushion and get back into the 'shoulds' voice.

Step 5 Continue to alternate between the two voices. Note who speaks loudest and longest, who has the best arguments, who gives in, who is stubborn and unyielding, who dominates and who needles.

Step 6 When the dialogue begins to sag, see if the two voices can negotiate some kind of agreement.

Step 7 If an agreement is reached, make a brief note of the key elements of it.

Now that you have returned from the party at the house in the meadow, you may find it useful to consider all the elements of what you saw and felt as a model or parable of your identity. The people at the party, including family and friends, amount to subdivisions of your personality. What it feels like is important. Did the characters get on well or badly with each other. Who did you get on with best; who did you dislike? Were you welcomed or rejected? How big was the house? What else did you notice? Were there any surprises? Try going back to the party and talk to the guests. See what they and you have to say to each other (see p. 202).

Goal: to reduce anxiety about making mistakes.
Number of people: alone.
Resources: none.
Time: as long as it takes.
Points to remember: very often it is through defining what is or is not a 'mistake' that supervisors, teachers and others who manage production and learning, hold and exercise their power.

Making mistakes

One of the ways in which you may undermine your self-esteem is to attach too great an importance to an error-free existence, at home or at work. While 'getting it right first time' is an admirable aim, the reality is that it is human to err. If you really need to avoid mistakes at work for technical or safety reasons, then check the control techniques that have been devised for this purpose. Paradoxically, if you give yourself permission to make mistakes, you are likely to make fewer of them because you reduce the anxiety caused by aiming for impossible perfection, and the tension caused by covering up mistakes when they do occur. To put yourself at ease with the idea that mistakes can be, if not desirable, then acceptable, try the following:

Any time you make a mistake:

Remind yourself that mistakes are an essential part of learning.
Keep a list of famous mistakes.
Remind yourself of people you know personally who have made big, or incredible or humorous mistakes.
If you have the idea that some people you live or work with never make mistakes, find a way of checking whether or not this is true.
If you are criticized for some mistake you can check whether it really matters or not by putting yourself in the other person's place. Would you object if you were them?

An expensive mistake
One of the costliest mistakes in motoring history was the 1958 Ford Edsel. Ford invested vast sums in customer research and public relations, advertising it as the 'Newest Expression of Fine Engineering'. But the project backfired. Only 35,000 cars sold (compared with 249,000 Mustangs sold in its first year of production). The investment was wasted. If you worry about your own mistakes, remember Ford's.

Goal: to build up your strengths.
Number of people: you and friends and family.
Resources: very large sheet of paper and felt pens.
Time: as long as it takes.
Points to remember: feeling good about yourself means knowing where yourstrengths lie. If people: make fun of this project ask yourself what they stand to lose if you become stronger.

Goal: to build your self-esteem.
Number of people: alone.
Resources: pen and paper or journal.
Time: as long as it takes.
Points to remember: if you can't think of any, or many entries, this is more likely to be caused by a habit of mind than a lack of strengths. Who would be threatened if you build up your strengths?

Goal: to focus on your strengths.
Number of people: alone.
Resources: quiet room and no interruptions.
Time: 30 minutes.
Points to remember: to be effective the exercise needs to be used repeatedly. Reach for the anchored feeling between challenges.

Poster of 'positives'

If your strengths are out of sight because you take them for granted or you don't believe you have many, one of the ways of bringing them out into the light of day is to make a poster that highlights your positive points.

Step 1 On a large sheet of paper write out all the things you like about yourself. It doesn't have to be a list, and some can be bigger than the others, but use the whole sheet.
Step 2 Put it up in a place where your friends or family can see it and ask them to add to it – but keep to strengths only.
Step 3 At the end of the day move it to your room and go to sleep mulling over what it says.
Step 4 Add any new strengths that you discover.

Memorable moments

Take the time to make a catalogue of your strengths under the following headings:

Qualities I like about myself.
Times I've felt loved.
Pleasant times and happy memories.
Difficulties I handled well.
Simple pleasures that are easily accessible.
Responsibilities that I shoulder successfully.
Times when I have been thanked or congratulated.

Calling up strength

Using a bit of light meditation you can learn to contradict feelings of low self-esteem. This involves building into yourself, through regular practice, a way of pushing self-doubts and excessive criticism into the background.

Step 1 Lie or sit down in your quiet place and make sure you won't be disturbed.
Step 2 Close your eyes, breathe steadily and let your body sink into a deeply relaxed state. If you are in any doubt about how to do this, see p. 192.
Step 3 When you are feeling relaxed, scan your mind for times when you were successful, confident or strong. Bring each situation to mind with all the sounds and colours that belong to it. Listen to your own voice, what you said and what others said.
Step 4 When you have got the good, strong feeling clearly in mind, anchor it to some part of your body by, for example, clasping your left shoulder or upper arm with your right hand. It doesn't matter where the feeling is anchored in your body except that there is a virtue in choosing somewhere that can be reached without unduly drawing attention to yourself!

Goal: to build self-esteem.
Number of people: alone or with a partner.
Resources: tape recorder to record the text for playback.
Time: 15-20 minutes.
Points to remember: just as other people have suggested that there is something problematic or wrong with you, through an exercise like this you can replace their suggestions with your own.

Step 5 Repeat this for several other images of strength and confidence.
Step 6 When you are ready to, open your eyes and come back out into the present moment.
Step 7 When you next feel inadequate or someone browbeats you or otherwise puts you down, repeat the anchoring movement to bring back the feeling of confidence and strength.

Treating yourself

This is a guided fantasy that you can use to reinforce your sense of yourself as a strong, valuable, well person. It does this by emphasizing that you are valuable, that you deserve the best, and that you can take care of yourself, love yourself and enjoy yourself.

Step 1 Sit or lie down in your quiet place and ensure that you won't be disturbed.
Step 2 Close your eyes and count yourself down: Ten . . . nine . . . you are sinking deeper and deeper with every breath you take . . . eight . . . seven . . . very relaxed . . . six . . . five . . . sinking deeper and deeper . . . with every breath . . . four . . . three . . . down . . . down . . . ever more relaxed . . . two . . . one . . . Now open the door or window into your own special, private, secret place that you alone can enter. Make yourself comfortable.
Step 3 Now visualize yourself taking a shower . . . Make the preparations that are familiar to you . . . the hot water on your body . . . soap . . . shampoo . . . towelling and drying . . . Now find your favourite clothes . . . they are recently washed and ironed . . . They smell fresh and sweet . . . dress in them . . . Brush your hair in your preferred style . . . Now move to the kitchen and take the ingredients for one of your favourite meals from the cupboards . . . Turn on the cooker and begin to prepare your meal . . . When it's ready . . . pour yourself a drink and eat what you have prepared . . . Notice the tastes and colours of what you are eating . . . When you have finished eating, clear away the dishes and wash them up. After you have cleared everything away, open the door and take a walk outside . . . Notice the trees and sky and the wind on your face and the traffic and other people coming and going. After a while you meet a friend . . . exchange a few words with her or him, then return to your home.
Step 4 When you are ready, take your leave of this private place to which you know you can return whenever you choose. Begin to count yourself back out again . . . one, two . . . slowly and without any hurry . . . three, four . . . up and out . . . five, six . . . coming up and into the present . . . seven, eight . . . almost there . . . nine, ten . . . Open your eyes . . . back to present time . . . here and now.

PRIORITIES

Having an accurate sense of what your priorities in life really are can be a considerable asset in planning what you are going to do and in making choices. However, because demands change from day to day, priorities can shift without us noticing. The following exercises invite you to bring your wants and needs out into the open and take a close look at them.

Identifying wants and needs

Since wants have a tendency to blur into needs, it's useful to make a distinction between them. Our needs sustain our personal and economic survival in the long term and our wants are ambitions, aspirations, yearnings, or desires that go beyond our basic needs.

Version one:
Step 1 Invite a friend to ask you repeatedly: 'What do you need ...?' followed by 'What do you want ...?'
Step 2 Reverse the roles to give your partner the same opportunity.

Version two:
Step 1 Take a pack of 20 or more file cards or small sheets of paper.
Step 2 On each card complete a phrase beginning: 'What I need is ...' Do this fast without censoring.
Step 3 Repeat on a fresh set of cards, with 'What I want is ...'
Step 4 Lay out the cards and look at them. Consider what they might be trying to tell you.

Goal: to surface and clarify your wants and needs.
Number of people: alone or with a partner.
Resources: pen and paper.
Time: 10 minutes.
Points to remember: if you keep a flow going you are likely to surface a wider range of needs and wants than if you consider them slowly. Keep up the momentum by including ridiculous items.

Sorting wants and needs

This exercise invites you to put in order of priority the wants and needs that you have identified in the previous one.

Step 1 Sort the needs and wants cards from the previous exercise into sets under the following headings:

Quality of life
Relationships
Creativity
Earning a living
Career progress
Wants or needs that really belong to someone else
Wants or needs that are caused by your early history

You may want to add categories of your own and copy some cards so that they can be in more than one set.
Step 2 Now put the cards in each category in order of priority.
Step 3 Look at the collection of cards as a whole. What does it tell you? Are there any gaps, excesses or surprises?

Goal: to clarify your priorities.
Number of people: alone or with a partner.
Resources: material from the previous exercise.
Time: as long as it takes.
Points to remember: When making this kind of mind map of yourself, comprehensiveness is more important than accuracy.

Goal: to identify your personal resources.

Number of people: alone or with a partner.

Resources: results of the previous two exercises.

Time: as long as it takes. You might want to come back to it a second or third time.

Points to remember: look for the overall pattern or trend.

Reviewing resources

This exercise enables you to assess the range of resources you can apply to the wants and needs you have identified in the last two exercises.

Step 1 Copy the chart below on to a piece of paper.

Step 2 List your most important needs and wants in the first column.

Step 3 Opposite them, make a note of your resources, including knowledge, skills, support and capacity for handling feelings. If you have extra resources not mentioned here, add another column. Knowledge and skills may be personal or professional; support can be financial, professional, or it might come from a partner or friends. Difficult feelings often accompany attempts to satisfy needs and wants and we often need resources such as counselling or training to help us handle them.

Step 4 Look at the overall pattern. How well or poorly do your resources match your needs and wants? Are there any obvious gaps? Are some needs and wants over-resourced?

Step 5 Make a note of the areas that are lacking in knowledge, skills and support or which you feel uncomfortable about.

Step 6 Take some action to improve your resources or to transfer skills from one area to another.

RESOURCES

NEEDS/WANTS	KNOWLEDGE	SKILLS	SUPPORT	FEELINGS

Goal: to identify personal priorities.
Number of people: alone or with a partner or family
Resources: pen and paper.
Time: as long as it takes.
Points to remember: accuracy and detail is less important than discovering the overall balance or lack of it.

Choices

A useful way of bringing your personal priorities to light is to make a series of maps of the choices you make in your life. A good method of doing this is to draw a pie chart – divide your circle up into 'pie slices', each representing the amount of time spent on an activity.

Here are some suggestions for useful pie charts:

How I spend my time
How we share out roles at home
How much of my life I spend in a submissive or dominant role
How much time I spend with others and how much on my own
How much time I spend doing things for others and how much of the time others do things for me

Or you could make several charts on one topic for different people – for example: 'When I am with X, how do we spend the time?'

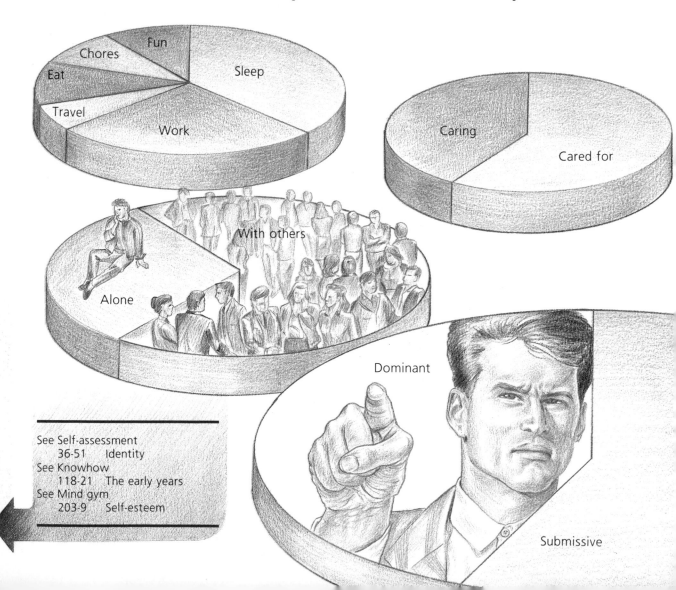

See Self-assessment
    36-51   Identity
See Knowhow
    118-21   The early years
See Mind gym
    203-9   Self-esteem

Goal: to enhance the possibilities in
your life.
Number of people: alone or with a
partner as a guide.
Resources: tape recorder and
comfortable chair or cushions.
Time: 15-20 minutes.
Points to remember: peak
experiences don't have to be
dramatic to qualify. They may have
been serene, light calm or ordinary
as well as surprising, ecstatic or
exciting.

Peak experiences

From time to time, for seconds, minutes or even days, you may slip
into a state of mind in which you feel perfectly at ease with yourself
and your surroundings. Recognizing and valuing these peak
experiences can provide a useful yardstick when you need to make
choices. Make a tape of the following sequences or ask a friend to read
it (see p. 191).

Step 1 *Sit or lie down in your quiet place and ensure that you won't be
disturbed. Make yourself comfortable.*
Step 2 *Close your eyes and count yourself down: 'Ten . . . nine . . . you are
sinking deeper and deeper with every breath you take . . . eight . . . seven . . .
very relaxed . . . six . . . five . . . sinking deeper and deeper with every breath
. . . four . . . three . . . down . . . down . . . and more relaxed . . . two . . . one
. . . Now focus on your own special secret place.*
Step 3 *Let your mind move around until it settles on an episode in your life
that stands out as a peak experience – a time when you felt well and at ease
with yourself and the world. Choose an event rather than a period of time.*
Step 4 *Bring the full intensity of the experience to mind again. Where are
you? What is happening? How did this event come to take place? How do
you feel? Accept the feeling.*
Step 5 *Now try to describe the event in the first person. 'I am standing with
George . . .', 'some camels are coming into sight over the horizon . . .'. This
will reinforce the freshness and reality of your peak experience.*
Step 6 *When you feel you have fully explored your peak experience you
can move on to another one or, alternatively, continue to* **Step 7**.
Step 7 *See if you can find a way of widening your perspective on what's
happening by stepping back a little from the event. Gently begin to evaluate
the experience without picking it to pieces. What did you value about it?
What was your contribution to it? Which of your strengths were in play?
Is there anything that would shut this out of your life now?*
Step 8 *When you are ready to . . . take your leave of this private place,
knowing that you can return whenever you choose . . . Begin to count
yourself back out again . . . one, two . . . slowly and without any hurry . . .
three, four . . . up and out . . . five, six . . . coming up and into the present
. . . seven, eight . . . almost there . . . nine, ten . . . open your eyes . . . back
to present time . . . here and now.*

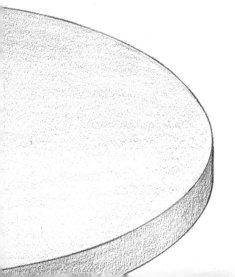

TRANSFORMATION

At the heart of the humanistic approach to the mind (see pp. 166-71) is the idea of transformation – working on yourself and making changes in your behaviour, attitudes and beliefs. Since transformation requires commitment and hard work, it presupposes a basic level of strength and well-being. A useful principle to keep in mind is that transformation that is rooted in broad physical change, often through emotional release, is likely to be deeper and more beneficial than superficial changes in lifestyle. However, moving out of an oppressive job or living arrangement may be the first very important step for some people. All the exercises in this section can be used for working on yourself and the ones that follow especially support transformation.

The need for transformation

Why should transformation or working on yourself be necessary or useful? It may be useful to have a reminder here of the three basic principles underlying the humanistic approach.

1 Unconscious motivation. Our frozen history shapes most of our behaviour.
2 Internalizing conflict. If your parents had substantial areas of unworked frozen history you will tend to act out their conflicts.
3 Reproducing conflict. You will tend, for example, to re-enact the conflict that is locked up in your frozen history in your daily life. You are likely to turn life situations into a repeat of the repressed conflicts or to choose situations that already mirror them.

Transformation implies bringing the hidden conflicts to the surface and resolving them. Two of the most fundamental ways of transforming yourself are through self-management and through recovery of your lost history. Both involve increasing your knowledge and understanding of how you became who you are.

Recovering your personal history

The point of recovering the details of the emotional landmarks in your childhood is that, as an adult, you can choose to make a different survival decision from the one that you made as a child (see pp. 18-35). Broadly, there are two approaches. One is to research what you and others know about the external facts and events of your history, perhaps by asking for information and feedback. The other is to seek the hidden knowledge and feelings within you that are usually inaccessible. Both are essential and they complement each other.

Goal: to map the extent of your self-knowledge.
Number of people: alone.
Resources: large sheet of paper and pens.
Time: as long as it takes.
Points to remember: you may need to come back to this map several times to add new material as it comes to light.

Window on yourself

The underlying issues of transformation and working on yourself can be seen very clearly through the window diagram below.

Step 1 Draw a version of this 'window' on a large sheet of paper.
Step 2 Begin to write down which elements of your behaviour belong in each area.
1 Open. Aspects of your behaviour that you and others know about, where you are most open.
2 Hidden. Aspects of your behaviour that you are aware of but that you keep hidden from others.
3 Blind. Aspects of your behaviour that others know about but that you remain unaware of. Other people's criticisms often point to these areas.
4 Unknown. Aspects of your behaviour of which both you and others are unaware.

The purpose of this exercise is to raise your awareness of these aspects of your behavior and its history. It is obviously not feasible to complete all four squares. However, the aim of transformation is to reduce the amount that is blind, hidden or unknown.

KNOWN TO OTHERS   UNKNOWN TO OTHERS

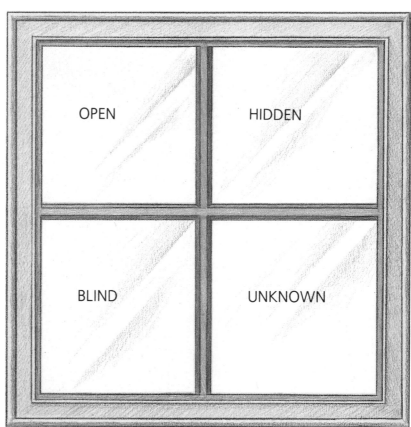

KNOWN TO SELF   OPEN   HIDDEN

UNKNOWN TO SELF   BLIND   UNKNOWN

Goal: to map the landmarks in your life.
Number of people: alone or with others doing the exercise for themselves.
Resources: a large sheet of paper, coloured pencils, pens or crayons.
Time: from an hour minimum to a whole evening.
Points to remember: mark periods when you can't remember what happened as a definite phase.

Life line

A very useful way of recovering your personal history is to draw a 'life line', a single line that represents the whole of your life from conception to the present day.

Step 1 Take a large sheet of paper and draw a point to mark the time of your conception.
Step 2 Now draw a line to represent the period from your conception to your birth and label it with your birth date.
Step 3 Continue to add short lengths of line and xs and notes to represent all the significant events of your life. Continue up to the present day.
Step 4 Perhaps using a different colour, add the names of the people who had the most influence on you, and how.
Step 5 Add another strand to represent your key interests in your early life and show how they changed with time.
Step 6 Review the whole life line as it becomes more complete and check that your key decisions are included.
Step 7 Hang the life line on the wall and add to it over the coming few weeks.
Step 8 What reactions or feelings do you have about your life line? What does it show? Decisive choosing? Drifting? Or control by other people? How important has your work been? How important have your friends been? What are the patterns or trends?

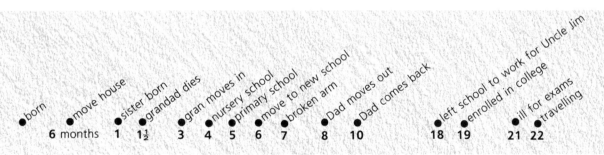

born • move house • sister born • grandad dies • gran moves in • nursery school • primary school • move to new school • broken arm • Dad moves out • Dad comes back • left school to work for Uncle Jim • enrolled in college • ill for exams • travelling

6 months   1   1½   3   4   5   6   7   8   10   18   19   21   22

Goal: to deal with difficult memories.
Number of people: alone or with a partner.
Resources: none.
Time: as long as it takes.
Points to remember: the early history has often been forgotten because it felt bad, so be prepared for a surge of feelings in this exercise.

Dealing with old pain

This exercise offers a way of beginning to deal with difficult or painful episodes from your past that at the moment you need to keep hidden. The aim is to go back intentionally to the event and recover a difficult memory, to see what you did about it at the time, how you coped, what your survival decision was, and then to make a new decision. The extent to which you can resolve this through a book alone may be limited, but if you are prepared to be patient and try it several times (see Learning from experience, p. 239), you will be able to get it to work for you.

Step 1 Scan your experience for a painful or difficult life event from your history that has echoes in, or is set off by, events in the present.
Step 2 Use literal description (see above) to re-enter the key scene.
Step 3 When the situation is fully in your mind, accept any feeling

Goal: to recover memories.
Number of people: alone.
Resources: none.
Time: as long as it takes.
Points to remember: this exercise will help to recover whatever was there to be recovered. If this is your first experience of recovering memories in this way, don't be surprised if a surge of feeling accompanies your description. If it feels too much, open your eyes and come out.

Recovering memories

If there is an episode from your childhood that you wish to recall more clearly, you can bring it into clearer focus by using literal description, as in *Step 3*.

Step 1 Sit comfortably and close your eyes. Pay attention to your breathing until you feel relaxed.

Step 2 Let the scene or episode come into your mind.

Step 3 When the scene is there with its people, colour, sounds and atmosphere, begin to describe it in fine detail in the present tense. 'I am standing in the doorway looking out into the garden. A car drives up and stops . . .' Continue, including everyone who is present, what they say, what you say, what you feel, how you react and how they react. Recreate the movements, smells, sound, music and tastes.

Step 4 When you have taken the scene as far as you want to, let it fade away and open your eyes.

Step 5 Describe in the present tense what is happening now. 'I am sitting here looking across the room. On the wall, I see a photograph and beside it there is a lamp and I can hear the birds singing outside the window . . .' (See Attention, p. 192.)

Jo moves in — bought apartment — new job — in hospital for three months — long holiday — July Nina born — Christmas with Nick and Sarah — New job — Jo in accident — financial crisis — Nina's first birthday
24   27 28   31   32

that may arise and try to see what you are doing to survive the experience. For example, the seven-year-old who repeatedly attempts and fails to get her parents' attention may survive this disappointment by deciding that it is best to read books and play on her own.

Step 4 When you have a good sense of the scene, open your eyes and come out into the present, accepting any feelings that may still be around.

Step 5 Consider when and how the way you survived then, in the past, is being re-enacted in the present.

Step 6 Make a new decision about how you choose to behave now. The new decision should acknowledge the history you carry but should put it firmly in the past.

Step 7 Consider how you can put this new decision into practice in your daily life.

EMOTIONAL INTELLIGENCE

Goal: to look at how you handle anger and fear.
Number of people: alone.
Resources: pen and paper.
Time: 15-30 minutes.
Points to remember: it is much more fruitful to look at *how* you handle these feelings. 'Why' questions tend to feed intellectual speculation.

To develop our emotional intelligence we need to learn how to handle our feelings. This can mean getting more closely in touch with fear, anger and grief, for example, and being able to express them appropriately at the right moment.

Identifying anger and fear

How you handle feelings of anger and fear influences how you live your life and who you choose to spend it with. We often gradually limit our world to one where anger and fear never arise. But if a lot of the fear and anger that we are trying to avoid actually belong to us personally, if they are entrenched in our past, then we may be unduly narrowing and limiting our intelligence.

Step 1 Take a pen and piece of paper and try to answer the following questions.

Step 2 When, where or how am I angry?

Step 3 When, where or how am I afraid?

Step 4 When, or with whom, do I feel safe enough to express anger?

Step 5 When, or with whom, do I feel safe enough to express fear?

Step 6 What messages do I have within myself about expressing anger or fear?

Step 7 What happens in my body when I feel angry or afraid?

Step 8 In what physical ways do I let off steam or run away?

Step 9 Whose example am I following?

Step 10 Do I know anyone who handles anger or fear better?

Step 11 What alternative could I try?

Step 12 Now look in close-up at a specific example of how you handle anger and fear. Seeing how you handle them can lead to useful modifications.

Step 13 What are the actions or words of the other person if someone else is involved?

Step 14 What is your verbal response?

Step 15 What is your body language saying?

Step 16 What are you feeling? What do you really want to say?

Step 17 Where do you keep the feeling if you have to hold on to it?

Step 18 How could you have been more assertive?

Goal: to pinpoint the connections between present-day and childhood emotion.
Number of people: alone.
Resources: paper and pen.
Time: one hour or more.
Points to remember: childhood anger is often related to interference with choice; childhood feelings of fear are often related to not understanding what was going on; and childhood grief is often related to a loss or lack of love.

Trigger wheel of emotions

Present-time emotions are often caused by a mixture of present and past events. Situations today that in some way mirror key events from the past may reactivate old feelings. This 'trigger wheel' will help you to examine your emotional life and see how much of what you feel today comes from the past.

Step 1 Copy the trigger wheel on to a large sheet of paper.
Step 2 In the inner circle fill in the people and situations that triggered the three kinds of emotion in you as a child – fear, anger and grief.
Step 3 In the outer circle fill in the people and situations that trigger the three kinds of emotion in you today.
Both circles may include friends, family and colleagues. Some may appear in two or more sections.
Step 4 Note and mark any links between the inner and outer circles.
Step 5 Note which emotions seem to cause you the most difficulty.
Step 6 Look at the situations in the outer circle. Is the actual situation now a reasonable cause for the emotion or is it reminding you of past occasions when you felt like that?
Step 7 Now look at your capacity to cope with what the trigger wheel shows. What resources do you have or can you create to deal with your own emotions? These may include a support group, a training course or a counsellor (see pp. 246-7).

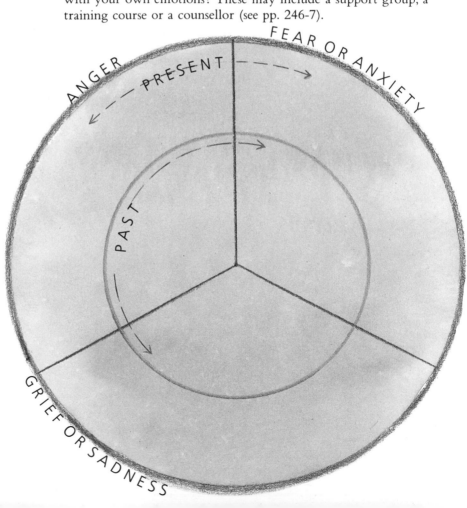

Goal: to surface hidden grief.
Number of people: alone or with a partner.
Resources: pen and paper.
Time: as long as it takes.
Points to remember: the healing that comes from dipping gently and intentionally into hidden grief may expand your intelligence in unsuspected ways.

Separation

Separation or death long ago can lead to a hidden sense of loss or resentment that colours present relationships and limits intelligent choice. You can check whether you are carrying significant amounts of hidden feelings through exploring lost love. Surfacing and releasing the hidden feelings may open up your intelligence, especially in areas around present-time separations, departures and endings.

Step 1 See if you can bring to mind a situation or person who has now gone from your life and left you feeling angry or resentful, or to whom you were never able to say goodbye.

Step 2 Write a letter detailing the things you wanted to say, but couldn't. Say how much you miss her or him and how much you would like to see them again or how angry you feel about their departure.

Step 3 Notice how you feel as you do this.

Step 4 If you begin to feel upset, this may point to the existence of an unworked area of lost love.

Step 5 You now have a choice. If the emotion feels a bit much, you can decide to note this underlying feeling and come out of it by, say, concentrating on the colours in the room (see Coming out, p. 192). If you feel you would like to continue, you can decide to accept the feeling, stay with it and let it run its healing course.

Referred from p. 198 (Life as a landscape)
The size, position, colouring, and especially the attention you gave to yourself as an image in the landscape may be a useful guide to your sense of self.

Goal: to begin to deal with unfinished business with your parents.
Number of people: alone.
Resources: none.
Time: 20-30 minutes.
Points to remember: this is not intended as a rehearsal for an actual dialogue. Because a high proportion of our learning arises through imitation, any tension between yourself and your parents is likely to mean that you are disowning the part of your intelligence that you associate with them.

Talking to parents

There are many reasons why, as children and later as adults, communication with our parents may have been unsatisfactory. The balance of power favours our parents. They had more experience of the world and they were legally responsible for our welfare. But as children we were unlikely to have had an accurate grasp of the emotional, economic and social pressures on our parents. At both infant and adolescent stages, learning to function separately from our parents, while at the same time being dependent on them, leads to tension and misunderstanding. The emotional wear and tear of parent-child conflicts, however unexpressed, can mean that love and mutual respect often get pushed into the background. This exercise provides an opportunity for you to begin to explore the 'unfinished business' you may have with your parents. Record the following text.

Step 1 Sit or lie down in your quiet place and ensure that you won't be disturbed.

Step 2 Close your eyes and count yourself down: 'Ten . . . nine . . . you are sinking deeper and deeper with every breath you take . . . eight . . . seven . . . very relaxed . . . six . . . five . . . sinking deeper and deeper with every breath . . . four . . . three . . . down . . . down . . . ever more relaxed . . . two . . . one . . . Now open the door or window into your own special, private, secret place that you alone can enter. Make yourself comfortable.

Step 3 Visualize one of your parents sitting facing you. Notice how your father or mother is sitting, what she or he is wearing, how you feel about her or him. Be completely honest and say all the things you wanted to say but never could. Hold nothing back. Tell your parent of your resentment, anger and fear and also of your love and appreciation. Be aware of any feelings that come up. Accept them but keep going with what you have to say. If very powerful emotions begin to come up, you can choose to come back into the here and now and return to the exercise another day. Or you can choose to stay with your feelings.

Step 4 Now be your parent. Respond to what you have said. Tell your child how you feel about it and how it was for you.

Step 5 Swap again. What do you want to say now? How do you respond to what your parent told you? How do you feel towards her or him?

Step 6 Now tell your parent what you need from the relationship.

Step 7 Become the parent again. How do you respond? What do you want from the child?

Step 8 Swap again and respond. Now tell your parent some things you appreciate about her or him.

Step 9 Swap and respond as parent. Tell the child things you appreciate about her or him.

Step 10 Let the dialogue run free. Go on to finish in a minute. Have parent and child each make one last statement. If you could never say anything else, what would it be?

Step 11 Return to the here and now (see p.192).

Goal: to learn to deal with anger, fear and grief.

Number of people: alone or with a partner.

Resources: a soundproof room and a number of large, soft cushions.

Time: as long as it takes.

Points to remember: the aim of this exercise is physical change – the release, discharge or healing of distress emotions – and the subsequent insight that comes through access to the intelligence it frees.

Handling anger, fear and grief

Becoming more emotionally competent means being able to express feelings such as these in appropriate circumstances, to hold on to them for a while when necessary and to tolerate other people expressing them. This is a task that takes time and is best undertaken in the company of someone who is already emotionally competent (see p. 186). However, given these limitations, if you feel ready for it you can begin to gain some experience of working with your feelings. This means expressing them appropriately in harmless ways. The underlying issue is to explore how far any strong feelings or lack of feeling in the present are entangled with remnants of your early history (see Self-defence, pp. 146-7). This exploration involves getting in touch with these feelings. If you can't get this process to work abandon it for the moment and come back to it again later.

The following suggestions presume that you have a private, reasonably soundproof room where you will not be disturbed. They also presume that the object of any of your strong feeling is not present. And they are not a rehearsal for dumping your feelings on to anyone at any time. They are your feelings (see pp. 148-51).

Anger

Choose a large cushion or pillow or a mattress and explore your angry feelings by vigorously pounding, kicking, pummelling or wringing them while making loud sounds. See if you can find a single phrase that encapsulates what you feel, such as 'leave me alone', or 'No, no, no'. The more your body movements resemble those of a champion tennis player's service (try using a tennis racket!), the more your body will be able to heal its angry feelings and the more likely it is that insight into the source of them will emerge.

Fear

If you occasionally feel afraid, anxious or panicky, you can help your body deal with these feelings and gain insight into what is driving them, through light shaking and trembling. These are the body's in-built mechanisms for dealing with and healing fear. The aim is to learn to let your body be taken over by the shaking while remaining aware that you are still in charge. To begin with you may feel more frightened but eventually the fear will subside, leaving you more relaxed and often with an insight into the origins of the fear.

Grief

Loss, bereavement, separation and disappointment all pose a challenge to the healing capacities of the human body. When you are alone and free of social constraints, you can express sadness through weeping. A major loss or disappointment will emerge as crying, and deep grief as sobbing. If you feel any of these versions of grief, give yourself permission to cry to whatever depth and length of time your body needs. Trust your body. When it has done what it needs to do it will stop. If you feel it's been going on too long, you can decide to stop at any time using the coming out exercise on p. 192.

PHYSICAL INTELLIGENCE

We are often not aware of the self-healing, self-balancing capacity of the body. Broadening and deepening this physical intelligence, through vision, touch and hearing, can open up a completely new and rich dimension in your daily life.

Colour sensitivity

Goal: to increase awareness of colour.
Number of people: alone.
Time: as often as you can.
Points to remember: your colour vision and colour perception can be greatly increased by drawing or painting in colour.

For a whole day notice a single colour, such as red. Look for the different tones of it. Make a collection of different red objects or images and arrange them in a display. Notice how inadequate words are for colours. How many names can you think of for red? Notice how subtle colour is and how rarely primary colours occur. On other days give your attention to, say, green or yellow or orange. As it gets dark in the evening, notice the difference between the daylight and the artificial light, and how colours change – how some glow and others fade almost to grey.

Pause and notice

Goal: to increase awareness of sound.
Number of people: alone.
Time: anytime.
Points to remember: try this in the places and times where your behaviour is most habitual - say, on regular journeys and meal times.

From time to time during the day stop what you are doing and listen to the sounds in the room, the sounds from nearby, the sounds from far away. Try this especially in places that you go to every day – in the street, the supermarket, the subway, the bus, the park. Notice how uncommon silence is. Try the same exercise for touch, smell and taste.

Mystery tour

Goal: to increase awareness of touch.
Number of people: you and a partner.
Resources: a variety of household materials and an apron or overall.
Time: 10-15 minutes to prepare, 5 minutes for the experience.
Points to remember: unusual juxtapositions are likely to give the most interesting results.

Take turns with someone else to arrange an experience for each other that explores the nature of touch. With the other person out of the room, prepare a variety of experiences – dry, wet, cold, hot, soft, hard, rough, smooth, solid, liquid. Blindfold your partner and lead her or him from one item to another. When your partner has had enough time to explore the different sensations, ask her or him to take you through the same exercise.

Blind meal

Goal: to increase awareness of taste and smell.
Number of people: you and a partner.
Resources: a wide variety of food.
Time: as long as it takes.
Points to remember: this exercise may reawaken childhood feeding experiences. Stay with it and see what you learn.

Take turns with a partner to feed each other. First put on a blindfold and let your partner feed you with a variety of foods. Then swap roles. If possible, make sure that neither of you knows what the range of foods is going to be for this extraordinary meal. This exercise also works very well without the blindfold.

Goal: to identify body tension.
Number of people: alone or with a partner.
Resources: an alarm clock.
Time: five or six interruptions during a morning would work very well.
Points to remember: if your body is preoccupied with holding on to tension, then your physical intelligence will be that much less open and responsive.

Stop and freeze

Physical tension often points to areas of unresolved conflict. By becoming more aware of specific areas of tension we can not only begin to identify emotional trouble spots but also prevent many aches and pains and improve our physical competence.

Step 1 Arrange to have your routine at home interrupted from time to time, either by your partner or by using an alarm clock set far enough ahead for you to forget that it's running.

Step 2 When you get the signal, pause in whatever you are doing and freeze motionless.

Step 3 While frozen, notice where your attention is. How much body awareness do you have at this point? Look at your posture, your eyes, feet, back, legs. Check to see where you might be holding tension.

Step 4 Exaggerate the posture and the tension, then let go of them.

Step 5 Pause and freeze again. This time contradict the posture or the tension – see if you can do the opposite.

Step 6 Repeat at intervals.

Physical tension
A history of painful or uncomfortable experiences, stored as disturbing memories, is often kept quiet through muscular tension. Freeing your activity from time to time can give an opportunity to notice how much inner tension inhibits or drives what you do.

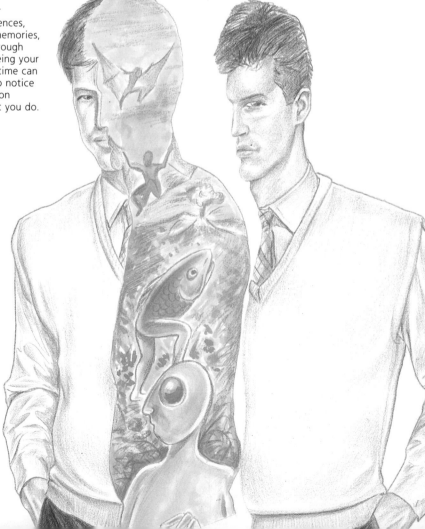

Goal: to increase awareness of breathing.
Number of people: alone.
Time: 2-3 minutes.
Points to remember: avoid over-breathing. It shifts the balance of carbon dioxide in the blood with unpleasant results.

Goal: to relax deeply.
Number of people: alone.
Time: 10-15 minutes maximum.
Points to remember: if you are not used to it the very deep state of relaxation that an exercise like this can produce may set free a variety of hidden feelings. Stay with them to see what there is to be learned from them.

Goal: to relax.
Number of people: alone.
Time: 1-2 minutes.
Points to remember: if you feel tense, an effective way of giving your body the chance to rest and recuperate is to acknowledge it and exaggerate the tension before letting it go.

Goal: to make friends with your body.
Number of people: alone.
Time: 5 minutes.
Points to remember: good access to your body signals enhances your intelligence through making it more likely that you will stay healthy.

Belly breathing

Rapid, shallow breathing opens you to anxiety and panic. If you aren't already familiar with it, learn to breathe at will with your abdomen. Breathing very deeply means exhaling fully. Try yelling to get the air out – a 'ha', 'ha' sound will help. Try taking an enormous breath, holding it for as long as is comfortable and then letting it out very slowly (see pp. 190-1).

Deep breathing

This exercise provides a good way to slow down and relax.

Step 1 Close your eyes and lean back into a comfortable chair that supports your body and head.
Step 2 Let your attention rest on your breathing.
Step 3 As you begin to settle, slowly and effortlessly, visualize breathing slowly in and then out a cloud of solid objects. Start with gold fish and the water they swim in, then move on to dry autumn leaves. Follow this with rain, sand from the sea shore, fire and flames, ocean waves, and fast-moving traffic (breathe in the lane coming towards you and breathe out the lane going away from you). Continue with trees, camels, the hot wind of the desert, steam, a whole beach full of pebbles, all the people from a crowded street.
Step 4 Then lastly, breathe in the air of the room you're in.
Step 5 Open your eyes.

Squeeze and stretch

This is another approach to relaxation.

Step 1 Contract your body into a very small tight space – you could squeeze yourself into a corner of the room. Keep breathing.
Step 2 Clench every part of you.
Step 3 Hold this position until it is unbearable, then slowly let it reverse until your body is open and stretched out flat on the floor.
Step 4 Open your mouth. Breathe. Put out your tongue. Breathe.
Step 5 Repeat.

Running commentary on your body

The more we ignore the messages from our body the more we are setting ourselves up for ailments and burn-out. Paying more attention to your body enhances your intelligence.

Step 1 For a period of 5 minutes verbalize every inner bodily reaction, every little twinge, sensation, feeling, discomfort or pain.
Step 2 Now talk to your body, tell it how you feel about it.
Step 3 Let it speak in turn. What does it want to say to you?

INTUITIVE INTELLIGENCE

Usually, our conscious awareness absorbs the world bit by bit, in chunks, naming and parking each part as it is recognized. This is the 'interpreter' function of the mind, which constantly and persistently seeks meaning in its step-by-step bites of life (see p. 133). But intuition, which provides direct access to the bodymind's non-verbal processing that precedes the interpreter, gives a different quality of knowledge. It comes in the form of hunches, gut feelings and inspired guesses. All the exercises in this chapter will enhance your intuitive intelligence by putting you in closer touch with what you feel. You gain access to your intuition by paying attention to your whole experience all at once. Generally this means learning to outwit, distract or reduce the activity of your interpreter, the bit of you that constantly asks 'why?' or 'what does this mean?'.

Goal: to enhance your intuition.
Number of people: alone.
Resources: an alarm clock or an excellent alternative is a tape with music that slowly fades at the end of the meditation period.
Time: 5-10 minutes to begin with, up to a maximum of 20 minutes.
Points to remember: this is a powerful and an effective way of opening to whatever there is for you to find. Treat the meditation with respect and it will respect you.

Meditation

Learning how to meditate and practising regularly is one of the most important ways of working with your mind and of developing your intuition. Cooling down the mind's activities means that its contents become fewer, the background more silent and the thoughts, ideas, feelings and intuitions that do arise become more susceptible to choice. Try it for yourself.

Step 1 Sit down in a comfortable chair where your body is well supported, in a room where you will not be interrupted. Set a timer to ring very quietly after 5-10 minutes or put on your tape.
Step 2 Close your eyes. Let any discomforts or twitches settle. After a few moments you will become aware of thoughts, images, ideas.
Step 3 Into the gentle whirl of thoughts, introduce the sound of the word 'shairing'. Let it chime lightly and completely effortlessly, like a bell.
Step 4 Eventually, you will find the sound has slipped away to become replaced by thoughts. When you notice that this has happened, lightly and effortlessly introduce the silent word again. The whole process should be effortless and without any sense of criticism or strain. Continue this process until the timer rings and then stop.
Step 5 After perhaps 30 seconds or a minute slowly open your eyes. Take your time as you move back into activity.

Dreamwork

One of the most important sources of insight into yourself is dreaming. Dreaming would appear to give more or less direct access to the activities of your non-verbal mind modules while your 'interpreter' is inactive (see Map of the mind, pp. 134-5). The practice of guided meditation appears to show that a form of dreaming is readily accessible during waking consciousness and dreamwork builds on this to encourage re-entering dreams. This involves continuing their action, inviting the characters to relate to each other and generally becoming used to using dreams as a way of extending your intuitive intelligence.

Goal: to enhance your intuitive intelligence.
Number of people: alone.
Resources: notebook or journal or tape recorder.
Time: as long as it takes.
Points to remember: dreams convey 'the unknown to you and others'. For that reason what they convey may seem unreasonable or crazy, but it may nonetheless be what you need to know.

Step 1 Keep a dreambook and a pen at your bedside. Or use a small tape recorder. This gives better recall because you can learn to recount your dream into it while you are still not quite awake.

Step 2 Play back the tape of your dream or read through your description of it.

Step 3 Take yourself back into the dream situation and continue it. See what the characters or objects in the dream want to say to each other and you. Let the dream unfold and transform in any way it wants.

Step 4 Look at the dream and any later development of it as a whole, and avoid getting lost in detail. Dreams make a lot of sense as symbols or maps of your present preoccupations or state of life.

What is the predominant feeling of the dream?

How does it relate to your present life situation? Dreams very often convey feelings such as apprehension, delight, awe, pleasure, humiliation, disappointment or disquiet that have been denied.

What might the dream be saying to you?

Does it point to something you are avoiding, or keeping quiet, or don't want to look at?

Step 5 Make a note of your conclusions.

Mind maps

A quite different but complementary strategy for enhancing your intuition is to learn to use the Mind maps, introduced by British writer and teacher Tony Buzan, as a way of visualizing processes, problems, situations, choices or patterns of behaviour as a whole. Mind maps allow for both sequential and parallel ways of organizing knowledge and information so that you can see the topic, or concern or process altogether.

Step 1 Take a large sheet of paper. In the centre of it draw an egg shape and inside it write the name of the process you want to map. It's a good idea to use a soft pencil so that you can easily rub out and change the map as you go along.

Step 2 For each of the sub-sections or subdivisions that you may be aware of, add a line from the central shape and add the name of the subdivision in one word.

Step 3 After you have done this, add another series of single lines and single words to represent the next layers of the map.

Step 4 Continue to explore the whole field that you want to map in this way.

Step 5 At the point where the map is fairly complete, it may be useful to make connections between the different parts of it in a colour, or to colour in some areas of the map to indicate the main groupings.

Step 6 Step back and look at the whole map. What does it tell you?

Goal: to increase your intuition.
Number of people: alone or with others.
Resources: sheet of paper, soft pencils, eraser and coloured pens.
Time: as long as it takes.
Points to remember: keep to the discipline of one word to a line, and a change of direction for a new idea or label.

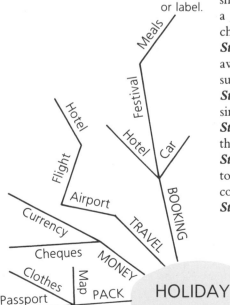

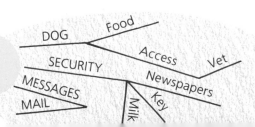

INTELLECTUAL INTELLIGENCE

In Western developed countries a minority of people, mostly men, have been educated to develop their intellect. The vast majority, including many women, are denied full intellectual development. However, stripped of its professional mystique, intellectual analysis, decision-making and problem-solving are accessible to us all.

Absorb and recall

One of the fundamental intellectual skills is to absorb large amounts of written or visual information and to gather the key elements of it into a brief summary, both accurately and comprehensibly. There is no mystery attached to this, anyone can do it. If it is new to you, try devising a summary of the contents of this book in two ways.

Step 1 Imagine you are phoning a friend who wants to include a description of this book in a newsletter. You have two minutes in which to tell her about it. Use a tape recorder to record what you say. Don't use notes, but do try it several times until you have a version you are happy with.

Step 2 Now try a different approach. Using the book to remind you, make a list of headings for the summary. Take as long as you like.

Step 3 Using these notes, write out the summary in five minutes flat.

Step 4 Now return to your recording and write it out. Don't edit it, but leave out any 'ums' and 'ers'.

Step 5 Compare the two summaries. You may find, as some people do, that the process of transcribing your speech suddenly makes you an articulate and engaging writer.

Reasoned discussion

Another important intellectual ability is to recognize and construct reasoned arguments. There are three kinds of argument. One involves taking a situation and seeking the causes of it. The second means looking at a series of events and reasoning through what the outcome will be. The third is to look at the sequence of argument to see if it contains any logical errors. We all do these all the time but we are usually not aware of how we do them. To bring the 'how' into view, try identifying and then listing the arguments put forward in *The Mind Gymnasium*.

Step 1 Seek the arguments that take a set of initial premises – if this . . . and this . . . and this . . . and this . . . then that and that is likely to happen. Then make a list of the key points.

Step 2 Seek the arguments that look at an end result and try to work back to how it happened. Make a list of the key points.

Step 3 Look at both sets of arguments. Note how they have become an analysis of the connections between the different strands in the book. See if you can spot any logical errors in them.

Goal: to enhance your thinking skills.
Number of people: alone.
Resources: pen and paper.
Time: as indicated.
Points to remember: set aside any ideas you may have about this exercise requiring special talent. It only needs practice and, if you can find it, good advice on your progress.

Goal: to enhance thinking skills.
Number of people: alone.
Resources: pen and paper.
Time: as long as it takes to make progress.
Points to remember: this is a first step. When you can recognize the kinds of argument, you will be in a better position to construct them for yourself and to know which type you need.

Goal: to enhance your thinking skills.
Number of people: alone.
Resources: pen and paper.
Time: as long as it takes.
Points to remember: sieving out the three basic stages of comparison is an important part of making choices.

Goal: to enhance problem-solving skills.
Number of people: alone or with others.
Resources: will depend on the nature of the problem but pen and paper at least.
Time: as long as it takes.
Points to remember: use this checklist as a skeleton for developing your own personalized version that suits your own specific needs.

Comparisons

Another form of intellectual activity involves making comparisons – seeing how a situation or series of proposals differ and how they are similar. The virtue of making comparisons is that it highlights the special qualities of each issue, item, proposition or choice.

Step 1 Look at the three main chapters in *The Mind Gymnasium* and compare them with each other.
Step 2 Make a note of the distinctive qualities of each chapter.
Step 3 Make a note of how they are similar and different.
Step 4 What conclusion do you reach?

Problem-solving

A branch of creativity that draws on the intellectual capacities of your mind is problem-solving. George Polya, an American mathematician, has put forward a very good recipe for problem-solving.

Step 1 *Understanding the problem*
What is it that you don't know? What information do you have? What is the aim? Is it possible to satisfy the aim?
Is the aim important enough or too trivial to justify looking for a solution? Is the aim beside the point, out of date or contradictory? Can you draw a diagram of the problem? Can you divide the aim into distinct sections and write them down?
Step 2 *Devising a plan*
Now try to find the connections between what you do know and what you don't know. You may need to sidestep the main problem temporarily if there is no other way forward. Aim to reach a plan of the solution. Have you seen the problem anywhere before – or the same problem in a slightly different form?
Do you know a related problem, or a similar, more specific or more general version of the problem?
Do any useful rules of thumb come to mind?
Could you restate the problem? How many different ways?
Are you developing some kind of map of the problem?
Could you solve a part of the problem?
Could you keep part of the aim and drop the rest of it?
Are you using all of what you know?
Are you keeping the whole of the aim fully in mind?
Step 3 *Carrying out the plan*
If your plan has several stages, can you check that each stage is being correctly implemented before moving on?
Are arrangements in place to carry out this check?
Step 4 *Looking back*
Examine the solution when it has been implemented; you may find a new and better solution.
Can you check that the solution fits the aim?
How will you know that this check is valid?
Can you use the solution for some other problem?

YOU AND OTHERS

None of us exists in isolation, and living and working with other people bring into play all the layers of your mind, from the deepest to the most superficial. In the exercises that follow, you will find two broad approaches. The first involves disentangling your personal history from that of other people – knowing where you stop and where they begin. The other consists of filling up the gaps in your relationship skills. The two are closely connected and working on one tends to lead to an improvement in the other.

CONFLICT

It seems to me that conflict is basic to life, it comes with growth. Dealing with it badly leads to escalation and polarization; dealing with it well can open up unsuspected creativity. Here are some guidelines for dealing with conflict that I have found useful. They are based on the map in the Knowhow chapter (see pp. 186-7).

Working on conflict
Whether you are already in conflict or you can see it coming you may find the following suggestions helpful.
1 Actively balance your own needs, feelings and rights with what is being asked of you.
2 Maintain clean communication. Avoid blame, don't criticize. Validate other people, they have needs and anxieties too. Do give feedback 'what I see you doing is . . .' Acknowledge feelings, 'I feel uncomfortable about . . .' 'I'm unhappy with . . .' 'I feel confused about . . .' (See I see, I imagine, I feel, p. 234.)
3 Give attention to the process. How are you and others 'running' the conflict? Are you or others tired? Is there an undercurrent of unacknowledged distress that is feeding the conflict by squeezing out creativity? Is this really your dispute?
4 If you have been energetic, zealous or highly committed to the issue in question, 'back off' – try to put some time and/or distance between yourself and the issue.
5 If you have been inclined to stand back from the conflict by avoiding it or accommodating other people's wishes, raise the energy of your input a bit. Make a virtue of the fact that your involvement is still lower than others. Draw attention to the process – interrupt it: 'Hang on a minute . . . What's happening here? What's going on? What are we trying to do?'
6 Do you assume that conflict is best dealt with by 'smoothing over' disputes, by being compliant and 'giving in' to others' demands? Or do you actively collude with others to keep off touchy subjects? If so you leave yourself vulnerable to 'going off at the deep end' if you find that your goodwill is being exploited. Instead of giving in, try 'backing off' and ask yourself what am I getting out of this? Is there a way of doing what is being asked and respecting my own needs?

Goal: to improve your handling of conflict.
Number of people: two ore more.
Resources: none.
Time: as long as it takes.
Points to remember: improving your emotional competence is an essential part of improving conflict resolution.

7 Do you assume that conflict inevitably means competing with or manipulating others to get what you want or to get your own way? If so you leave yourself vulnerable to being excluded or rejected as hostile and aggressive. As well as pursuing your own interests, try 'backing off' a bit. Put yourself in the other person's shoes, how would you feel if you were them? Is there some way in which you can have what you want without exploiting other people?

8 Do you feel compelled to face up to conflict only in certain ways? Developing your emotional competence and encouraging people you live or work with to do the same will greatly extend your repertoire of ways of handling conflict.

CONFIDENCE

Self-esteem and confidence are closely connected. If you feel good about yourself and value your abilities, this is likely to be reflected in a confident, assertive approach to other people and situations. Improving your self-esteem is an important part of building your confidence, but there are a number of exercises that specifically help to promote confident self-presentation.

Active listening

Listening brings out the qualities of your mind like few other activities. Active listening means being fully there for the other person. It means suspending judgments, opinions and your own inner chat so that you hear what is being said with a minimum of interference.

Goal: to improve your listening skills.
Number of people: yourself and one other.
Resources: none.
Time: build up from 5 minutes each to longer stretches of listening.
Points to remember: the relative formality of this exercise is essential – when it becomes a conversation, development of skills is likely to have stopped.

Step 1 Ask a friend to join you in improving your listening skills. Tell your partner that it won't be a conversation, that you want her or him to talk while you practise listening.

Step 2 Ask your partner to tell you about some episode from her or his life, something a little difficult or problematic. Don't join in the conversation, just listen. Keep good eye contact, but don't stare. Give light, wide attention so that you can notice what your partner's body may be saying, too. Let go of any opinions, judgments or interpretations that you may have about what she or he is saying. Limit what you say, too. Ask your partner to expand on what she or he is saying, reflect back to your partner what you believe she or he means and check that you have understood if you are in any doubt.

Step 3 Now give your partner equal time if she or he wants it.

Goal: to build your confidence.
Number of people: yourself and one other.
Resources: none.
Time: try a series of short practices.
Points to remember: once you pick it up, changing the quality of your eye contact will rapidly alter the way you come over to people, because you will seem more 'present' for them.

Eye contact

Perhaps the single most effective way in which you signal your self-confidence to other people is through the quality of your eye contact. Staring at the floor or ceiling limits the amount of contact between you and other people.

Step 1 Check the quality of your eye contact.
How often do you avoid people's eyes when talking to them?
Do you do it with everyone or just certain people?
Which people?
Can you see how you do it?
Some people have difficulty in talking or thinking while maintaining intermittent eye contact. Are you one of them?
Step 2 If you feel that your eye contact is uncertain, and also feel up to taking the risk, ask your partner or a friend to mimic how they see you doing it.
Step 3 Ask your friends to help you practise meeting their eyes.
Step 4 After you have had some practice, ask them to give you feedback on how you come over to them now.

Goal: to build your confidence.
Number of people: alone or with a partner.
Resources: none.
Time: as long as it takes.
Points to remember: keep a moderate, steady tone of voice when delivering your request.

Making requests

An adaptation of the exercise (See False assumptions, p. 235.) can be used to help make it more feasible to ask for what you want.

Step 1 When you need to ask someone for something, separate what you see, think or perceive from what you feel and what you want, such as: 'I see that I am carrying out the garbage again. I feel that my goodwill is being exploited. From now on I want you to take an equal share of the messy jobs.'
Step 2 When you have developed a request, test it against the following list:
Can you get the other person to agree to a convenient time and place to hear your request?
Can you reduce your request to a size that will minimize resistance?
Is your request simple enough, involving not more than, say, two actions that can be easily remembered?
Will you avoid blaming or attacking the other person?
Will you be specific enough, giving times and dates?
Are you asking for a change of attitude? If so, bear in mind that a change of behaviour is much more feasible.
Step 3 When you have got a clear request worked out, try it on the people who can give you what you want.

Goal: to build your confidence.
Number of people: alone.
Resources: paper and pens.
Time: as long as it takes.
Points to remember: confidence is often related to self-esteem, if you often tend to feel unconfident see the self-esteem exercises on pp. 203-9.

Powerful people

Your confidence is likely to vary according to the power you give to other people, as well as the power that is vested in them. It's easy to under- or over-estimate your own and other people's power.

Step 1 Make a list of the people you know for whom confidence or lack of it is an issue.
Step 2 Look at each person in turn, then at yourself in terms of their:

Decision-making power – can they hire and fire and dispose of resources? Are they accessible?
Information power – do they own information, such as books or publications, have sole access to databases, or to wide-ranging contacts.
Dependence power – how strong are your obligations to them?
Expert power – are they publicly licensed holders of qualifications, knowledge, skills or duties?
Personal power – are they spontaneous, authentic, honest, open, trusting and relatively free from distress?
Status power – are they famous, wealthy or the heads of organizations?
Reward and punishment power – do they use the stick and carrot to ensure compliance?
Synergy (growth-oriented power) – do they facilitate the needs and interests of others.

Step 3 Draw a pie chart for each person including yourself, divided according to your view of these subdivisions of their power.
Step 4 Look at how your personal pie chart matches those of other people. Does the size of each 'good' or 'poor' correspond with how confident you feel when relating to them?
Step 5 Look at what action you can take to improve any imbalance of power between you and the other people.

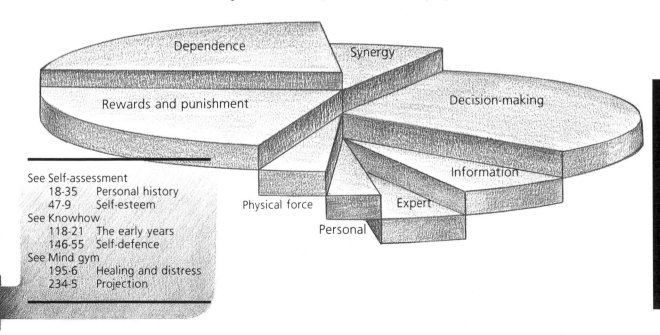

Goal: to respond well to criticism.
Number of people: alone.
Resources: may need pen and paper.
Time: as long as it takes.
Points to remember: if you avoid criticism by over-using any of these strategies, you run the risk of cutting yourself off from vital information.

Responding to criticism

Criticism can be difficult, if it comes in an offensive or resistible form, and it may be that the critic is dealing with what they feel by projecting the blame or complaint on to the nearest person. But criticism may also contain vital information. If you find yourself being criticized, try one of these strategies for dealing with it.

Strategy 1 – Acknowledging
Agree with the critic. The purpose of this is to stop or interrupt the criticism. Use this when the criticism seems plausible.
1 Tell them that they are right.
2 Reflect back to them what you hear them saying.
3 If it is appropriate, thank them for their criticism.
4 If it is appropriate, explain yourself, but without apologizing.

Strategy 2 – Token agreement
Use this when the criticism is neither constructive nor accurate.
1 Agree in part with what they say.
2 Agree that it is possible that what they say could be correct.
3 Agree that in principle what they say is correct.

Strategy 3 – Probing
If the criticism is vague, ask for clarification. What do they intend? What do they mean? What are they trying to say?

Strategy 4 – Delay
It takes time to register what you are feeling. Don't be hurried into any of these responses. Reserve the right to respond later.

PROJECTION

Projection means disowning some bit of ourselves that we don't accept, by attaching it to other people. We then come to believe that they possess this quality, which in fact belongs to us.

Goal: to avoid projecting on to others.
Number of people: two or more.
Resources: none.
Time: as often as necessary.
Points to remember: if you do this diligently you will begin to pick up the shadow of both your own and other people's frozen history. Bear in mind that today, as in the past, you and other people are trying to survive in your own way, as best you can.

I see, I imagine, I feel

Learning to recognize and withdraw projections on to those around you are possibly the most important gifts you have to give people. A good way of approaching this task is to learn to separate what you see happening – the observation – from any ideas or fantasies you have about it and, in turn, to distinguish both of these from any feelings. This means other people do not need to be defensive.

Step 1 Engage the support of your partner or of a friend and explain what you will be trying to do (ideally they take a turn as well).
Step 2 At any point where there is a flurry of uncertainty about the other person's actions or motivations check each of the three stages. For example: 'I notice that when you came home you went straight out into the garden and stood staring into space (I see). I imagine you are upset about something (I imagine) and I feel anxious that you might take it out on me' (I feel).

Goal: to deal with projection.
Number of people: alone.
Resources: none.
Time: not relevant.
Points to remember: this simple check can have very profound effects. Use it with people who you can't stand or you have a crush on, with anyone who sets off an extreme reaction, either positive or negative.

False assumptions

Use this exercise when you notice your feelings being triggered by someone else's presence.

Step 1 Ask yourself 'Who does this person remind me of? How do they remind me? What do I want to say to the person they bring to mind? And how do I feel about that?'

Step 2 Ask yourself 'How is this person actually different from the person they remind me of?' Make a clear distinction between the person in the present and the past memory. 'This woman reminds me of the shopkeeper who accused me of stealing when I was little. But I know she is a different person with a different history, and she hasn't accused me of stealing but just looks a bit cross.'

SELF-DISCLOSURE

Self-disclosure is an essential part of our connections with others because it gives them more insight into our own minds. An appropriate amount of self-disclosure usually leads to warmer relationships. Too little may leave other people with the impression that you are secretive or have something to hide from them; too much can be a burden, if it is not in some way reciprocal.

Goal: to ease self disclosure between friends and partners.
Number of people: two or more.
Resources: none.
Time: should be agreed in advance.
Points to remember: this apparently innocuous exercise has a lot of potential for fun and openness, but it may be a little risky.

Flipping the truth

This exercise can lead to a surprising increase in openness between you and your partner or friends. It also makes an excellent party game. With your partner or a friend or friends agree to put aside a set amount of time – a few minutes or an hour – to say the opposite of what you believe to be true. Track the undulations of thought and feeling very exactly, but say the reverse of what is true. For example: 'I'm not at all interested in what we're going to have for lunch. I'm delighted that you've thrown away the magazine I was reading. I'm perfectly happy to work through the night, and all next weekend.'

Goal: to increase your capacity for self-disclosure.
Number of people: two.
Resources: none.
Time: up to 30 minutes each.
Points to remember: several short periods may be better than one long one each. Take equal time even if it means silence.

Clearing the air

Quite often a disagreement or row reveals that there are areas of misunderstanding or confusion between you and your partner or colleagues. In an emotionally charged discussion, people often exaggerate or become defensive. However, there can often be an urgent need to deal with misunderstandings when making decisions or responding to some demand or other. If you have been involved in a messy disagreement, then this is a good way of cleaning up afterwards.

Step 1 After a 'cooling off' period, find a place to meet with each other away from interruptions or other people.
Step 2 Person One takes a timed period to say what he or she resents and appreciates about the other person. Try to keep both negatives and positives in balance with each other.
Step 3 Person Two then does the same.

RELATIONSHIPS

In the past, when social arrangements were more static, marital and working relationships had a fixed quality. But with a faster rate of change it is becoming increasingly important to assess the ways in which we relate to other people continuously.

Goal: to ask for help.
Number of people: whoever you can trust to support you.
Time: for as long as it seems useful.
Points to remember: feedback is something that you may choose to accept or to ignore.

Friendly reminders

If you are attempting to change your mind, it's a pity to assume that unless you do it all on your own it won't somehow be valid. Enlist the help of your partner or friends.

Step 1 Make a mini-contract with them in which they agree to help you identify or interrupt unaware behaviour. For example: 'If you see me biting my lower lip, will you ask me what I'm thinking?'
Step 2 Ask for feedback: 'Will you keep an eye on me in this situation and afterwards tell me how good my eye contact was?'

Goal: to find a true perspective on your relationships.
Number of people: alone.
Resources: pen and paper.
Time: as long as it takes.
Points to remember: look for a pattern in your relationships – what is over-represented or under-represented?

Relationship styles (see Communication, pp. 180-1)
In your relationships with other people you can be:
A friend – supportive or cathartic
An adviser – prescriptive or informative
A critic – confronting or catalytic

Step 1 For the significant people in your life, draw a pie chart showing how you relate to each of them, and how they relate to you.
Step 2 Compare the different pie charts. What do they tell you about your relationships?

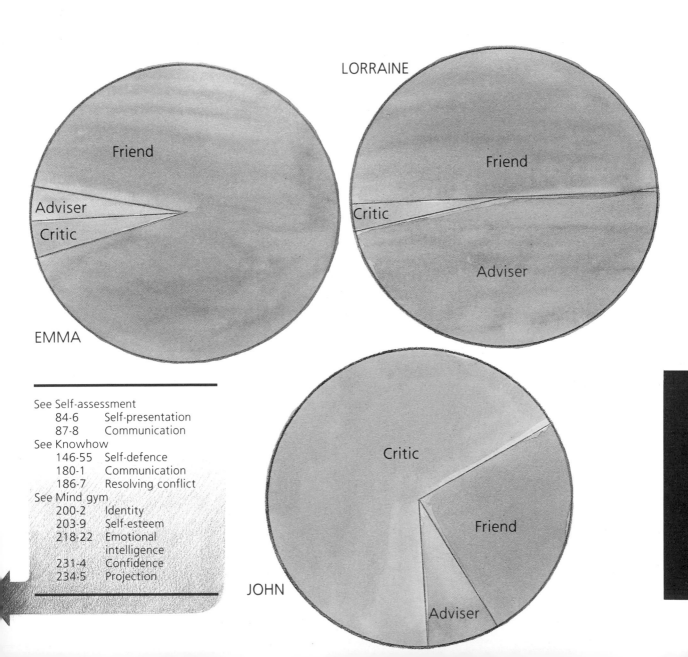

Goal: to assess how a relationship works.
Number of people: two or more.
Resources: sound recorder and video camera and recorder.
Time: try an hour.
Points to remember: giving attention to how you interact is likely to be more useful than discussing what is said.

Record and playback

If you have access to a tape recorder or a video recorder and camera, then a very powerful way of looking at your relationships is to record yourselves and then play back the tape and review what you see or hear later on.

Step 1 Avoid prejudging what you are going to look for. Run a tape long enough so that you get the chance to forget that it's on.
Step 2 Review the tape and assess yourself before hearing what your partner or friend has to say. Look for body language, tone of voice or hesitations, Who was dominant or submissive? Was there a balance between your contributions? When you have given your own reactions, ask for feedback from your friend.

Goal: to learn how to use feedback.
Number of people: two or more.
Resources: none.
Time: not relevant.
Points to remember: feedback is a powerful form of communication and it should not be given unless it is asked for.

Giving and receiving feedback

While conversation and discussion are indispensable to human communication, both tend to become competitive, with each person striving to make their point. From time to time a slightly more formal approach can be very useful.

Asking for feedback Specify what you want your partner or friend to look for and when; also what if anything is off-limits.
Giving feedback Distinguish between positives and negatives and give the positives first. Make sure that giving negative feedback does not become an excuse for dumping negative feelings. You can avoid this by distinguishing between the person and their behaviour and by making a clear distinction between what you see, imagine and feel (see p. 234).
Receiving feedback Remember, feedback is for your use. What you make of it is your business. Do not respond or justify yourself. Thank your partner or friend and move on.

SYNERGY

Synergy – high-energy collaboration between people living or working with each other – brings to mind such words as intensive, active, creative, flexible, responsive, reciprocal and power-sharing. Moving towards synergy and away from competitiveness, withdrawal, accommodation, smoothing and compromise, involves becoming more emotionally competent and learning to share power. But it is now beginning to fall within our reach. In practical terms, achieving synergy means constantly giving attention to process (how things are done) as well as to content or production (what is done).

Goal: effective, shared decision-making and problem-solving.
Number of people: group.
Resources: writing materials, charts.
Time: as long as it takes.
Points to remember: shared decision-making demands a reasonable degree of emotional competence in all involved.

Learning from experience

'Learning from experience' is a recipe for moving any group towards synergy and power-sharing. You can apply it, for example, to a department, a small company, a store, a neighbourhood action group, a flat-share or a co-operative. We all learn from experience, but in human affairs the content of what we have to say often obscures the underlying dynamics of what is happening. This exercise will help you to improve group decision-making, problem-solving and productivity, by concentrating on the process stage by stage, instead of on the detail of what you are producing, selling, deciding or initiating.

1 *Current procedure*

Take a close look at what usually happens in your organization. Do you keep your future PLANS separate from both your ACTIONS – such as supplying goods and/or services – and from your REVIEW of the result? Are there three stages? Do you have a review stage at all?

Action 2
Does the action phase squeeze out the review and plan phases? Are those concerned with action included in review and planning? Is the action undermined by doubts about usefulness and quality?

Plan 1
Is everyone involved in the action invited to contribute to future planning? Are there taboos against certain kinds of problem? Are all discussions about new action kept public and open?

Review 3
Is the review phase usually informal, casual and private, involving only a few members of the group? Are the review and planning stages indistinguishable?

2 *How to make it work*

When you are joining a new project or re-organizing or initiating one, introduce the following steps and the checklist below. You'll find that it will gradually give a clear understandable shape to your working process. It's important to ensure that everyone is synchronized – confusion will arise at meetings if some people are planning while others are reviewing.

Review 3

Begin by airing your feelings about the last action phase. Take it in turns and ensure that everyone has their say. Collect all the information before evaluating what went wrong and what went right. Before you go on to the planning stage, check that you are satisfied that the review phase is complete.

Action 2

During your new action phase try to exclude all planning and review. This may mean setting up a system of data collection as a basis for the review phase. If problems arise you may need to pause for a fresh review and plan before resuming the action.

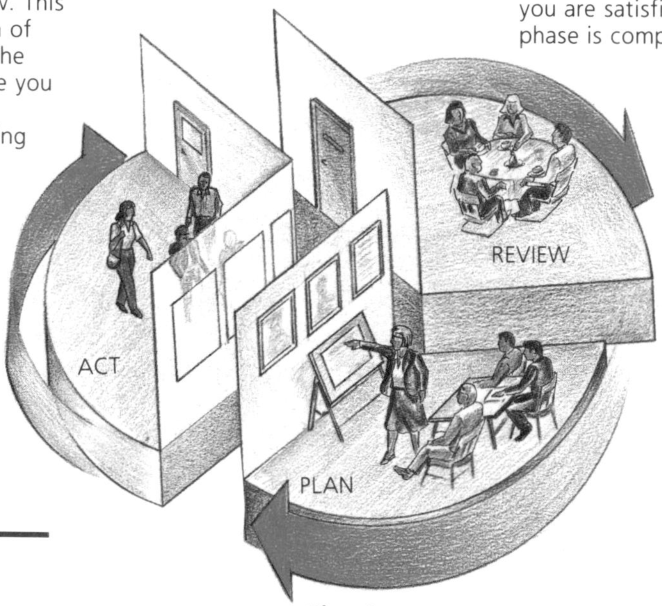

REVIEW

ACT

PLAN

Plan 1

Consider all the possible courses of action, bearing in mind what your previous review phases revealed. You may want to subject each plan to a short plan, action, review test before making a final decision.

Power sharing

Learning from experience is an excellent way of moving towards power sharing. The benefits, however, are greatly enhanced if the level of emotional competence (see p. 186) in all the members of your group is developing simultaneously. Feelings and emotions that arise in the process may need to be worked through and issues around power will also need to be acknowledged and resolved as the gaps between boss or expert, and employee or lay person are bridged, abolished or dissolved. Collusion and self-deception will certainly creep in, but once they are recognized, they can be minimized. If it is to work well, everyone will need to internalize the method fully and to contribute to the decision-making processes that relate to their own responsibilities or obligations. (See Conflict resolution, pp.186-7.)

3 *Checks and counterchecks*

To ensure the best possible results, it is essential to introduce a series of checks into each review phase. These are questions that everyone considers individually before and during the review sessions. Anyone can call for a further check when they personally see the need for one.

Use the following checklist and add others according to specific needs.

Responsibility: Has everyone internalized the whole action, plan, review process?
Collusion: Is there a secret agreement between some members to avoid looking at 'touchy' issues?
Distress: Is emotional distress distorting the process? Are resources available to help resolve it, such as support groups or training?
Range: Have enough different plans of action and approaches been thoroughly explored?
Perspective: Is there a good balance between immediate needs and long-term aims?
Timing: Is the cycle being repeated often enough? Is too much time being spent in one phase?
Contributions: Who talks? Who stays silent? (See Work without experts, pp. 184-5.)
Agreement: Is the process meeting people's needs and staying within the initial agreement?
Chaos: Is the need for a certain amount of chaos in reviews recognized, to avoid finishing prematurely?
Discrimination: Is the planned action sexist, racist, ageist or in any way discriminatory?

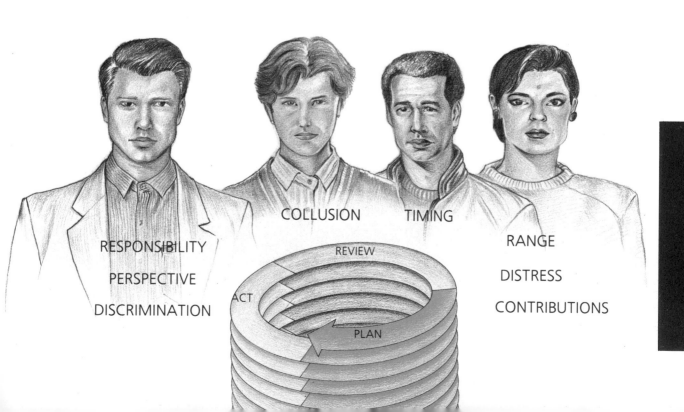

RESPONSIBILITY
PERSPECTIVE
DISCRIMINATION

COLLUSION   TIMING

RANGE
DISTRESS
CONTRIBUTIONS

REVIEW
ACT
PLAN

YOU AND THE PLANET

The technology that brings us the image of the whole earth from space also brings images of earthquakes, floods, hurricanes and terrorism. A special corner of your mind is likely to be devoted to your reactions to world events such as these, and especially the threat of nuclear or ecological disaster. If you are not aware of these elements in your mind, this is probably because they often include feelings of powerlessness and despair. The numbness that results from keeping these feelings quiet is one of the things that keeps us separate from each other. Recognizing and beginning to dispel this numbness opens your mind to the people around you and also the populations over the horizon. It also makes it easier to see what you can do to lessen the crisis. If you don't feel ready to look at this aspect of your mind yet, that's fine. The following exercises will give you a taste of what's involved. Several come from 'Despair and Empowerment' workshops offered by Joanna Macy, an American peace worker.

OUR FRAGILE FUTURE

Working with the pain you may feel about the dangers of the world we live in can provoke difficult feelings. If you are in doubt about how to handle them, leave it until you have more confidence in your ability to work with your mind. Either way, 'Coming out' (see p. 192) and the 'Deep breathing' exercise (see p. 225) are useful whenever there is a danger of your attention becoming swamped by despair. These exercises involve: gradually approaching and experiencing the denied feelings that otherwise may leave us numb, acknowledging them as a human and wholesome response, and realizing that it is precisely these feelings that provide the deepest connections with other people.

Goal: to enhance your ability to deal with despair and oppression.
Number of people: two or more.
Resources: writing materials.
Time: as long as it takes.
Points to remember: you may find that difficult feelings come up, but they will give rise to increased awareness.

Confession of sorrows

Write out, or share verbally with a partner or friend, a comprehensive catalogue of sorrows about the world as you experience it.
And/or
Use a clipboard, dress like a market researcher, stop people in the street, and say you're doing research or a survey. Ask them what troubles them about the world today. Use active listening and help them to talk. Don't give your opinion at any stage.
And/or
Repeat the following statements several times in a deliberately confident, cheery way that contradicts what you know to be true.
'All of the nuclear plants ever built are very safe. Nothing could happen to them that will ever affect my children, born or unborn.'
'Looking at the smile of a tiny infant, who could imagine anyone ever flying a mission that would put even one baby at risk.'
'World leaders are psychologically sophisticated and possess all the facts. We can trust them to ensure that the world is kept safe for all.'
'Look at the blue sky up there and the green of the grass and the flowers and all the leaves on the trees. Nobody would do anything to put all of that at risk.'

Creative writing

After surfacing something of your depth of concern for the planetary crisis that we are involved in, move on to begin to consider what can be done about it. Here is a well-tried way of approaching this next stage. Take your pen and freely, spontaneously and without censoring take ten minutes to complete this sentence. If you are inclined to, make it a poem, a song or a story. 'Out of this dark and painful stuff my task is to . . .'

Experiencing your power

Version 1

Sit down and make yourself comfortable. Close your eyes and go inwards. As you settle down, visualize the times, recently or in the distant past, when you were personally powerful and effective. Bring to mind the situations, places and times, the people who were there, how you felt, what you said and the strategies that you used. See if you can anchor the feeling so that it is accessible when you need it.

Version 2

Take a large sheet of paper and make a drawing of your power. Let it take any shape or form that works for you.

Talking to a child in the future

Sit down in a comfortable place. Close your eyes and go in. Breathe. Become still. Let yourself drift off into the future. Visualize a child of, say, thirty, fifty, or a hundred years hence. Let her or him come into your mind. Perhaps its your grandchild. Tell her or him about what you are doing to make it a better world.

Obstacles to change

This can be done alone but it works better if you do it with a partner or several others.

Take time to write out a list of all the obstacles that you are aware of that seem to prevent you from making changes in the world around you. Make it a comprehensive list. Don't hold back on the scale of the obstacles you face in bringing about the changes you would like to see. When everyone has completed their list, slowly and with full attention to what you are doing, take it in turns to set light to the piece of paper your obstacles are written on and burn it to a cinder.

In touch with life (The Cradling)

This guided meditation increases our awareness of the state of the planet and what it means to be human, and it is also deeply relaxing. You need two or more people and a tape recorder to record the text below. Use a gentle matter-of-fact tone and leave a space after each statement. For the exercise, lie down and close your eyes. Your partner sits beside you, starts the tape and takes one of your hands. Then follow the tape. As you relax, give your attention to the point of contact between you. At the end of the tape, rewind it, change places and then run it again for your partner.

Goal: to increase your connection with humanity and the planet.
Number of people: two.
Resources: a tape recorder.
Time: about an hour.
Points to remember: this is a powerful exercise both when you are the active and the passive partner.

Gently lift your partner's hand.
Cradle it.
Look at it as though you were a
visitor from another world.
This hand is unique in the cosmos.
Its special shape has evolved
across aeons of time.
Feel the weight of it.
Flex the elbow and wrist and
fingers.
See how the joints are hinged to
enable it to move.
Feel the heat in it, the same
temperature as every other human
on this planet.
Feel the texture of the skin beneath
your touch. It's growing.
It can be so easily hurt and yet it
heals itself through bruising and
scarring.
This hand can act.
It is capable of the most
intricately precise movements and
actions.
And it can hold.
It can caress and soothe and
comfort.
Lay the hand down and move to
your partner's leg.

Lift the leg and foot.
Feel the weight of it,
the solidity of bone and sinew.
Bend the knee and ankle.
Notice the strength and the
flexibility.
It allows this person to walk or run
or climb or jump or kick.
Or just stand.
It was once little and uncertain,
proud to be able to stand alone.
Now it has stamina that sustains it
for hours of movement.
And it knows what it is to be tired.
Put it down very gently and move
to the other leg.

This companion leg was also once
small and unsure of itself.
Now, for all its strength, it is
easily hurt, broken, crushed.
It has no armour, just skin that can
tear and burn, bones that can
fracture.
This leg has many years of life
ahead of it.
It will take your partner on
countless journeys,
both risky and routine.

Lay the leg down with the
gentleness due to one of the most
precious objects in the cosmos.
Move to your partner's other hand.
Take hold of it and lift it.
Observe the difference. It's unique.
Turn it over.
Feel the life in it,
the glow of cells burning oxygen.
Notice its vulnerability,
how easily it can be hurt,
the countless millions of nerve
endings that bring sensitivity
but also openness to pain.
Notice how much you want this
hand and all other hands like it to
stay whole in the time that they
have left to them.
This hand has many tasks still to
undertake -
writing,
making music,
making love,
making lunch.
This hand could be the one that
comforts you in the last moments of
your life.
Put it gently down and move to
your
partner's head.

Place a hand under your partner's
neck and another under the skull.

Now slowly lift your partner's head.
Cradle it gently.
What you hold in your hand is
perhaps the most extraordinary
object in the whole universe.
A living human head of a person
from Planet Earth,
more complex, more intricate and
more subtle than any other known
object,
a treasure chest of plans, ideas,
faces and feelings,
symphonies and songs.
The head you hold in your hands is
the flower of human evolution,
it's a blossom with a strong
perfume,
the human mind.
This mind can choose and love and
understand,
and if it has been hurt, it can lose
sight of how wonderful it is.
In the life of this planet the work
of this mind has barely begun.
In the days to come do what you can
to ensure that it can continue what
it has to do,
so that the children of this mind
and their children's children
live to see and feel and make love
and imagine and hope as we have
done.

Feel the weight of this head in your
hands.
It could be a Chinese farmer
or a Brazilian midwife
or an American general
or an African teacher.
It could be yours.

Lay your partner's head down
gently,
sit back for a moment and stay with
your sense of awe and wonder.

RESOURCES

UK
Association of Humanistic
Psychology
12 Southcote Road
Tufnell Park
London N19 5BJ
01 607 7852
*A supportive network for people
exploring personal growth. Operates
a referrals service.*

Human Potential Resource Group
Department of Educational Studies
University of Surrey
Guildford GU2 5XH
0583 509191
*Long-established growth centre.
Offers a large number of humanistic
psychology based courses covering
a wide range of interests.*
Personal effectiveness programme
    Co-counselling, assertiveness
    training, stress management
Professional development
    6 Category Intervention Analysis,
    Dimensions of Facilitator Style,
Self- and Peer-Assessment
Management and Training
    Leadership skills, team-building,
    organizational dynamics, stress
    management, appraisal, self-
    presentation, vision-building,
    women in management.

Parent Network
44-46 Caversham Rd
London NW5 2DS
01 485 8535
*Aims to improve the quality of life
and relationships for children and
their parents. Education for
parenting through a national
network of parent support groups.*

Brunel Management Programme
Brunel University
Uxbridge
Middlesex
0895 56461 x 215
*Stress at work, courses in
interpersonal skills in management.*

Metanoia
13 North Common Road
Ealing Common
London W5
01 579 2505

*Mostly professional training but
courses on health and healing,
female sexuality, and burnout.*

Caer Centre for Alternative
Education and Research
Rosemerryn
Lamorna
Penzance
Cornwall TR19 6BN
0736 810 530

Findhorn Foundation
Cluny Hill College
Forres IU36 0RD
Scotland
0309 73655

Gerda Boyesen Centre for
    Biodynamic Psychology and
    Psychotherapy
Acacia House
Centre Avenue
Acton Park
London W3 7JX

Human Potential Research Project
Department of Educational Studies
University of Surrey
Guildford
Surrey GU2 5XH
0483 509191

Redwood Women's Training
Association
Invergarry
Kitlings Lane
Walton-on-the-Hill
Stafford
ST7 0LE
0785 662823
*Sexuality courses for women.
Assertiveness courses for women
and men.*

Open Centre
188 Old Street
London EC1V 9BP
*Wide range of workshops, including
bioenergetics, psychodrama, gestalt,
intuitive massage, primal integration
and encounter.*

Karuna
Curtisknowle House
Curtisknowle
Totnes
Devon TQ9 7JX
054 882 583

Spectrum
49 Croftdown Rd
Gospel Oak
London NW5 1EL
01 485 5259

Institute of Psychosynthesis
1 Cambridge Gate
Regent's Park
London NW1 4JN
01 486 2588
*Short courses for the integration of
transpersonal and personal
psychology*

Women's Therapy Centre
6 Manor Gardens
Holloway
London N7 6LA
01 263 6200

Changes Bookshop
242 Belsize Road
Kilburn
London NW6 3BT
01 328 5161
*Specialist psychology bookseller
with an excellent stock of foreign
books. Mail order.*

Wentworth Institute
68a Church Road
Richmond
Surrey
01 940 6181
*Co-counselling, psychotherapy, new
paradigm research.*

Unit for Research into Changing
Institutions
115 Poplar High Street
London E14 0AE
01 987 3600
*Researches ways to implement and
advance the capacity of society and
its associated institutions to adapt
to change in a functional and
realistic manner.*

London Co-counselling Community
17 Lisburne Road
Hampstead
London NW3 2NS
01 485 0005
*Offers courses in the fundamentals
of co-counselling.*

Co-counselling Phoenix
Change Strategies
5 Victoria Rd
Sheffield S10 2DJ
Publishes a directory of UK co-counselling teachers. Contact for fundamentals of co-counselling.

Co-counselling International (CCI)
International liaison between autonomous co-counselling communities. Source of contact for co-counselling courses and teachers.

USA
Carol Driscoll
144 Smith St, Middletown
Connecticut 06457
203 632 1327

UK
Jean Trewick
Westerley, Prestwick Lane,
Chiddingfold
Surrey GU8 4XW
042 879 2882

CANADA
Stuart Hill,
Associate Professor,
P.O. Box 191
McDonald College
Lakeshore Rd
Ste. Anne Bellevue
Quebec. H9X 1C0

AUSTRALIA
Kay Barr
26 Surrey Rd
Wilson
Perth
Western Australia
458 1200

Re-evaluation Counselling
Has a bigger membership than CCI co-counselling. Dozens of local organizers in 14 countries. For details contact:
International Reference Person
719 Second Avenue
North Seattle
Wa 98109
206 284 0311
Re-evaluation counselling has very centralized organization. Apart from this it is in most respects identical to co-counselling, which split off from it over a decade ago.

Colleges offering contract learning or independent study or where student autonomy is high

UK
School for Independent Study
North East London Polytechnic
Holbrook Rd
London E15 3EA
01 590 7722
Offers a variety of opportunities for do-it-yourself courses where you can design your own study programme and choose your own subject or combination of subjects including psychology and counselling. BA, BSc, MA by Independent Study.

USA
Alverno College
3401 South 39th St
Milwaukee
Wi. 53215
Women's college with a feminist approach.

Antioch University West
3663 Sacramento Street
San Francisco
Calif. 94118
415 931 6170
Humanistic education.

California Institute of Integral studies
3494 21st St
San Francisco
Calif. 94110
415 648 1489
Post graduate courses in humanistic psychology.

Teacher's College
Columbia University
Box 50
New York
NY10027
212 678 3760
Independent study for adults.

Evergreen State College
Olympia
Wa. 98505
202 866 6300

The Fielding Institute
2112 Santa Barbara St
Calif. 93105
805 678 1099

Union Graduate School
PO Box 85315
Cincinatti
Ohio 45201
513 621 6444

Temple University
Department of Education
Broad Street and Montgomery
Avenue
Philadelphia
Penn 19122

Whatcom Community College
5217 Northwest Rd
Bellingham
Wa. 98226

CANADA
Department of Adult Education
Ontario Institute for Studies in Education
225 Bloor St West
Toronto
Canada

AUSTRALIA
Tertiary Education Resource Centre,
University of New South Wales
Kensington,
NSW
Australia

RECOMMENDED READING

Banton, Michael (1965) *Roles: An Introduction to the Study of Human Relations*, Tavistock

Boadella, David (1987) *Lifestreams*, RKP

Buzan, Tony (1982) *Use Your Head*, Ariel Books

Bailey, Diane and Parkinson, Tony (1987) *Be Fair*, Institute of Personnel Management
(A useful collection of ways to eliminate discrimination in employment.)

Chorover, Stephan L. (1980) *From Genesis to Genocide: the meaning of human nature and the power of behaviour control*, MIT Press
(An excellent account of who benefits and who suffers from theories about human nature.)

Chamberlain, David B. (1983) *Consciousness at Birth: a review of the empirical evidence*, Chamberlain Publications, San Diego
(A very extensive account of how newborn babies love, understand and choose).

Coover, Virginia (1981) *Resource manual for a living revolution*, New Society Publishers
(A full and well worked out account of how our own personal development is related to the organizations and societies we live in. Many useful exercises based on counselling and groupwork principles and hints on running successful meetings.)

de Mause, Lloyd (1982) *Foundations of Psychohistory*, Creative Books Inc
(A fascinating presentation of how different styles of child-rearing shape historical change. Closely argued linking of traumatic foetal and birth experience with the group fantasies of politics and religion that we use to keep them quiet.)
ed. (1980) *History of Childhood*, Souvenir Press
(Harrowing but essential account of the evolution of the parent-child relationship.)

Dickson, Anne (1983) *A Woman in Her Own Right*, Quartet Books
(An excellent handbook on how to be more assertive. Down to earth and practical. Based on extensive experience of teaching assertiveness and training others to teach it.)
(1985) *The Mirror Within*, Quartet Books
(Also excellent, a no-nonsense guide to women's sexuality.)

Erikson, Erik H. (1971) *Identity: Youth and Crisis*

Ernst, Sheila and Goodison, Lucy (1981) *In Our Own Hands: a book of self-help therapy*, Women's Press
(An indispensable compendium of different approaches to self-help therapy. Written by women for women, its underlying political orientation underlines selected approaches but remains generous to others.)

Fodor, Nandor (1949) *The Search for the Beloved: A clinical investigation of the trauma of birth and pre-natal conditioning*, University Books
(Possibly the earliest comprehensive theoretical presentation of the effects of foetal and birth trauma. Despite some psychoanalytic fantasies on dreams, this book is a cornerstone of psychology that has yet to be absorbed by the mainstream.)

Fromm, Eric (1963) *The Art of Loving*, Unwin Books (1966) *Fear of Freedom*, RKP

Gazzaniga, Michael (1985) *The Social Brain: discovering the networks of the mind*, Basic Books
(A friendly narrative that shows how brain science is largely a matter of opportunity and personality. Threaded through the experiments and meetings is a model of human functioning that shows how the structure of the brain drives social behaviour.)

Grof, Stanislav (1985) *Beyond the Brain: birth, death and transcendence in psychotherapy*, State University of New York Press
(Solid and detailed presentation of Grof's three decades of research into how birth experiences influence an individual's development. Although this research is valuable in suggesting that formative influences begin earlier than imagined, Grof also reaches conclusions about transcendent realms that, for me, remain unconvincing.)

Hampden-Turner, Charles (1981) *Maps of the Mind*, Mitchell Beazley
(This is a comprehensive compendium of sixty different approaches to the mind. It is succinct and dense, but a very useful and accessible survey.)

Heron, John (1971-83) *Experience and Method*
Catharsis in Human Development
Experiential Research – A new Paradigm Assessment
Revisited Empirical Validity in Experiential Research
Co-counselling
Dimensions of Facilitator Style
Six Category Intervention Analysis
Education of the Affect
University of Surrey Human Potential Research Project
(A selection of papers in pamphlet form reporting on ten years of very fruitful research into facilitation, interpersonal skills and self-help therapy.)

Hodson, Phillip (1984) *Men . . . an investigation into the emotional male*, Ariel Books

Jackins, Harvey (1977) *The Human Side of Human Beings: the theory of re-evaluation counselling*, Rational Island Publishers
(A very accessible exposition of how human intelligence is limited by early distress and what can be done about it.)

Janov, Arthur (1983) *Imprints: the lifelong effects of the birth experience*, Coward-McCann

Jung, Carl G. (1975) *The Portable Jung*, Viking Press

Kaplan, J. Louise (1978) *Oneness and Separateness: from infant to individual*, Simon and Schuster
(Although it is psychoanalytically based and asserts that life begins at birth, this is otherwise a reliable account of early psychological development.)

Keleman, Stanley (1979) *Somatic Reality: bodily experience and emotional truth*, Center Press Berkeley
(An almost poetic description of the process of physical transformation. Very good about the middle

ground where old ways of behaving have become obsolete but the new has not yet fully emerged.)

Lake, Frank *Studies in Constricted Confusion: exploration of a pre- and peri-natal paradigm* (Hard to read but fascinating notes of another pioneer of birth and foetal development.)

Lincoln, Yvonna S. and Guba, Egon G. (1985) *Naturalistic Enquiry*, Sage Publications (A very academic but sound book about the philosophy and practice of co-operative research.)

Macy, Joanna Rogers (1983) *Despair and Empowerment in the Nuclear Age* (A comprehensive approach to contemporary spirituality that links the personal and the political in a common action approach. Unique and excellent.)

Maslow, A. H. (1987) *Motivation and personality* (3rd ed), Harper and Row (Maslow is the main originator of humanistic psychology; this new edition of his classic work has been completely updated by four of his colleagues and is excellent.)

McKay, Michael and Fanning, Peter (1987) *Self-Esteem*, New Harbinger (A very thorough and systematic compilation of theory and practical recipes for assessing and improving self-esteem.)

Miller, Jean Baker (1976) *Towards a New Psychology of Women*, Penguin (A classic treatment of the inequalities between men and women. Excellent on the difficulties and virtues of connecting knowledge, work and personal life.)

Nelson-Jones, Richard (1986) *Human Relationship Skills: training and self-help*, Cassel Educational

Pietroni, Patrick (1986) *Holistic Living: a guide to self-care by a leading practitioner*, Dent

Postle, Denis (1980) *Catastrophe Theory*, Fontana (1978) *Fabric of the Universe*, Macmillan (Sub-atomic physics and the eastern religious tradition, in pictures.)

Reason, Peter and Rowan, John (eds) (1981) *Human Enquiry: a sourcebook of New Paradigm research*, John Wiley (Academic but readable collection of articles on the background, theory and practice of doing research with people instead of on them.)

Restak, Richard M. (1979) *The Brain: the last frontier*, Warner Books

Rogers, Carl R. (1961) *On becoming a person*, Constable (This is a very personal and readable book about the various aspects of self-development. Read anything by Rogers; after Maslow, he is the main classic writer on humanistic psychology.)

Rogers, Carl R. and Stevens, Barry (eds) (1967) *Person to person: The problem of being human*, Real People Press (Contains papers by Rogers, Gendlin, Schlien and Van Dusen, set in a series of musings and commentaries by Barry Stevens, a woman who seems an actual example of Maslow's self-actualizing person.)

Rossi, Ernest Lawrence (1986) *Psychobiology of Mind-Body Healing*, W. W.Norton (Thorough treatment of how current developments in biology and medicine are consolidating existing techniques in hypnosis.)

Rowan, John (1988) *Ordinary Ecstasy: humanistic psychology in action*, RKP revised (Attempts to give a complete account of what humanistic psychology is and does. It includes its origins, fields of application, directions for the future, theory and research.)

Rowan, John and Dryden, Windy (1987) *Innovative Therapy in Britain*,Open University Press (This has chapters on primal integration, feminist therapy, psychosynthesis, transpersonal psychotherapy and Neuro-Linguistic Programming.)

Shohet, Robin (19865) *Dream sharing*, Turnstone Press (An excellent book on dreams from many different angles, practically useful. Tells you how to make the most of your dreams from the point of view of self-development.)

Stone, Hal and Winkelman, Sidra (1985) *Embracing Ourselves*, Devorrs and Co (A very homely and accessible account of the phenomenon of sub-personalities. It includes typical examples, their effects and how to work with them.)

Trungpa, Chogyam (1973) *Cutting Through Spiritual Materialism*, Watkins London (A Tibetan Buddhist emigré. Very good on the way that high spiritual ideals can become secure psychological defences.)

Tuan, Yi-Fu (1984) *Dominance and Affection: the making of pets*, Yale University Press (Fascinating examination of the way that dominance is built into everyday life. Very good about the oppression of women, children and pets.)

Verny, Thomas (1982) *The Secret Life of the Unborn Child*, Sphere Books (Highly readable explanation of the need to take better care of the foetus during pregnancy and birth.)

Wasdell, David *Dynamics of Disarmament Primal Matrix of Social Process Foundations of Psychosocial Analysis* Unit for Research into Changing Institutions (Three of numerous papers and reviews that offer insight into how and why social structures form a defence against personal anxiety.)

Watts, Alan (1971) *Psychotherapy East and West*, Vintage Books (Usefully links the core of two broad traditions of working with the mind.)

Zimbardo, Philip G (1977) *Shyness: what it is, what to do about it*, Addison-Wesley (A very thorough and practical approach to dealing with shyness.)

Author's acknowledgements
For Gaia Books Rosanne Hooper has sieved out the imponderables and irrelevancies from my writing and nudged it into a more accessible structure and style. Peggy Sadler has worked patiently and tirelessly to keep the illustration both appetizing and illuminating. Lucy Lidell's trust of what must often have seemed to be an unusual creative process has been especially fruitful.

The loving support of my partner, Jill Anderson has been vital. She has made decisive interventions at every stage of the conception and writing of the book.

Several consultants have been generous with their time and commitment. John Rowan has supported the book throughout, contributing a long list of practical suggestions and improvements. Dr John Tomlinson's down to earth, practical general practitioner's eye, has done much to keep the book relevant to your experience as well as mine. Bob Young's political and historical perspective underlines many areas of the content. Dick Saxton has contributed both critical feedback and a cornucopia of exercises. Dr Windy Dryden, Anne Dickson and David Wasdell have both read and made valuable comments on the text as it has emerged.

The many other people who have contributed indirectly to the book range from Michael Griffiths who taught me about interactive design, to innumerable co-counselling partners and members of several co-operative enquiry groups with whom much of what you have read was developed and tested.

Lastly, the book draws heavily on John Heron's research and experience. His loving support at critical times in the past have contributed to making the book possible.

While in many ways *The Mind Gymnasium* has been a collective effort, nevertheless the responsibility for what appears here and for any errors or omissions that there may be, lies with me.

Gaia Books would like to extend thanks to all of the following. First, to Denis Postle who generously shared his knowledge, experience, insight and energy; to John Rowan who patiently read the entire book at various stages, gave valuable feedback and contributed two of the spreads on humanistic psychology; to Anne Dickson, Dr Robert Young, Dr John Tomlinson, Dr Windy Dryden and Jill Anderson who all contributed helpful comments and suggestions; and to Dick Saxton who also gathered together many of the exercises. We would also like to thank Lucy Lidell, Joss Pearson and Patrick Nugent for their support and guidance Casey Horton and Joanna Godfrey Wood for good-humoured editorial help; Lesley Gilbert for copy preparation; Lucy Oliver for design assistance; Jane Parker for the index; also Eve Webster, Odile Louis-Sidney, Toby Flannagan, Magnum Photos Ltd., and On Yer Bike.

Photographic credits
Title page Hag
p.6-7 Eve Arnold/Magnum
p.19 Josef Koudelka/Magnum
p.37 René Burri/Magnum
p.53 Constantine
  Manos/Magnum
p.67 Burt Glinn/Magnum
p.72 top left: Denis Postle
  top right: Chris Kenney
  bottom left: NASA

bottom right: Gustav Doré
p.73 top left: Denis Postle
  top right: Chris Kenney
  bottom left: Denis Postle
  bottom right: Denis
  Postle
p.85 Richard Kalvar/Magnum
p.103 Peter Marlow/Magnum
p.207 Ford Motor Company
  Limited

Typesetting
Filmset in Sabon by S.B. Datagraphics Limited, Colchester, Essex

Colour reproduction
N.S. Plates Ltd, London

Several other books along the lines of The Mind Gymnasium *are being planned. Do write in to tell how you get on with it. Do send, for example, your 'life as a fairy story', or your 'life as a landscape'. I don't promise to respond personally but the feedback will go towards improving the later books.*